Vital Statistics
on Congress
1995-1996

Vital Statistics on Congress 1995-1996

Norman J. Ornstein
American Enterprise Institute

Thomas E. Mann
The Brookings Institution

Michael J. Malbin
State University of New York at Albany

With
Amy Schenkenberg

Congressional Quarterly Inc.
Washington, D.C.

Library of Congress Catalog No. 87-659232
ISBN 0-87187-845-3; 0-87187-846-1 (pbk.)
ISSN 0896-9469

Contents

Tables and Figures

Figures

Preface

With media coverage moving from one controversy to the next and heightened public disdain toward its members and its work, the contemporary Congress seems in constant tumult. Members themselves, often unsure of their status at any given moment, regularly shift their legislative focus. And the 1994 Republican takeover of both chambers for the first time since 1952 has brought promises of more fundamental change. But exactly how different is the contemporary Congress from its predecessors in terms of its work product, its membership, its political orientation, or its performance? This eighth edition of *Vital Statistics on Congress, 1995-1996* is your lens through which to observe and evaluate the changing shape of politics and the legislative branch of government.

Vital Statistics has been published and regularly updated for sixteen years, beginning in the last year of the Carter administration. A glance at any table shows that a member who left in 1980 and won election again in 1994 would scarcely recognize the place. All the turmoil of the 1980s in Congress is chronicled here, including the obsession with budget-related issues through most of the Reagan years, the fracture and reconsolidation of the Democrats in the House, the sharp swings in partisan control of the Senate, and the changing role of political action committees in congressional campaigns. Other changes in the 1980s, such as reform of the seniority system, the development of a budget process, and the changing numbers of blacks, women, and younger members in Congress, evolved from those of the 1970s. Many of the areas that were most fluid in 1980 now seem more settled—the number of committees, for example, and size of staffs have both stabilized—and even begun to decline. *Vital Statistics* serves to rebut the common misconception that such growth has been ongoing, but it also points out the emerging trends of the 1990s. After an explosive growth of government in the 1970s, there is a new focus on downsizing the federal government—including the legislative branch—coupled with a resurgence of concern over the federal budget deficit.

The characteristics of the members themselves have also been changing. Increased retirement and incumbent defeats in the House have resulted in the greatest number in modern times of members in their first three terms. And the 1994 midterm elections witnessed a dramatic shift in the Democratic-Republican ratio within the different regions of the country.

After the 1994 elections another trend emerged. As of mid-August 1995, five Democratic members had switched to the Republican Party. In the tables that are relevant we note the party change of Senators Richard Shelby (Ala.) and Ben Nighthorse Campbell (Colo.) as well as the change in the House by Nathan Deal (Ga.). Two other Democratic House members who have changed parties, Billy Tauzin (La.) and Greg Laughlin (Texas), are counted as Democrats in the tables. There will likely be other changes in party affiliation before the 104th Congress ends.

The framers of the Constitution intended for Congress to be the branch of government most immediately responsive to changes in society, the House more so than the Senate. Even when many of the members remain the same, the statistics in this book show that Congress fulfills its role well. Its approach to governing changed in each year of the Reagan presidency and throughout the Bush administration, appearing to follow shifts in public opinion about taxation, defense spending, and social services. The Republican majority of the 104th Congress, whether it lasts or not, has already brought dramatic change to the institution and will surely have an impact on many Congresses to come.

Today Congress finds itself responding to an increasingly energized, yet hostile, public that is demanding change as well as greater accountability from all its elected officials. How Congress reacts to the public, and has reacted to it in the past, can teach us a great deal about politics in America. This book is intended for all those who watch Congress for that reason, or who observe it as journalists, political scientists, students, lobbyists, citizens, or even as staff and members of the institution.

A good portion of the data here can be found in various congressional reports or publications. Our intention in *Vital Statistics on Congress* is to bring it all together in one convenient volume. The book would not be possible without its many indirect contributors and those who helped us locate some piece of data or other. They include Congressional Quarterly, the Congressional Research Service, the Federal Election Commission, and the staffs of many House and Senate committees and offices. We are also indebted to Julie Frank, Carey Macdonald, Lisa

Norrett, Justin Oberman, and Kevin Yingling for their help in counting, compiling, checking, and rechecking data. A special debt is owed to Amy Schenkenberg, who compiled much of the data for this volume, organized and directed the research efforts, and added her own contributions and insights. And thanks to Jeanne Ferris, Congressional Quarterly's acquisitions editor for this book, and to Ann O'Malley for her accurate and thorough editing.

Members of Congress   1

Chapter One provides data on the regional distribution, partisanship, and seniority of members of Congress. Table 1-1 and Figure 1-1 examine congressional apportionment within eight regions from 1910 (when the U.S. House of Representatives reached its permanent size of 435) through 1990. Between 1910 and 1990 the South and the West consistently gained seats, while the Border, New England, Mid-Atlantic, and Plains regions consistently lost them. In addition, the 1980 census brought a major gain to the Rocky Mountain states. Since 1960 the most notable losses have come in the Mid-Atlantic, the Midwest, and the Plains regions, led by New York (down from a high of forty-five seats in the 1940s to thirty-one in the 1990s) and Pennsylvania (down from thirty-three to twenty-one seats in the same period). The 1990 census revealed that these trends continued unabated, with considerable gains for Florida, Texas, and California, and notable losses for several Northeast and Midwest states. In the 1990s California has by far the largest congressional delegation followed by New York, Texas, and Florida. (In the 1940s New York had the largest congressional delegation, followed by Pennsylvania, Illinois, Ohio, and California.)

Shifts in the number of House seats have been accompanied by changes in the ratio of Democrats to Republicans within all the various regions (see Tables 1-2 and 1-3 and Figure 1-2). In the 1920s, for example, the Democrats completely dominated the South and had a substantial edge in the Border states, while the Republicans were dominant in six other regions, particularly New England, the Midwest, and the Plains states. By the mid-1930s, the Democrats had taken control of every region except New England and the Plains (which together had only 63 of the 435 seats). Although Democratic strength in several of these regions fell during the 1940s and 1950s, they held onto their domination into the 1960s. Only in the sparsely populated Plains states did the Republicans have a marked advantage; they also maintained a sizable majority in the Midwest.

By 1980 the regional map of party strength had changed again, and it continued to change throughout the decade. The Democratic proportion of southern and Border state seats fell from the 90 percent to the 65 percent range, reflecting the increased competitiveness of the parties in these areas. Similarly, Democratic Party strength in the Rocky Mountain states fell from 73.3 percent of the seats in 1960 to 36.8 percent after the 1980 election and to 29.2 percent after 1984, indicating a marked Republican resurgence. But the Democrats rebounded, reaching near parity with Republicans in 1990, with 45.8 percent of the seats and maintaining that level following the 1992 election.

The 1994 elections altered the House map dramatically when Republicans won seats almost across the board and reached an overall majority. The only region where the GOP did not capture at least 50 percent of the House seats was New England, where Democrats gained 3 percentage points to reach 63.6. The most significant GOP advancements came in the Rocky Mountain, Pacific Coast, Border, and southern states. Republicans had slowly been making advancements in the South until, in this election, they handily won a majority of the seats for the first time since Reconstruction. Prior to the election, the only southern state in which Republicans held a majority of House seats was Florida. Whether Republicans will be able to maintain these gains is uncertain, but many signs suggest that a durable realignment has occurred in the South, with the GOP likely to dominate its politics for years to come.

As Table 1-3 demonstrates, the changes in state apportionments and party strength across regions have important implications for the regional composition of the political parties within Congress. In the 1920s the Democratic Party in the House was dominated by the Deep South. Most Republican members of the House were from the East and the Midwest. By the 1940s representatives from the South no longer constituted a majority of the Democratic Party but a sizable plurality (a majority if one includes Border states), while Republican strength remained concentrated in the East and the Midwest.

By 1990 both parties had changed substantially in regional character. House Democrats still include more members from the South than from any other region, but the proportion had dropped to only 29.8 percent in 1992 with increased shares from the Mid-Atlantic, the Midwest, and the Pacific Coast regions. Together these three regions made up 47.7 percent of House Democrats. Republicans had gained an increased proportion of members from the South (27.2 percent of Republican House members up from 1.2 percent in 1948) and the Rocky Mountain states. There has been some decline in the proportion of

Republicans from the Mid-Atlantic, Plains, and New England regions. In fact Republicans lost considerable ground in New England in the 1990 election, capturing only seven seats, their weakest showing since 1978. They gained back one seat in 1992, bringing the GOP total to eight for the New England region. Republicans made significant gains in the South in 1992, capturing several of the newly created seats in that region, making it the largest Republican base in the House. Although the Democrats lost seats in the South in 1994, southern Democrats make up a slightly greater percentage of House Democrats than in 1992 (30 percent versus 29.8 percent) because the total number of Democrats sharply declined. But House Republicans gained fourteen seats in the South and also find their greatest regional concentration there, 27.7 percent. The Republican percentage of midwestern representatives increased as well, from 17.6 percent to 18.2 percent. It is clear from Table 1-3 that in the past several decades there has been a transformation of the South and several other regions that has changed the nature of both parties in Congress.

Tables 1-4 and 1-5 reveal similar trends in the Senate. The tables show the changes in the Senate with the advent of Republican control in 1980, the Democrats' return to power in 1986, and then the Republican takeover in 1994. The shifting party fortunes in the South are particularly noteworthy. The Republican majority in the Senate now rests upon its dominance of the Rocky Mountain and southern states.

A comparison of Table 1-5 with Table 1-3 shows that although broad party trends over time are similar for the House and the Senate, the different bases of elections for the two bodies lead to significant differences in the regional makeup of the House and Senate Democratic and Republican parties. Both Senate parties (but especially the Republicans) show considerably more Plains, Rocky Mountain, and New England influence than their House counterparts do because these two regions, although sparsely populated, elect twenty-eight senators.

Conversely, the House Democratic and Republican parties have greater proportions of members from the Mid-Atlantic and Midwest regions than the Senate parties do. Only 7.5 percent of the Republican members of the post-1994 Senate were from the Midwest and 7.5 percent from the Mid-Atlantic regions compared with 18.2 and 14.3 percent for the House Republican Party in the Midwest and Mid-Atlantic regions, respectively. Another interesting element of the Senate party configurations is that Republicans from the southern and Rocky Mountain states make up more than 45 percent of Senate Republicans while Senate Democrats are more evenly divided among the eight regions. Regional differences within parties and across chambers have interesting implications for House-versus-Senate responses to future Sunbelt-Frostbelt or other regional tensions that may flare in the coming decade: energy, economics, and the environment.

Tables 1-6 and 1-7 show the seniority of members of the House and Senate since 1953. Throughout the 1960s there was a steady increase in the proportion of very senior House members—"careerists"—and an intermittent but real decline in the proportion of very junior legislators (see Table 1-6). Both trends peaked at the beginning of the Ninety-second Congress (1971)—the twenty-year club reached 20 percent of the House membership, while the proportion that had served six years or less fell to 34 percent. It was the peak as well in mean terms served.

These trends reversed dramatically during the 1970s. In the Ninety-seventh Congress (1981-1982), junior members made up 47 percent of the House and the careerists only 11 percent. A 1.7-to-1 ratio of juniors to seniors in 1971 had changed to a 4.3-to-1 ratio in only a decade. The record number of retirements after the Vietnam War was the major factor in this decline of seniority in the House. Clearly these changes contributed to the reforms enacted in the House during the same period. However, by 1991 the cycle had nearly come full circle; the ratio was down to 1.8-to-1 (approaching the 1.7-to-1 ratio from 1971) reflecting the low turnover in 1984-1990 House elections. In the 102d Congress, the number of senior members reached its highest level (17 percent of the members having served ten or more terms) since 1973. This trend would not continue, however, as 1992 marked a year of significant change in Congress. A near record number of retirements, as well as a significant number of primary and general election defeats, paved the way for a large influx of new members. The 110-member freshman class of the 103d Congress was the largest of its kind since 1949. The number of senior members decreased somewhat, from 17 percent in the 102d Congress to 15 percent in the 103d, as did the percentage of members serving four to six and seven to nine terms.

The shift toward a more junior House continued in 1994. The members serving their second term leapt from 9 percent in 1992 to 23 percent in 1994. There were eighty-six freshmen in 1994 so that over half of the representatives are serving their first, second, or third term. In other words, 52 percent have been elected in the 1990s. The number of members serving four to six terms declined from 25 percent in 1992 to 16 percent.

Table 1-7 shows years of service in the Senate over the same time span. In contrast to the House, a smaller proportion of the members of the Senate of the 1950s could be considered careerists. Senior senators with three terms or more made up only 6 percent to 10 percent of the Senate. This pattern began to change in the late 1950s and early 1960s, as the number of senators in their third term grew, and in the late 1960s, as the same people swelled the ranks of the most senior group.

At the low end of the seniority scale, other patterns prevail. The number of first-term senators, which averaged about forty in the 1950s and early 1960s, dropped markedly to an average of about thirty in the mid-1960s and reached a low point of twenty-five in 1971. The number of freshmen climbed again in the 1970s and, paralleling the House, hit a post-World War II high of forty-eight in 1979, then jumped to a remarkable fifty-five after the 1980 election. While there was a good size freshman class in 1992 (thirteen), the mean and median years of service in the Senate continued to rise, with the mean reaching its highest level since 1975 and the median surpassing its previous high of eleven years.

In 1994 the number of senior senators reached twenty-five members—the highest number since at least 1953 (the earliest year we tabulated). Those senators serving seven to twelve years also increased sharply from seventeen to twenty-six. Conversely, the 1992 junior retirements combined with the 1994 departures and defeats cut the number of members in their second term by twelve, from thirty-two to twenty.

Tables 1-8 through 1-13 list prior occupations of members of Congress by body and party from the 83d through the 104th Congresses. Overall, it is clear that lawyers, business executives, and bankers continue to dominate both houses of Congress, though in proportions somewhat different from those in earlier times: 39 percent of the current House membership and 54 percent of the senators are lawyers. Although these numbers are high, they do not compare with the Ninetieth Congress, when 56 percent of House members and 68 percent of the senators were lawyers. In fact while the number of lawyers has decreased in the last three congresses, the 1994 elections brought the share of House members with experience in business or banking to 37 percent, up from thirty percent in 1992. This is almost equal to the percentage of lawyers.

Among other significant occupations, the House and Senate have seen the number of farmers decline since the 1950s and 1960s, from an average of 11 or 12 percent in the House to less than 5 percent and from 18 to 20 percent in the Senate to 9 percent. The number of educators in the House, which seemed to be on the decline in the 1980s, increased significantly with the election of the 102d Congress and has continued to rise. The figure now stands at 17 percent, up from less than 9 percent in the 100th Congress. Educators make up 10 percent of the current Senate.

There are party differences, though not startling ones, in occupation. More House Republicans than House Democrats come from the world of business and banking. And the gap seems to be widening. Currently, business people and bankers make up more than 50 percent of Republican House members and only 23 percent of Democratic members. More Democrats than Republicans in the House are lawyers and educators, though these disparities seem to be getting less extreme.

Tables 1-14 and 1-15 show the religious affiliations of members of both houses of Congress. Note the increase, since the 1960s, in the number of Catholics and Jews and the decline in the number of Methodists and Presbyterians. Patterns remained stable in the 1980s and 1990s, but with a steady increase in the number of Baptists.

Tables 1-16 and 1-17 show the number of blacks and women, respectively, in Congress. Of particular interest is the party shift from the nineteenth century to the mid-twentieth for black members, their steep increase in the Ninety-first and Ninety-second Congresses, and the steep increases in the 1980s of blacks and Republican women. The 1990 election marked the first time a black Republican had been elected to the House of Representatives in more than a half century. Blacks made significant gains with the 1992 elections, due in large part to redistricting and the creation of new black majority districts mandated by the Voting Rights Act of 1965. They held onto these gains in 1994. Women also made substantial gains with the election of 1992. While the total number of women in the House (forty-eight) remained the same in the 104th Congress, there was a significant party line shift of five more Republican women. Women make up 11 percent of the House in the 104th Congress, compared with 6.4 percent in the 102d. There are a total of eight women in the Senate, an all time high in that chamber.

Table 1-18 traces the shifts in party members and partisan control in the House and Senate since the Thirty-fourth Congress in 1855-1857. The respective eras of Republican and Democratic dominance of Congress are clearly shown in this table. The consistent Democratic majorities in the past few decades makes the Republican 1994 takeover of both the House and Senate all the more striking.

Table 1-1   Apportionment of Congressional Seats, by Region and State, 1910-1990 (435 seats)

Region and state	1910	1930	1940	1950	1960	1970	1980	1990
South	104	102	105	106	106	108	116	125
Alabama	10	9	9	9	8	7	7	7
Arkansas	7	7	7	6	4	4	4	4
Florida	4	5	6	8	12	15	19	23
Georgia	12	10	10	10	10	10	10	11
Louisiana	8	8	8	8	8	8	8	7
Mississippi	8	7	7	6	5	5	5	5
North Carolina	10	11	12	12	11	11	11	12
South Carolina	7	6	6	6	6	6	6	6
Tennessee	10	9	10	9	9	8	9	9
Texas	18	21	21	22	23	24	27	30
Virginia	10	9	9	10	10	10	10	11
Border	47	43	42	38	36	35	34	32
Kentucky	11	9	9	8	7	7	7	6
Maryland	6	6	6	7	8	8	8	8
Missouri	16	13	13	11	10	10	9	9
Oklahoma	8	9	8	6	6	6	6	6
West Virginia	6	6	6	6	5	4	4	3
New England	32	29	28	28	25	25	24	23
Connecticut	5	6	6	6	6	6	6	6
Maine	4	3	3	3	2	2	2	2
Massachusetts	16	15	14	14	12	12	11	10
New Hampshire	2	2	2	2	2	2	2	2
Rhode Island	3	2	2	2	2	2	2	2
Vermont	2	1	1	1	1	1	1	1
Mid-Atlantic	92	94	93	88	84	80	72	66
Delaware	1	1	1	1	1	1	1	1
New Jersey	12	14	14	14	15	15	14	13
New York	43	45	45	43	41	39	34	31
Pennsylvania	36	34	33	30	27	25	23	21
Midwest	86	90	87	87	88	86	80	74
Illinois	27	27	26	25	24	24	22	20
Indiana	13	12	11	11	11	11	10	10
Michigan	13	17	17	18	19	19	18	16
Ohio	22	24	23	23	24	23	21	19
Wisconsin	11	10	10	10	10	9	9	9
Plains	41	34	31	31	27	25	24	22
Iowa	11	9	8	8	7	6	6	5
Kansas	8	7	6	6	5	5	5	4

(Table continues)

Table 1-1   (continued)

Region and state	1910	1930	1940	1950	1960	1970	1980	1990
Minnesota	10	9	9	9	8	8	8	8
Nebraska	6	5	4	4	3	3	3	3
North Dakota	3	2	2	2	2	1	1	1
South Dakota	3	2	2	2	2	2	1	1
Rocky Mountain	14	14	16	16	17	19	24	24
Arizona	1	1	2	2	3	4	5	6
Colorado	4	4	4	4	4	5	6	6
Idaho	2	2	2	2	2	2	2	2
Montana	2	2	2	2	2	2	2	1
Nevada	1	1	1	1	1	1	2	2
New Mexico	1[a]	1	2	2	2	2	3	3
Utah	2	2	2	2	2	2	3	3
Wyoming	1	1	1	1	1	1	1	1
Pacific Coast	19	29	33	43	52	57	61	69
Alaska	—	—	—	1[b]	1	1	1	1
California	11	20	23	30	38	43	45	52
Hawaii	—	—	—	1[b]	2	2	2	2
Oregon	3	3	4	4	4	4	5	5
Washington	5	6	6	7	7	7	8	9

[a] New Mexico became a state in 1912; in 1910 it had a nonvoting delegate in Congress.
[b] Alaska became a state on January 3, 1959, Hawaii on August 21, 1959. In 1950 each had a nonvoting delegate in Congress, making the total for that year 437; subsequent reapportionment reduced the total to 435.

Sources: Congressional Quarterly's Guide to U.S. Elections (Washington, D.C.: Congressional Quarterly, 1975), 531; *Congressional Quarterly's Guide to U.S. Elections,* 2d ed. (Washington, D.C.: Congressional Quarterly, 1985), 1125; Richard E. Cohen, "House Headed for a Big Reshuffling," *National Journal,* January 7, 1989, 25; *Congressional Quarterly Weekly Report,* December 29, 1990, 4240.

9

Figure 1-1 Apportionment of Congressional Seats by Region, 1910 and 1990

Source: Table 1-1.

Table 1-2 Democratic Party Strength in the House, by Region, 1924-1994

Region	1924	1936	1948	1960	1972	1978	1980	1982	1986	1988	1990	1992	1994
South													
Percent	97.1	98.0	98.1	94.2	68.2	71.3	64.5	71.2	66.4	66.4	66.4	61.6	48.8
Seats	104	101	105	104	107	108	107	116	116	116	116	125	125
Border													
Percent	58.7	95.2	88.1	84.2	77.1	77.1	67.6	76.4	67.6	67.6	67.6	65.6	50.0
Seats	46	42	42	38	35	35	34	34	34	34	34	32	32
New England													
Percent	12.5	44.8	39.3	50.0	64.0	72.0	64.0	66.6	62.5	58.3	69.6	63.6	63.6
Seats	32	29	28	28	25	25	25	24	24	24	23[a]	22[a]	22[a]
Mid-Atlantic													
Percent	26.7	68.0	48.9	49.4	53.8	63.8	53.8	58.3	56.9	58.3	56.9	54.5	50.0
Seats	90[b]	94	92[c]	87	80	80	80	72	72	72	72	66	66
Midwest													
Percent	16.9	78.3	43.7	40.7	38.4	55.3	51.2	55.0	57.5	58.8	61.2	58.1	43.2
Seats	83[d]	83[e]	87	86	86	85	84	80	80	80	80	74	74
Plains													
Percent	15.4	44.8	16.1	19.4	33.3	40.0	36.0	54.2	45.8	50.0	54.2	54.5	36.4
Seats	39[f]	29[g]	31	31	24	25	25	24	24	24	24	22	22

Rocky Mountain													
Percent	28.6	93.3	75.0	73.3	42.1	47.4	36.8	33.3	37.5	37.5	45.8	45.8	25.0
Seats	14	15	16	15	19	19	19	24	24	24	24	24	24
Pacific Coast													
Percent	19.0	80.0	36.3	51.2	57.9	66.1	56.1	62.3	59.0	59.0	60.6	63.8	49.3
Seats	21	30[h]	33	43	57	56	57	61	61	61	61	69	69

Note: Numbers refer to the Congress that followed the election. Number of seats is total for all parties in the region (exceptions noted below). Does not include vacant seats. Discrepancy in the number of regional seats before and after 1980 is caused by post-1980 redistricting.

[a] Excludes one seat held by an Independent from Vermont.
[b] Excludes one seat held by a Socialist from New York.
[c] Excludes one seat occupied by a representative from New York who was a member of the American Labor Party.
[d] Excludes one seat held by a Socialist from Wisconsin.
[e] Excludes seven seats held by Progressives from Wisconsin.
[f] Excludes two seats occupied by representatives from Minnesota who were members of the Farmer Labor Party.
[g] Excludes five seats occupied by representatives from Minnesota who were members of the Farmer Labor Party.
[h] Excludes one seat held by a Progressive from California.

Sources: Congressional Directory (Washington, D.C.: U.S. Government Printing Office, 1925, 1937, 1949, 1961, 1973, 1979, 1981, 1983, 1985); *Congressional Quarterly Weekly Report,* November 8, 1986, 2843; November 22, 1986, 2958; November 12, 1988, 3269; November 10, 1990, 3802; November 7, 1992, 3571; November 12, 1994, 3236.

Table 1-3 Democratic and Republican Seats in the House, by Region, 1924–1994

Region	1924 D	1924 R	1936 D	1936 R	1948 D	1948 R	1960 D	1960 R	1972 D	1972 R	1978 D	1978 R	1980 D	1980 R	1988 D	1988 R	1990 D	1990 R	1992 D	1992 R	1994 D	1994 R
South																						
Percent	54.9	1.2	29.8	2.2	39.2	1.2	37.5	3.5	30.3	17.7	27.9	19.7	28.5	20.1	29.6	22.2	28.9	23.3	29.8	27.2	30.0	27.7
Seats	101	3	99	2	103	2	98	6	73	34	77	31	69	38	77	39	77	39	77	48	61	64
Border																						
Percent	14.7	7.8	12.0	2.2	14.1	2.9	12.3	3.5	11.2	4.2	9.8	5.1	9.5	5.8	8.8	6.2	8.6	6.6	8.1	6.2	7.9	6.9
Seats	27	19	40	2	37	5	32	6	27	8	27	8	23	11	23	11	23	11	21	11	16	16
New England																						
Percent	2.2	11.4	3.9	17.6	4.2	9.9	5.4	8.2	6.6	4.7	6.5	4.5	6.6	4.8	5.4	5.7	6.0	4.3	5.4	4.5	6.9	3.5
Seats	4	28	13	16	11	17	14	14	16	9	18	7	16	9	14	10	16	7	14	8	14	8
Mid-Atlantic																						
Percent	13.0	26.9	19.3	33.0	17.1	27.5	16.5	25.7	17.8	19.3	18.5	18.5	17.8	19.6	16.2	17.1	15.3	18.6	14.0	17.0	16.2	14.3
Seats	24	66	64	30	45	47	43	44	43	37	51	29	43	37	42	30	41	31	36	30	33	33
Midwest																						
Percent	7.6	28.2	19.6	19.8	14.4	28.7	13.4	29.8	13.7	27.6	17.0	24.2	17.8	21.7	18.1	18.9	18.4	18.6	16.7	17.6	15.8	18.2
Seats	14	69	65	18	38	49	35	51	33	53	47	38	43	41	47	33	49	31	43	31	32	42
Plains																						
Percent	3.3	13.5	4.0	17.6	1.9	15.2	2.3	14.6	3.3	8.3	3.6	9.6	3.7	8.5	4.6	6.9	4.9	6.6	4.6	5.7	3.9	6.1
Seats	6	33	13	16	5	26	6	25	8	16	10	15	9	16	12	12	13	11	12	10	8	14

Rocky Mountain																						
Percent	2.2	4.1	4.2	1.1	4.6	2.3	4.2	2.3	3.3	5.7	3.3	6.4	2.9	6.3	3.5	8.6	4.1	7.8	4.3	7.4	3.0	7.8
Seats	4	10	14	1	12	4	11	4	8	11	9	10	7	12	9	15	11	13	11	13	6	18
Pacific Coast																						
Percent	2.2	6.9	7.2	6.6	4.6	12.3	8.4	12.3	13.7	12.5	13.4	12.1	13.2	13.2	13.8	14.3	13.8	14.4	17.0	14.2	16.7	15.2
Seats	4	17	24	6	12	21	22	21	33	24	37	19	32	25	36	25	37	24	44	25	34	35
Total seats	184	245	332	91	263	171[a]	261	171	241	192	276	157	242	189	260	175	267	167[b]	258	176	204	230

Note: D indicates Democrats; R indicates Republicans. Third-party members and vacant seats have been excluded. Percentages may not add to 100.0 because of rounding.

[a] There was one Independent elected in 1948.
[b] Bernard Sanders was elected as an Independent from Vermont.

Sources: Congressional Directory, 1925, 1937, 1949, 1961, 1973, 1979, 1981, 1983, 1985; *Congressional Quarterly Weekly Report,* November 12, 1988, 3269; November 10, 1990, 3802; November 7, 1992, 3571; November 12, 1994, 3236.

Table 1-4 Democratic Party Strength in the Senate, by Region, 1924-1994

Region	1924	1936	1948	1960	1972	1978	1980	1982	1984	1986	1988	1990	1992	1994
South														
Percent	100.0	100.0	100.0	100.0	68.2	72.7	54.4	50.0	54.5	72.7	68.2	68.2	59.1	40.9[a]
Seats	22	22	22	22	22	22	22	22	22	22	22	22	22	22
Border														
Percent	50.0	100.0	80.0	60.0	50.0	70.0	70.0	70.0	60.0	60.0	60.0	60.0	60.0	50.0
Seats	10	10	10	10	10	10	10	10	10	10	10	10	10	10
New England														
Percent	8.3	50.0	25.0	41.7	58.3	58.3	50.0	50.0	50.0	50.0	58.3	58.3	58.3	50.0
Seats	12	12	12	12	12	12	12	12	12	12	12	12	12	12
Mid-Atlantic														
Percent	37.5	75.0	37.5	25.0	25.0	50.0	50.0	50.0	50.0	50.0	50.0	50.0	62.5	50.0
Seats	8	8	8	8	8	8	8	8	8	8	8	8	8	8
Midwest														
Percent	10.0	88.9	20.0	70.0	60.0	80.0	60.0	60.0	70.0	70.0	70.0	70.0	80.0	60.0
Seats	10	9[b]	10	10	10	10	10	10	10	10	10	10	10	10
Plains														
Percent	0.0	66.7	16.7	25.0	58.3	41.7	25.0	25.0	33.3	50.0	50.0	58.3	58.3	58.3
Seats	11[c]	9[d]	12	12	12	12	12	12	12	12	12	12	12	12

Rocky Mountain

Percent	50.0	93.8	75.0	75.0	56.2	37.5	31.3	31.3	31.3	37.5	37.5	37.5	37.5	31.2[e]
Seats	6	16	16	16	16	16	16	16	16	16	16	16	16	16

Pacific Coast

Percent	16.7	50.0	33.3	80.0	60.0	60.0	40.0	40.0	30.0	40.0	40.0	40.0	50.0	50.0
Seats	6	6	6	10	10	10	10	10	10	10	10	10	10	10

Note: Number of seats is total for all parties in the region (exceptions noted below).

[a]Includes Sen. Richard Shelby (Ala.) who switched from the Democratic to the Republican Party on the day following the election.
[b]Excludes one Progressive from Wisconsin.
[c]Excludes one senator from Minnesota who was a member of the Farmer Labor Party.
[d]Excludes two senators from Minnesota and one senator from Nebraska who were members of the Farmer Labor Party.
[e]Does not include Sen. Ben Nighthorse Campbell (Colo.) who switched from the Democratic to the Republican Party March 3, 1995.

Sources: Congressional Directory, 1925, 1937, 1949, 1961, 1973, 1979, 1981, 1983, 1985; *Congressional Quarterly Weekly Report,* November 8, 1986, 2812, 2839; November 12, 1988, 3264; November 10, 1990, 3826; November 7, 1992, 3558; November 12, 1994, 3236.

Figure 1-2   Democratic Party Strength in Congress, by Region, 1924–1994
(percentage of Democratic seats in regional delegation)

Percent

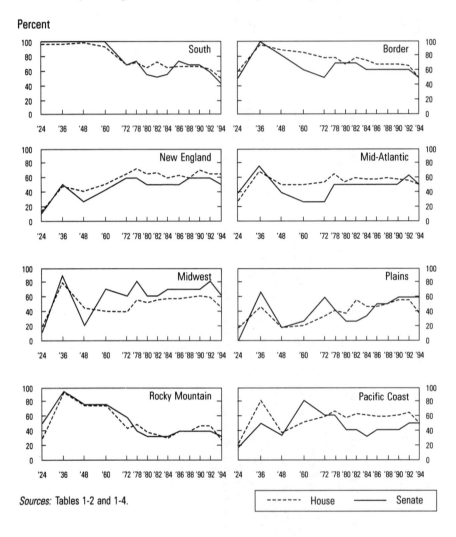

Sources: Tables 1-2 and 1-4.

------- House   ——— Senate

Table 1-5 Democratic and Republican Seats in the Senate, by Region, 1924-1994

Region	1924 D	1924 R	1936 D	1936 R	1948 D	1948 R	1960 D	1960 R	1972 D	1972 R	1978 D	1978 R	1980 D	1980 R	1988 D	1988 R	1990 D	1990 R	1992 D	1992 R	1994 D	1994 R
South																						
Percent	53.7	0.0	28.9	0.0	40.7	0.0	33.8	0.0	26.3	16.3	27.1	14.6	25.5	18.9	27.3	15.6	26.8	15.9	22.8	20.9	19.1	24.5[a]
Seats	22	0	22	0	22	0	22	0	15	7	16	6	12	10	15	7	15	7	13	9	9	13
Border																						
Percent	12.2	9.3	13.2	0.0	14.8	4.8	9.2	11.4	8.8	11.6	11.9	7.3	14.9	5.7	10.6	8.9	10.7	9.1	10.5	7.3	10.6	9.4
Seats	5	5	10	0	8	2	6	4	5	5	7	3	7	3	6	4	6	4	6	4	5	5
New England																						
Percent	2.4	20.4	7.9	37.5	5.6	21.4	7.7	20.0	12.3	11.6	11.9	12.2	12.8	11.3	12.7	11.1	12.5	11.4	12.3	11.6	12.8	11.3
Seats	1	11	6	6	3	9	5	7	7	5	7	5	6	6	7	5	7	5	7	5	6	6
Mid-Atlantic																						
Percent	7.3	9.3	7.9	12.5	5.6	11.9	3.1	17.1	3.5	13.9	6.8	9.8	8.5	7.5	7.3	8.9	7.1	9.1	8.8	7.0	8.5	7.5
Seats	3	5	6	2	3	5	2	6	2	6	4	4	4	4	4	4	4	4	5	3	4	4
Midwest																						
Percent	2.4	16.7	10.5	6.3	3.7	19.0	10.8	8.6	10.5	9.3	13.6	4.9	12.8	7.5	12.7	6.7	12.5	6.8	14.0	4.6	12.8	7.5
Seats	1	9	8	1	2	8	7	3	6	4	8	2	6	4	7	3	7	3	8	2	6	4
Plains																						
Percent	0.0	20.4	7.9	18.8	3.7	23.8	4.6	25.7	12.3	11.6	8.5	17.1	6.4	17.0	10.9	13.3	12.5	11.4	12.3	11.6	14.9	9.4
Seats	0	11	6	3	2	10	3	9	7	5	5	7	3	9	6	6	7	5	7	5	7	5

(Table continues)

Table 1-5 (continued)

Region	1924 D	1924 R	1936 D	1936 R	1948 D	1948 R	1960 D	1960 R	1972 D	1972 R	1978 D	1978 R	1980 D	1980 R	1988 D	1988 R	1990 D	1990 R	1992 D	1992 R	1994 D	1994 R
Rocky Mountain																						
Percent	19.5	14.8	19.7	6.3	22.2	9.5	18.5	11.4	15.8	16.3	10.2	24.4	10.6	20.8	10.9	22.2	10.7	22.7	10.5	23.2	10.6	20.8[b]
Seats	8	8	15	1	12	4	12	4	9	7	6	10	5	11	6	10	6	10	6	10	5	11
Pacific Coast																						
Percent	2.4	9.3	3.9	18.8	3.7	9.5	12.3	5.7	10.5	9.3	10.2	9.8	8.5	11.3	7.3	13.3	7.1	13.6	8.8	11.6	10.6	9.4
Seats	1	5	3	3	2	4	8	2	6	4	6	4	4	6	4	6	4	6	5	5	5	5
Total seats	41	54	76	16	54	42	65	35	57	43	59	41	47	53	55	45	56	44	57	43	47	53

Note: D indicates Democrats; R indicates Republicans. Third-party members who did not caucus with either major party have been excluded. Percentages may not add to 100.0 because of rounding.

[a] Includes Sen. Richard Shelby (Ala.) who switched from the Democratic to the Republican Party on the day following the election.

[b] Does not include Sen. Ben Nighthorse Campbell (Colo.) who switched from the Democratic to the Republican Party on March 3, 1995.

Sources: Congressional Directory, 1925, 1937, 1949, 1961, 1973, 1979, 1981, 1983, 1985; *Congressional Quarterly Weekly Report,* November 12, 1988, 3264; November 10, 1990, 3826; November 7, 1992, 3558; November 12, 1994, 3236.

Table 1-6   Seniority of Representatives, 1953-1995

Congress	Percentage of representatives serving								Mean term	Median term
	1 term	2 terms	3 terms	1-3 terms	4-6 terms	7-9 terms	10+ terms	Total		
83d (1953)										
Percent	18	14	12	44	29	16	10	100	4.9	4
Seats	78	61	53	192	127	70	42	431		
84th (1955)										
Percent	11	17	13	42	26	19	12	100	5.2	4
Seats	50	74	58	182	115	84	54	435		
85th (1957)										
Percent	9	11	16	36	31	17	16	100	5.5	5
Seats	40	46	69	155	133	74	71	433		
86th (1959)										
Percent	18	10	10	38	30	17	15	100	5.6	4
Seats	79	43	43	165	131	74	66	436		
88th (1963)										
Percent	15	13	13	41	24	19	17	100	5.7	5
Seats	66	55	55	176	104	81	74	435		
89th (1965)										
Percent	19	14	11	44	22	18	17	100	5.5	4
Seats	83	60	47	190	94	78	72	434		
90th (1967)										
Percent	14	15	12	41	25	16	17	100	5.6	4
Seats	60	65	54	179	110	70	75	434		
91st (1969)										
Percent	8	15	14	37	31	15	18	100	5.7	5
Seats	36	65	58	159	132	64	76	431		
92d (1971)										
Percent	11	10	13	34	29	16	20	100	6.0	5
Seats	48	45	57	150	127	69	87	433		
93d (1973)										
Percent	16	11	10	37	30	16	18	100	5.7	5
Seats	67	49	41	157	131	67	78	433		
94th (1975)										
Percent	20	14	10	44	24	·19	14	100	5.4	4
Seats	86	61	42	189	102	81	61	433		

(Table continues)

Table 1-6   (continued)

Congress	Percentage of representatives serving							Total	Mean term	Median term
	1 term	2 terms	3 terms	1-3 terms	4-6 terms	7-9 terms	10+ terms			
95th (1977)										
Percent	15	21	12	48	21	17	14	100	4.6	4
Seats	64	92	54	210	90	73	60	433		
96th (1979)										
Percent	18	14	17	49	22	16	13	100	5.0	4
Seats	77	61	76	214	96	70	55	435		
97th (1981)										
Percent	17	17	13	47	28	14	11	100	4.9	4
Seats	73	75	57	205	120	60	50	435		
98th (1983)										
Percent	18	14	16	49	28	11	13	100	4.6	4
Seats	80	63	68	211	121	48	55	435		
99th (1985)										
Percent	9	19	14	41	32	13	14	100	4.7	4
Seats	39	81	60	180	141	55	59	435		
100th (1987)										
Percent	11	8	17	37	33	14	16	100	5.6	5
Seats	48	37	74	159	144	63	69	435		
101st (1989)										
Percent	8	12	8	28	38	20	14	100	5.8	5
Seats	33	54	33	120	167	86	60	433		
102d (1991)										
Percent	10	9	11	30	31	21	17	100	6.2	5
Seats	42	41	47	130	137	92	76	435		
103d (1993)										
Percent	25	9	9	43	25	16	15	100	5.3	4
Seats	110	39	38	187	109	72	67	435		
104th (1995)										
Percent	20	23	9	52	16	18	14	100	4.8	3
Seats	86	102	38	225	72	78	59	435		

Note: Terms are consecutive full terms. Percentages may not add to totals because of rounding.

Sources: Congressional Directory, 1953 through 1985; *Congressional Quarterly Weekly Report,* October 11, 1986; November 8, 1986; January 7, 1989; November 10, 1990; November 7, 1992; November 12, 1994; *The Almanac of American Politics 1990* (Washington, D.C.: National Journal, 1989).

Table 1-7   Seniority of Senators, 1953-1995

Congress	Number of senators serving				Total	Mean years service	Median years service
	6 years or less	7-12 years	13-18 years	19 years or more			
83d (1953)	46 (16)	29	14	7	96	8.5	7
84th (1955)	42 (14)	37	8	9	96	8.4	7
85th (1957)	37 (10)	36	13	10	96	9.6	9
86th (1959)	42 (20)	30	14	12	98	9.4	8
87th (1961)	42 (7)	25	22	11	100	9.7	9
88th (1963)	42 (12)	26	18	14	100	9.9	7
89th (1965)	29 (8)	36	16	19	100	11.1	9
90th (1967)	28 (7)	34	19	19	100	11.6	9
91st (1969)	32 (14)	32	17	19	100	11.2	11
92d (1971)	25 (10)	24	29	22	100	11.5	11
93d (1973)	40 (13)	20	20	20	100	11.2	9
94th (1975)	35 (11)	22	23	19	99	11.5	9
95th (1977)	42 (17)	25	13	20	100	10.6	9
96th (1979)	48 (20)	24	10	18	100	9.6	7
97th (1981)	55 (18)	20	10	15	100	8.5	5
98th (1983)	43 (5)	28	16	13	100	9.6	7
99th (1985)	32 (7)	38	18	12	100	10.1	9
100th (1987)	26 (13)	44	16	14	100	9.6	8
101st (1989)	31 (10)	26	29	14	100	9.8	10
102d (1991)	30 (5)	23	28	19	100	11.1	11
103d (1993)	30 (13)	17	32	21	100	11.3	12
104th (1995)	29 (11)	26	20	25	100	12.3	11

Note: Figures in parentheses are the number of freshmen senators. Senators who are currently in their first full term are listed under the "6 years or less" column.

Sources: Congressional Directory, 1953 through 1985; *Congressional Quarterly Almanac* (Washington, D.C.: Congressional Quarterly, various years); *Congressional Quarterly Weekly Report,* October 11, 1986; November 8, 1986; November 12, 1988; November 19, 1988; November 10, 1990; *National Journal,* November 7, 1992, 2562; November 12, 1994, 2644.

Table 1-8   Prior Occupations of Representatives, 83d-104th Congresses, 1953-1995

Occupation	83d 1953	84th 1955	86th 1959	88th 1963	89th 1965	90th 1967	91st 1969	92d 1971	93d 1973
Acting/ entertainer	—	—	—	—	—	—	—	—	—
Aeronautics	—	—	—	—	—	—	—	—	—
Agriculture	53	51	45	45	44	39	34	36	38
Business or banking	131	127	130	134	156	161	159	145	155
Clergy	—	—	—	3	3	3	2	2	4
Congressional aide	—	—	—	—	—	—	—	—	—
Education	46	47	41	36	68	57	59	61	59
Engineering	5	5	3	3	9	6	6	3	2
Journalism	36	33	35	33	43	39	39	30	23
Labor leader	—	—	—	3	3	2	3	3	3
Law	247	245	242	250	247	246	242	236	221
Law enforcement	—	—	—	—	—	—	2	1	2
Medicine	6	5	4	3	3	3	5	6	5
Military	—	—	—	—	—	—	—	—	—
Professional sports	—	—	—	—	—	—	—	—	—
Public service/ politics	—	—	—	—	—	—	—	—	—
Veteran	246	261	261	291	310	320	320	316	317

Note: Dashes indicate years and occupations for which Congressional Quarterly did not compile data.

[a] Includes Bernard Sanders (I-Vt.).

Sources: Congressional Quarterly Almanac; Congressional Quarterly Weekly Report, November 8, 1986, 2862; November 12, 1988, 3295; November 10, 1990, 3837; November 7, 1992, Supplement, 9; November 12, 1994, Supplement, 11.

94th 1975	95th 1977	96th 1979	97th 1981	98th 1983	99th 1985	100th 1987	101st 1989	102d 1991	103d 1993	104th 1995
—	—	—	—	—	—	1	2	2	1	1
—	—	—	—	3	4	3	3	1	2	1
31	16	19	28	26	29	20	19	20	19	20
140	118	127	134	138	147	142	138	157	131	162
5	6	6	3	2	2	2	2	2	2	2
—	5	10	11	16	16	—	—	—	—	—
64	70	57	59	43	37	38	42	57[a]	66[a]	75[a]
3	2	2	5	5	6	4	4	7	5	6
24	27	11	21	22	20	20	17	25[a]	24[a]	15[a]
3	6	4	5	2	2	2	2	3	2	2
221	222	205	194	200	190	184	184	183	181	171
2	7	5	5	5	8	7	8	5	10	11
5	2	6	6	6	5	3	4	5	6	10
—	—	—	—	1	1	0	0	1	0	0
—	—	—	—	3	3	5	4	3	1	2
—	—	—	—	—	—	94	94	61	87	102
307	—	—	—	—	—	—	—	—	—	—

Table 1-9   Prior Occupations of Democratic Representatives, 83d-104th Congresses, 1953-1995

Occupation	83d 1953	84th 1955	86th 1959	88th 1963	89th 1965	90th 1967	91st 1969	92d 1971	93d 1973
Acting/ entertainer	—	—	—	—	—	—	—	—	—
Aeronautics	—	—	—	—	—	—	—	—	—
Agriculture	21	22	28	21	26	17	14	19	14
Business or banking	55	59	71	67	98	82	76	70	72
Clergy	—	—	—	1	2	1	1	1	2
Congressional aide	—	—	—	—	—	—	—	—	—
Education	18	26	30	24	54	43	40	39	41
Engineering	3	3	2	2	6	4	3	2	1
Journalism	18	16	21	18	27	22	22	17	16
Labor leader	—	—	—	3	3	2	3	3	3
Law	130	136	168	158	171	150	150	150	137
Law en- forcement	—	—	—	—	—	—	1	1	1
Medicine	2	2	2	1	1	1	2	4	3
Military	—	—	—	—	—	—	—	—	—
Professional sports	—	—	—	—	—	—	—	—	—
Public service/ politics	—	—	—	—	—	—	—	—	—
Veteran	118	131	175	175	210	183	181	185	175
Total number of Democratic members	213	232	283	258	295	248	243	255	243

Note: Dashes indicate years and occupations for which Congressional Quarterly did not compile data.

Sources: Congressional Quarterly Almanac, various years; *Congressional Quarterly Weekly Report,* November 8, 1986, 2862; November 12, 1988, 3295; November 10, 1990, 3837; November 7, 1992, Supplement, 9; November 12, 1994, Supplement 11.

94th 1975	95th 1977	96th 1979	97th 1981	98th 1983	99th 1985	100th 1987	101st 1989	102d 1991	103d 1993	104th 1995
—	—	—	—	—	—	0	1	1	0	0
—	—	—	—	0	1	0	0	0	0	0
13	6	10	11	13	13	10	8	11	7	6
84	69	71	58	73	72	66	66	77	56	46
4	4	4	2	2	2	2	2	2	1	1
—	3	7	9	10	10	—	—	—	—	—
51	56	44	39	29	24	24	25	37	45	39
1	0	0	2	2	2	2	2	4	2	1
19	15	6	9	13	10	11	9	14	11	4
3	6	3	4	2	2	2	2	3	2	1
158	154	135	121	132	122	122	122	126	122	93
2	7	4	4	2	6	6	6	4	8	7
3	1	1	2	2	3	1	2	3	4	2
—	—	—	—	0	0	0	0	0	0	0
—	—	—	—	2	2	3	3	2	0	0
—	—	—	—	—	—	59	58	41	51	53
198	—	—	—	—	—	—	—	—	—	—
291	292	277	243	267	253	258	260	267	258	204

Table 1-10   Prior Occupations of Republican Representatives, 83d-104th Congresses, 1953-1995

Occupation	83d 1953	84th 1955	86th 1959	88th 1963	89th 1965	90th 1967	91st 1969	92d 1971	93d 1973
Acting/ entertainer	—	—	—	—	—	—	—	—	—
Aeronautics	—	—	—	—	—	—	—	—	—
Agriculture	32	29	17	24	18	22	20	17	24
Business or banking	76	68	59	67	58	79	83	75	83
Clergy	—	—	—	2	1	2	1	1	2
Congressional aide	—	—	—	—	—	—	—	—	—
Education	28	21	11	12	14	14	19	22	18
Engineering	2	2	1	1	3	2	3	1	1
Journalism	18	17	14	15	16	17	17	13	7
Labor leader	—	—	—	0	0	0	0	0	0
Law	117	109	74	92	76	96	92	86	84
Law en- forcement	—	—	—	—	—	—	1	0	1
Medicine	4	3	2	2	2	2	3	2	2
Military	—	—	—	—	—	—	—	—	—
Professional sports	—	—	—	—	—	—	—	—	—
Public service/ politics	—	—	—	—	—	—	—	—	—
Veteran	128	130	86	116	100	137	139	131	142
Total number of Republican members	221	203	153	176	140	187	192	180	192

Note: Dashes indicate years and occupations for which Congressional Quarterly did not compile data.

Sources: Congressional Quarterly Almanac, various years; Congressional Quarterly Weekly Report, November 8, 1986, 2862; November 12, 1988, 3295; November 10, 1990, 3837; November 7, 1992, Supplement, 9; November 12, 1994, Supplement, 11.

94th 1975	95th 1977	96th 1979	97th 1981	98th 1983	99th 1985	100th 1987	101st 1989	102d 1991	103d 1993	104th 1995
—	—	—	—	—	—	1	1	1	1	1
—	—	—	—	3	3	3	3	1	2	1
18	10	9	17	13	16	10	11	9	12	14
56	49	56	76	65	75	76	72	80	75	116
1	2	2	1	0	0	0	0	0	1	1
—	2	3	2	6	6	—	—	—	—	—
13	14	13	20	14	13	14	17	19	20	35
2	2	2	3	3	4	2	2	3	3	5
5	12	5	12	9	10	9	8	10	12	10
0	0	1	1	0	0	0	0	0	0	1
63	68	70	73	68	68	62	62	57	59	78
0	0	1	1	3	2	1	2	1	2	4
2	1	5	4	4	2	2	2	2	2	8
—	—	—	—	1	1	0	0	1	0	0
—	—	—	—	1	1	2	1	1	1	2
—	—	—	—	—	—	35	36	20	36	49
109	—	—	—	—	—	—	—	—	—	—
144	143	158	192	167	182	177	175	167	176	230

Table 1-11   Prior Occupations of Senators, 83d-104th Congresses, 1953-1995

Occupation	83d 1953	84th 1955	86th 1959	88th 1963	89th 1965	90th 1967	91st 1969	92d 1971	93d 1973
Acting/ entertainer	—	—	—	—	—	—	—	—	—
Aeronautics	—	—	—	—	—	—	—	—	—
Agriculture	22	21	17	16	18	18	16	13	11
Business or banking	28	28	28	23	25	23	25	27	22
Clergy	—	—	—	0	0	0	0	0	0
Congressional aide	—	—	—	—	—	—	—	—	—
Education	17	17	16	15	16	15	14	11	10
Engineering	5	2	2	2	2	2	2	2	2
Journalism	10	10	13	8	10	10	8	7	5
Labor leader	—	—	—	1	1	0	0	0	0
Law	59	60	61	66	67	68	68	65	68
Law enforcement	—	—	—	—	—	—	0	0	0
Medicine	1	2	1	1	1	1	0	1	1
Military	—	—	—	—	—	—	—	—	—
Professional sports	—	—	—	—	—	—	—	—	—
Public service/ politics	—	—	—	—	—	—	—	—	—
Veteran	63	62	61	62	63	65	69	73	73

Note: Dashes indicate years and occupations for which Congressional Quarterly did not compile data.

Sources: Congressional Quarterly Almanac, various years; *Congressional Quarterly Weekly Report,* November 8, 1986, 2862; November 12, 1988, 3295; November 10, 1990, 3837; November 7, 1992, Supplement, 9; November 12, 1994, Supplement, 11.

	94th 1975	95th 1977	96th 1979	97th 1981	98th 1983	99th 1985	100th 1987	101st 1989	102d 1991	103d 1993	104th 1995
	—	—	—	—	—	—	0	0	0	0	1
	—	—	—	—	2	2	2	2	1	1	1
	10	9	6	9	9	10	5	4	8	8	9
	22	24	29	28	29	31	28	28	32	24	24
	0	1	1	1	1	1	1	1	1	1	0
	—	0	0	0	0	0	—	—	—	—	—
	8	13	7	10	12	12	12	11	10	11	10
	2	0	0	2	0	1	1	0	0	0	0
	5	6	2	7	7	8	8	8	10	9	8
	0	0	0	0	0	0	0	0	0	0	0
	67	68	65	59	61	61	62	63	61	58	54
	0	0	0	0	0	0	0	0	0	0	0
	1	1	1	1	1	1	1	0	0	0	1
	—	—	—	—	1	1	1	1	1	1	1
	—	—	—	—	1	1	1	1	1	1	1
	—	—	—	—	—	—	20	20	5	10	12
	73	—	—	—	—	—	—	—	—	—	—

Table 1-12   Prior Occupations of Democratic Senators, 83d-104th
Congresses, 1953-1995

Occupation	83d 1953	84th 1955	86th 1959	88th 1963	89th 1965	90th 1967	91st 1969	92d 1971	93d 1973
Acting/ entertainer	—	—	—	—	—	—	—	—	—
Aeronautics	—	—	—	—	—	—	—	—	—
Agriculture	8	7	7	9	10	9	7	5	4
Business or banking	11	10	14	12	14	12	12	15	12
Clergy	—	—	—	0	0	0	0	0	0
Congressional aide	—	—	—	—	—	—	—	—	—
Education	11	11	13	12	12	10	9	6	7
Engineering	2	0	2	2	2	2	2	2	2
Journalism	5	6	10	7	7	7	5	5	4
Labor leader	—	—	—	1	1	0	0	0	0
Law	34	27	43	46	48	48	42	41	42
Law en- forcement	—	—	—	—	—	—	—	0	0
Medicine	1	2	1	1	1	1	0	1	1
Military	—	—	—	—	—	—	—	—	—
Professional sports	—	—	—	—	—	—	—	—	—
Public service/ politics	—	—	—	—	—	—	—	—	—
Veteran	31	32	40	41	44	43	41	41	42
Total number of Democratic members	46	48	64	67	68	64	58	54	56

Note: Dashes indicate years and occupations for which Congressional Quarterly did not compile data.

Sources: Congressional Quarterly Almanac, various years; *Congressional Quarterly Weekly Report,* November 8, 1986, 2862; November 12, 1988, 3295; November 10, 1990, 3837; November 7, 1992, Supplement, 9; November 12, 1994, Supplement, 11.

94th 1975	95th 1977	96th 1979	97th 1981	98th 1983	99th 1985	100th 1987	101st 1989	102d 1991	103d 1993	104th 1995
—	—	—	—	—	—	0	0	0	0	0
—	—	—	—	1	1	1	1	1	1	1
5	3	2	2	2	3	2	1	3	3	4
12	14	15	13	14	12	13	13	15	12	11
0	0	0	0	0	0	0	0	0	0	0
—	0	0	0	0	0	—	—	—	—	—
6	8	4	5	5	4	6	6	6	6	5
2	0	0	1	0	0	0	0	0	0	0
4	4	2	4	5	6	6	5	8	7	5
0	0	0	0	0	0	0	0	0	0	0
45	46	43	33	32	32	35	36	35	33	26
0	0	0	0	0	0	0	0	0	0	0
1	1	1	1	1	1	1	0	0	0	0
—	—	—	—	0	1	0	0	0	0	0
—	—	—	—	1	0	1	1	1	1	1
—	—	—	—	—	—	13	14	4	8	7
45	—	—	—	—	—	—	—	—	—	—
60	61	58	46	46	47	55	55	56	57	47

Table 1-13   Prior Occupations of Republican Senators, 83d-104th
Congresses, 1953-1995

Occupation	83d 1953	84th 1955	86th 1959	88th 1963	89th 1965	90th 1967	91st 1969	92d 1971	93d 1973
Acting/ entertainer	—	—	—	—	—	—	—	—	—
Aeronautics	—	—	—	—	—	—	—	—	—
Agriculture	14	14	10	7	8	9	9	8	7
Business or banking	17	18	14	11	11	11	13	12	10
Clergy	—	—	—	0	0	0	0	0	0
Congressional aide	—	—	—	—	—	—	—	—	—
Education	6	6	3	3	4	5	5	5	3
Engineering	3	2	0	0	0	0	0	0	0
Journalism	5	4	3	1	3	3	3	2	1
Labor leader	—	—	—	0	0	0	0	0	0
Law	25	33	18	20	19	20	26	24	26
Law en- forcement	—	—	—	—	—	0	0	0	0
Medicine	0	0	0	0	0	0	0	0	0
Military	—	—	—	—	—	—	—	—	—
Professional sports	—	—	—	—	—	—	—	—	—
Public service/ politics	—	—	—	—	—	—	—	—	—
Veteran	32	30	21	21	19	22	28	32	31
Total number of Republican members	48	47	34	33	32	36	42	44	42

Note: Dashes indicate years and occupations for which Congressional Quarterly did not compile data.

Sources: Congressional Quarterly Almanac, various years; *Congressional Quarterly Weekly Report,* November 8, 1986, 2862; November 12, 1988, 3295; November 10, 1990, 3837; November 7, 1992, Supplement, 9; November 12, 1994, Supplement, 11.

94th 1975	95th 1977	96th 1979	97th 1981	98th 1983	99th 1985	100th 1987	101st 1989	102d 1991	103d 1993	104th 1995
—	—	—	—	—	—	0	0	0	0	1
—	—	—	—	1	1	1	1	0	0	0
5	6	4	7	7	7	3	3	5	5	5
10	10	14	15	15	19	15	15	17	12	13
0	1	1	1	1	1	1	1	1	1	0
—	0	0	0	0	0	—	—	—	—	—
2	5	3	5	7	8	6	5	4	5	5
0	0	0	1	0	1	1	0	0	0	0
1	2	0	3	2	2	2	3	2	2	3
0	0	0	0	0	0	0	0	0	0	0
22	22	22	26	29	29	27	27	26	25	28
0	0	0	0	0	0	0	0	0	0	0
0	0	0	0	0	0	0	0	0	0	1
—	—	—	—	1	1	1	1	1	1	1
—	—	—	—	0	0	0	0	0	0	0
—	—	—	—	—	—	7	6	1	2	5
28	—	—	—	—	—	—	—	—	—	—
37	38	41	53	54	53	45	45	44	43	53

Table 1-14 Religious Affiliations of Representatives, 89th-104th Congresses, 1965-1995

	89th (1965)			90th (1967)			91st (1969)			92d (1971)			93d (1973)			94th (1975)			95th (1977)		
	D	R	Total	D	R	Total	D	R	Total	D	R	Total	D	R	Total	D	R	Total	D	R	Total
Catholic	81	13	94	73	22	95	72	24	96	77	24	101	69	30	99	88	22	110	95	24	119
Jewish	14	1	15	14	2	16	15	2	17	10	2	12	10	2	12	17	3	20	20	3	23
Protestant																					
Baptist	33	9	42	30	12	42	30	13	43	32	10	42	33	12	45	37	10	47	36	10	46
Episcopalian	29	25	54	25	25	50	22	27	49	27	22	49	25	25	50	29	21	50	26	22	48
Methodist	46	23	69	37	32	69	34	32	66	33	32	65	30	33	63	40	23	63	36	24	60
Presbyterian	30	26	56	27	37	64	26	38	64	26	41	67	25	35	60	25	25	50	23	22	45
All other	62	43	105	43	54	97	44	56	100	49	49	98	50	55	105	55	40	95	56	38	94
Total	295	140	435	249	184	433	243	192	435	254	180	434	242	192	434	291	144	435	292	143	435

(Table continues)

Table 1-14 (continued)

	96th (1979)			97th (1981)			99th (1985)			101st (1989)			102d (1991)			103th (1993)			104th (1995)		
	D	R	Total	D	R	Total	D	R	Total	D	R	Total	D	R	Total	D	R	Total	D	R	Total
Catholic	93	23	116	81	38	119	82	43	125	81	39	120	85	37	122	77	41	118	71	54	125
Jewish	18	5	23	21	6	27	24	6	30	26	5	31	26	6	33[a]	26	5	32[a]	20	4	25[a]
Protestant																					
Baptist	33	10	43	28	13	41	27	9	36	33	10	43	35	12	47	38	13	51	30	27	57
Episcopalian	29	22	51	25	27	52	22	22	44	22	21	43	24	17	41	18	17	35	13	21	34
Methodist	32	26	58	26	30	56	35	27	62	38	25	63	38	24	62	31	23	54	21	29	50
Presbyterian	25	27	52	18	28	46	22	25	47	16	26	42	15	27	42	20	26	46	17	30	47
All other	47	45	92	44	50	94	41	50	91	44	49	93	44	44	88	49	50	99	32	65	97
Total	277	158	435	243	192	435	253	182	435	260	175	435	267	167	435[a]	258	176	435[a]	204	230	435[a]

Note: D indicates Democrats; R indicates Republicans.

[a] Totals include Bernard Sanders (I-Vt.).

Sources: Congressional Quarterly Almanac, various years; *Congressional Quarterly Weekly Report,* November 10, 1984, 2922; November 12, 1988, 3295; November 10, 1990, 3837; November 7, 1992, Supplement, 9; November 12, 1994, Supplement, 11.

Table 1-15 Religious Affiliations of Senators, 89th-104th Congresses, 1965-1995

	89th (1965)			90th (1967)			91st (1969)			92d (1971)			93d (1973)			94th (1975)			95th (1977)		
	D	R	Total	D	R	Total	D	R	Total	D	R	Total	D	R	Total	D	R	Total	D	R	Total
Catholic	12	2	14	11	2	13	10	3	13	9	3	12	10	4	14	11	4	15	10	3	13
Jewish	1	1	2	1	1	2	1	1	2	1	1	2	1	1	2	2	1	3	4	1	5
Protestant																					
Baptist	9	3	12	7	4	11	6	3	9	5	3	8	5	3	8	6	3	9	6	3	9
Episcopalian	8	7	15	8	7	15	5	10	15	4	13	17	6	11	17	6	9	15	6	11	17
Methodist	15	7	22	15	8	23	14	8	22	13	7	20	13	5	18	11	5	16	13	7	20
Presbyterian	8	3	11	8	4	12	8	5	13	10	6	16	8	6	14	10	7	17	9	5	14
All other	15	9	24	14	10	24	14	12	26	13	12	25	15	12	27	15	9	24	14	8	22
Total	68	32	100	64	36	100	58	42	100	55	45	100	58	42	100	61	38	99	62	38	100

(Table continues)

Table 1-15 (continued)

	96th (1979)			97th (1981)			99th (1985)			101st (1989)			102d (1991)			103th (1993)			104th (1995)		
	D	R	Total	D	R	Total	D	R	Total	D	R	Total	D	R	Total	D	R	Total	D	R	Total
Catholic	9	4	13	9	8	17	11	8	19	12	7	19	12	8	20	15	8	23	12	8	20
Jewish	5	2	7	3	3	6	4	4	8	5	3	8	6	2	8	9	1	10	8	1	9
Protestant																					
Baptist	6	5	11	3	6	9	4	7	11	4	8	12	4	8	12	4	7	11	3	7	10
Episcopalian	5	12	17	5	15	20	4	17	21	7	13	20	6	12	18	4	11	15	4	10	14
Methodist	13	6	19	9	9	18	9	7	16	9	4	13	9	4	13	7	5	12	5	6	11
Presbyterian	10	2	12	8	2	10	8	1	9	7	2	9	7	2	9	5	3	8	4	4	8
All other	11	10	21	10	10	20	7	9	16	11	8	19	11	9	20	13	8	21	11	17	28
Total	59	41	100	47	53	100	47	53	100	55	45	100	55	45	100	57	43	100	47	53	100

Note: D indicates Democrats; R indicates Republicans.

Sources: Congressional Quarterly Almanac, various years; *Congressional Quarterly Weekly Report,* November 10, 1984, 2922; November 12, 1988, 3295; November 10, 1990, 3837; November 7, 1992, Supplement, 9; November 12, 1994, Supplement, 11.

Table 1-16   Blacks in Congress, 41st-104th Congresses, 1869-1995

Congress	House D	House R	Senate D	Senate R	Congress	House D	House R	Senate D	Senate R
41st (1869)	—	2	—	1	80th (1947)	2	—	—	—
42d (1871)	—	5	—	—	81st (1949)	2	—	—	—
43d (1873)	—	7	—	—	82d (1951)	2	—	—	—
44th (1875)	—	7	—	1	83d (1953)	2	—	—	—
45th (1877)	—	3	—	1	84th (1955)	3	—	—	—
46th (1879)	—	—	—	1	85th (1957)	3	—	—	—
47th (1881)	—	2	—	—	86th (1959)	3	—	—	—
48th (1883)	—	2	—	—	87th (1961)	3	—	—	—
49th (1885)	—	2	—	—	88th (1963)	4	—	—	—
50th (1887)	—	—	—	—	89th (1965)	5	—	—	—
51st (1889)	—	3	—	—	90th (1967)	5	—	—	1
52d (1891)	—	1	—	—	91st (1969)	9	—	—	1
53d (1893)	—	1	—	—	92d (1971)	13	—	—	1
54th (1895)	—	1	—	—	93d (1973)	16	—	—	1
55th (1897)	—	1	—	—	94th (1975)	16	—	—	1
56th (1899)[a]	—	1	—	—	95th (1977)	15	—	—	1
71st (1929)	—	1	—	—	96th (1979)	15	—	—	—
72d (1931)	—	1	—	—	97th (1981)	17	—	—	—
73d (1933)	—	1	—	—	98th (1983)	20	—	—	—
74th (1935)	1	—	—	—	99th (1985)	20	—	—	—
75th (1937)	1	—	—	—	100th (1987)	22	—	—	—
76th (1939)	1	—	—	—	101st (1989)	23	—	—	—
77th (1941)	1	—	—	—	102d (1991)	25	1	—	—
78th (1943)	1	—	—	—	103d (1993)	38	1	1	—
79th (1945)	2	—	—	—	104th (1995)	37	2	1	—

Note: Does not include Eleanor Holmes Norton, a nonvoting delegate who represents Washington, D.C.

[a] After the Fifty-sixth Congress, there were no black members in either the House or Senate until the Seventy-first Congress.

Sources: Black Americans in Congress, 1870-1977, H.Doc. 95-258, 95th Cong., 1st sess., 1977; *Congressional Quarterly Almanac,* various years; *Congressional Quarterly Weekly Report,* November 10, 1984, 2921; November 8, 1986, 2863; November 12, 1988, 3294; November 10, 1990, 3836; November 7, 1992, Supplement, 8; November 12, 1994, Supplement, 10.

Table 1-17   Women in Congress, 65th-104th Congresses, 1917-1995

Congress	House D	House R	Senate D	Senate R	Congress	House D	House R	Senate D	Senate R
65th (1917)	—	1	—	—	85th (1957)	9	6	—	1
66th (1919)	—	—	—	—	86th (1959)	9	8	—	1
67th (1921)	—	2	—	1	87th (1961)	11	7	1	1
68th (1923)	—	1	—	—	88th (1963)	6	6	1	1
69th (1925)	1	2	—	—	89th (1965)	7	4	1	1
70th (1927)	2	3	—	—	90th (1967)	5	5	—	1
71st (1929)	4	5	—	—	91st (1969)	6	4	—	1
72d (1931)	4	3	1	—	92d (1971)	10	3	—	1
73d (1933)	4	3	1	—	93d (1973)	14	2	1	—
74th (1935)	4	2	2	—	94th (1975)	14	5	—	—
75th (1937)	4	1	2	—	95th (1977)	13	5	—	—
76th (1939)	4	4	1	—	96th (1979)	11	5	1	1
77th (1941)	4	5	1	—	97th (1981)	10	9	—	2
78th (1943)	2	6	1	—	98th (1983)	13	9	—	2
79th (1945)	6	5	—	—	99th (1985)	13	9	—	2
80th (1947)	3	4	—	1	100th (1987)	12[a]	11	1	1
81st (1949)	5	4	—	1	101st (1989)	14	11	1	1
82d (1951)	4	6	—	1	102d (1991)	19	9	1	1
83d (1953)	5	7	—	1	103d (1993)	36	12	5	1
84th (1955)	10	7	—	1	104th (1995)	31	17	5	3

Note: Includes only women who were sworn in as members and served more than one day.

[a] Includes the late Sala Burton, who died after being sworn into the 100th Congress, and who was replaced by another Democratic woman, Nancy Pelosi.

Sources: Women in Congress, H. Rept. 94-1732, 94th Cong., 2d sess., 1976; *Congressional Quarterly Almanac,* various years; *Congressional Quarterly Weekly Report,* November 10, 1984, 2921; November 8, 1986, 2863; November 12, 1988, 3294; November 10, 1990, 3836; November 7, 1992, Supplement, 8; November 12, 1994, Supplement, 10.

Table 1-18 Political Parties of Senators and Representatives, 34th-104th Congresses, 1855-1995

Congress		Senate					House of Representatives				
		Number of senators	Demo-crats	Repub-licans	Other parties	Vacant	Number of repre-sentatives	Demo-crats	Repub-licans	Other parties	Vacant
34th	(1855-1857)	62	42	15	5	—	234	83	108	43	—
35th	(1857-1859)	64	39	20	5	—	237	131	92	14	—
36th	(1859-1861)	66	38	26	2	—	237	101	113	23	—
37th	(1861-1863)	50	11	31	7	1	178	42	106	28	2
38th	(1863-1865)	51	12	39	—	—	183	80	103	—	—
39th	(1865-1867)	52	10	42	—	—	191	46	145	—	—
40th	(1867-1869)	53	11	42	—	2	193	49	143	—	1
41st	(1869-1871)	74	11	61	—	—	243	73	170	—	—
42d	(1871-1873)	74	17	57	—	1	243	104	139	—	2
43d	(1873-1875)	74	19	54	—	1	293	88	203	3	2
44th	(1875-1877)	76	29	46	—	—	293	181	107	—	—
45th	(1877-1879)	76	36	39	1	—	293	156	137	14	1
46th	(1879-1881)	76	43	33	—	—	293	150	128	11	—
47th	(1881-1883)	76	37	37	2	—	293	130	152	6	—
48th	(1883-1885)	76	36	40	—	—	325	200	119	2	1
49th	(1885-1887)	76	34	41	—	1	325	182	140	4	—
50th	(1887-1889)	76	37	39	—	—	325	170	151	1	—
51st	(1889-1891)	84	37	47	—	—	330	156	173	14	—
52d	(1891-1893)	88	39	47	2	—	333	231	88	10	—
53d	(1893-1895)	88	44	38	3	3	356	220	126	7	—
54th	(1895-1897)	88	39	44	5	—	357	104	246	16	1
55th	(1897-1899)	90	34	46	10	—	357	134	206	9	—
56th	(1899-1901)	90	26	53	11	—	357	163	185	5	—
57th	(1901-1903)	90	29	56	3	2	357	153	198	—	1
58th	(1903-1905)	90	32	58	—	—	386	178	207	—	1
59th	(1905-1907)	90	32	58	—	—	386	136	250	—	1

60th	(1907-1909)	92	29	61	—	2	386	164	222	—	—
61st	(1909-1911)	92	32	59	—	1	391	172	219	—	—
62d	(1911-1913)	92	42	49	1	1	391	228	162	1	—
63d	(1913-1915)	96	51	44	1	—	435	290	127	18	3
64th	(1915-1917)	96	56	39	1	—	435	231	193	8	—
65th	(1917-1919)	96	53	42	1	—	435	210[a]	216	9	—
66th	(1919-1921)	96	47	48	1	—	435	191	237	7	—
67th	(1921-1923)	96	37	59	—	—	435	132	300	1	2
68th	(1923-1925)	96	43	51	2	—	435	207	225	3	—
69th	(1925-1927)	96	40	54	1	1	435	183	247	5	—
70th	(1927-1929)	96	47	48	1	—	435	195	237	3	—
71st	(1929-1931)	96	39	56	1	—	435	163	267	1	4
72d	(1931-1933)	96	47	48	1	—	435	216[b]	218	1	—
73d	(1933-1935)	96	59	36	1	—	435	313	117	5	—
74th	(1935-1937)	96	69	25	2	—	435	322	103	10	—
75th	(1937-1939)	96	75	17	4	—	435	333	89	13	—
76th	(1939-1941)	96	69	23	4	—	435	262	169	4	—
77th	(1941-1943)	96	66	28	2	—	435	267	162	6	—
78th	(1943-1945)	96	57	38	1	—	435	222	209	4	—
79th	(1945-1947)	96	57	38	1	—	435	243	190	2	—
80th	(1947-1949)	96	45	51	—	—	435	188	246	1	—
81st	(1949-1951)	96	54	42	1	—	435	263	171	1	—
82d	(1951-1953)	96	48	47	2	—	435	234	199	2	—
83d	(1953-1955)	96	46	48	1	—	435	213	221	1	—
84th	(1955-1957)	96	48	47	1	—	435	232	203	—	—
85th	(1957-1959)	96	49	47	—	—	435	234	201	—	—
86th	(1959-1961)	98	64	34	—	—	436[c]	283	153	—	—
87th	(1961-1963)	100	64	36	—	—	437[d]	262	175	—	1
88th	(1963-1965)	100	67	33	—	—	435	258	176	1	—
89th	(1965-1967)	100	68	32	—	—	435	295	140	—	—
90th	(1967-1969)	100	64	36	—	—	435	248	187	—	—

(Table continues)

41

Table 1-18 (continued)

Congress		Senate					House of Representatives				
		Number of senators	Demo-crats	Repub-licans	Other parties	Vacant	Number of repre-sentatives	Demo-crats	Repub-licans	Other parties	Vacant
91st	(1969-1971)	100	58	42	—	—	435	243	192	—	—
92d	(1971-1973)	100	54	44	2	—	435	255	180	—	—
93d	(1973-1975)	100	56	42	2	—	435	242	192	1	—
94th	(1975-1977)	100	61	37	2	—	435	291	144	—	—
95th	(1977-1979)	100	61	38	1	—	435	292	143	—	—
96th	(1979-1981)	100	58	41	1	—	435	277	158	—	—
97th	(1981-1983)	100	46	53	1	—	435	243	192	—	—
98th	(1983-1985)	100	46	54	—	—	435	268	167	—	—
99th	(1985-1987)	100	47	53	—	—	435	253	182	—	—
100th	(1987-1989)	100	55e	45	—	—	435	258	177f	—	—
101st	(1989-1991)	100	55	45	—	—	435	260	175	—	—
102d	(1991-1993)	100	56	44	—	—	435	267	167	1	—
103d	(1993-1995)	100	57	43	—	—	435	258	176	1	—
104th	(1995-1997)	100	47g	53	—	—	435	204	230	1	—

Note: All figures reflect immediate election results.

a Democrats organized House with help of other parties.

b Democrats organized House because of Republican deaths.

c Proclamation declaring Alaska a state issued January 3, 1959.

d Proclamation declaring Hawaii a state issued August 21, 1959.

e Includes the late Sen. Edward Zorinsky (D-Nev.) who was replaced by Sen. David Karnes, a Republican, thus changing the ratio when he was sworn in on March 11, 1987, to 54 Democrats and 46 Republicans.

f Includes the late Stewart McKinney (R-Conn.).

g Sen. Ben Nighthorse Campbell (Colo.) switched from the Democratic to Republican Party March 3, 1995, making the ratio 46-54.

Sources: Statistics of the Presidential and Congressional Elections of November 4, 1980, compiled from official sources by Thomas E. Ladd, under direction of Edmund L. Henshaw, Jr., clerk of the House of Representatives (Washington, D.C., 1981); *Congressional Directory* (1983, 1985); *Congressional Quarterly Weekly Report,* November 8, 1986, 2812, 2839, 2843, 2856-2857; November 22, 1986; March 14, 1987, 483; November 12, 1988; November 10, 1990; November 7, 1992; November 12, 1994.

Elections 2

For the members of the House and Senate, there are no more vital statistics than those on congressional elections. Whatever their personal goals within Congress, members must first win reelection. Yet, as the dramatic change in party control of the Senate in the 1980 elections and both chambers in the 1994 elections made clear, individual electoral success is not enough—the fate of party colleagues is extraordinarily important in shaping the internal character of Congress and therefore the ability of individual members to accomplish their legislative and political goals.

The data in Table 2-1 document the steady decline in turnout in presidential and congressional elections after 1960, reaching a modern-day low for presidential elections in 1988 and for congressional elections in 1990. That trend was reversed in 1992, when a five percentage point jump in turnout brought it back to the 1972 level. Turnout in subsequent midterm elections also registered a modest increase.

Table 2-2 relates the party's popular vote to the percentage of seats in the House of Representatives actually won over the past five decades. The long-term Democratic control of Congress is evident in this table, although Democratic support appears slightly less robust when looking at the national popular vote for the parties rather than the seats won. In the mid-1960s and again in 1980, the Republicans came within striking distance of the Democrats in national popular vote; yet they never won more than 44 percent of the seats in those years. This malapportionment, in which the majority party enjoys seat margins much more favorable than its vote margins—shown clearly by the figures in the last column of Table 2-2—is common to electoral systems with single-member districts. A gain of a certain percentage in a party's popular vote usually allows it to pick up two or three times that percentage in seats. 43

Republican successes in the 1980 House elections cut the Democratic majority party seat bonus to half what it had been in 1976 and 1978. In 1982 an impressive effort by the national Republican Party held the Democratic seat pick-up to twenty-six (or 5.9 percent) in spite of a 5.2 percent increase in votes. In 1984, however, the Republicans failed to convert a sizable vote gain into seats, and in 1988 they actually lost seats while gaining votes, a malady typical of minority parties in this form of electoral system. In 1990 the Democrats managed to pick up a few seats without winning any additional popular votes.

In 1992 Republicans made gains in both the percentage of major party vote and in the number of seats won over their 1990 margins. Democrats, on the other hand, drew their lowest share of the aggregate nationwide vote since 1980. These numbers provided only a modest foreshadowing of what was to come in 1994. The Republican increase in votes and seats was the most sizable gain by either party since 1948. The Republican sweep almost eliminated the Democratic seat bonus, producing for the first time in four decades a rough parity between both parties' votes and seats.

Net seats picked up by each party as a result of House and Senate general and special elections are shown in Table 2-3. The election of 1958 was especially important to Senate Democrats in maintaining their majority during the subsequent two decades, a majority that ended abruptly with the surprising pickup of twelve seats by the Republicans in the 1980 elections. The Republican majority proved much less durable, ending after only six years with the Democratic sweep of the 1986 Senate elections. House Democrats, however, saw their strength wax and wane in pairs of elections until the Watergate year of 1974, which gave them a margin sufficient to protect their majority in the face of Republican gains in 1978 and 1980. The 1992 election marked the first net gain by House Republicans since 1984. After displaying the potential for substantial gains after the 1993 special elections, Republicans shocked the political community by gaining fifty-two House and eight Senate seats in the 1994 general election. This was the largest gain in House seats by either party since the Democrats gained seventy-five seats in 1948, and it ended a forty-year reign by the Democrats.

Table 2-4 presents the number of seats lost or gained by the president's party in midterm elections, data that have long fascinated analysts of U.S. politics. In every midterm election but one since the Civil War, the party of the president has lost ground in the House of Representatives. The exception was 1934, which signaled the last major realignment in the party system. The number of seats changing party hands has varied widely over time, but in recent midterms prior to 1994, a trend of smaller losses had been established. In the previous five midterm elections occurring in the first term of a president, the average loss was only thirteen seats. Then in 1994 this pattern ended with a presidential party loss of fifty-two seats in the House, the greatest midterm loss in more than five decades.

The 1994 elections were even more surprising to analysts because the magnitude of the loss is generally determined by the previous presidential election: smaller numbers of candidates elected on the coattails of the president result in more modest midterm losses. But in 1992, the Democrats had actually lost ten seats—making their huge loss in 1994 a much bigger shock.

The midterm pattern of Senate elections is different from that of the House, chiefly because only a third of the Senate is up for reelection at a time, with tremendous variation in the proportion of those seats held by the president's party. In the thirty-three midterm elections since the Civil War, the president's party gained seats in ten of them.

Table 2-5 and Figure 2-1 demonstrate that although more seats change party control than the net shifts in Table 2-3 suggest, the stabilizing impact of House elections remains impressive: in no election since 1954 have more than 14 percent of the 435 seats changed party hands. Nevertheless, the last three elections reflect an increased trend in seats switching party control. The election of 1988 had fewer seats (nine) change hands than at any time in American history. But in 1990, twenty-one seats switched party control and in 1992 forty-three—roughly 10 percent of the House membership. The 1994 elections had an even larger shift, sixty seats or 13.8 percent of the House. Though this percentage is still small, it is the largest shift recorded in this table— even greater than the watershed year of 1974. Further, much of this turnover was inspired by a growing public dissatisfaction with government, the abatement of which remains uncertain for 1996.

The numbers in this table also confirm that the 1994 elections were not a vote against the status quo, regardless of party. It was aimed directly at the Democrats. Fifty-six of the sixty seats that switched party hands went from Democratic to Republican control; not one Republican-held incumbent seat went Democratic.

In contrast to the small percentage of change in the House, as many as one-third of the Senate seats up for election in any one year have changed party control. However, change is not always the rule; in 1992 a mere four seats changed hands (see Table 2-6 and Figure 2-2). In addition, despite the impressive advantages of incumbency, parties have, in most cases, picked up more of their gains not in open seats but in races against incumbents. Yet again, 1994 proved to be unconventional with six open seats switching party control—all from Democratic to Republican.

Finally, one is struck again by the importance of particular elections for long-term party control. In 1958 for the Senate and in 1974 for the

House, the Democrats posted impressive gains that were maintained in subsequent elections. We must wait and see whether 1994 will lead to longterm Republican control in either one or both of the chambers.

Tables 2-7 and 2-8 chronicle the fate of House and Senate incumbents. In most years of the modern Congress, the bulk of House incumbents who sought reelection usually succeeded. Even landslides in the general election ordinarily led to the defeat of only 10 percent of the incumbents seeking reelection. A substantial increase in retirements in the 1970s was largely responsible for the relatively high turnover during that period. As presented in Table 2-7, reelection rates in 1986 and 1988 were extraordinarily high—only six incumbents defeated in each general election—generating outcries from groups who believed that campaigns and election rules unfairly favored incumbents. But the elections of 1992 and 1994 have shown a reversed trend: more and more incumbents are being voted out of office by their constituents.

Election year 1992 saw the largest number of voluntary retirements (sixty-five) from the House in the post-war era. And another forty-three incumbents were defeated (nineteen in primaries, the highest in more than fifty years), producing the most turnover in a single election since 1948. The 1994 elections, though not having as many retirements or primary defeats as in 1992, had the most members defeated in the general elections since the 1974 post-Watergate upsurge.

Senate incumbents usually have not fared as well as their House counterparts because the level of competition in statewide races is generally higher. That pattern held true in 1992, when 82.1 percent of those senators seeking reelection were reelected, compared with 88.3 percent of House members. The contrast was stark in 1986: 7 of 28 senators seeking reelection were defeated in the general election, while only 6 of 391 representatives met the same fate. The 1994 elections upset this trend as Senate incumbents fared better than their House counterparts. Senators had a reelection rate of 92.3 percent.

Still, both renomination and reelection have proven to be more difficult hurdles for senators than for representatives. Table 2-9 provides a party breakdown of those House and Senate retirements.

Tables 2-10 and 2-11 examine the number of terms served by incumbents defeated in primary and general elections of the House and Senate, respectively. Table 2-10 shows that in the early years most defeated House incumbents were in their first term. Fifty-four percent of those defeated in 1946, 55 percent of those defeated in 1948, and 60 percent of those defeated in 1966 were in their first terms. Then the pattern changed, and from 1974 through 1992 the number of years members had served was spread much more evenly, especially within the first to fourth terms. In 1992 the largest number of defeated incumbents were in their fifth term. But in 1994 voters again ousted more first termers, seventeen of the thirty-eight defeated incumbents. While a handful of highly visible, senior members lost in 1994, including Dan Rostenkowski and Jack Brooks, the number of "old bulls" defeated was actually far less than in 1992.

Table 2-11 shows a slightly different pattern in the Senate. While the total number of defeated incumbents varied over time, the members were consistently in their first or second terms. Of the thirteen incumbents who lost in 1946, more than 50 percent (seven) were in their first term. Nine of the ten defeated incumbents in 1948 were first-termers, as were six of the ten in 1958 and 1978. The defeated incumbents in 1980 fell across a wider range of service years—five in their first term and three in their third and fourth terms. But then in 1992 all five of the defeated were in their first or second term.

In terms of the margin of victory rather than the rate of reelection, some change has occurred in the electoral standing of House and Senate incumbents. The proportion of House incumbents who have won reelection with at least 60 percent of the major party vote increased from about three-fifths in the 1950s and early 1960s to three-fourths in the 1970s, and to almost nine-tenths in the late 1980s (see Table 2-12). This trend began to change in 1990, however, when the percentage of incumbents reelected with at least 60 percent of the major party vote dropped from 88.5 to 76.4. The 1992 elections saw even fewer incumbents, 65.6 percent reelected by a so-called "safe" margin. And in 1994 that number dropped another percentage point to 64.5 percent, the lowest percentage since 1964. Most experts attribute the increased competitiveness to a combination of factors including redistricting, anti-incumbent sentiment, fewer uncontested seats, and the growing number of voters who call themselves Independent.[1]

Table 2-13 demonstrates fluctuation in the Senate margins of victory as well, highlighting the different patterns in the South and the North. From the 1940s through the mid 1970s, the percentage of incumbents in the South with 60 percent or more of the major party vote fell from 100 to 57.1 percent while those in the rest of the country increased about fifteen percentage points. From 1980-1990 there was a significant increase nationwide. Then in 1992 and 1994 the percentage of those within the "safe margin" stabilized in the South but sharply declined in the rest of the country, back to the levels of the 1960s.

Viewed from the perspective of congressional careers, elections still pose a significant challenge to incumbents. Table 2-14 reveals that more than two-thirds of the senators and over half of the representatives serving in the 104th Congress received less than 55 percent of the vote, and even more of them less than 60 percent, in at least one election. Moreover, when the conditions of initial election to Congress are examined (Table 2-15), it is apparent that many representatives and a majority of senators have themselves either defeated incumbents or replaced retiring incumbents of the other party.

Tables 2-16 and 2-17 point to the substantial divergence between presidential and congressional voting. Since 1956, when the Democrats in the House and Senate withstood Dwight D. Eisenhower's sweeping victory in the presidential election, more than one-fourth of all congressional districts have supported a presidential candidate of one party and a House candidate of the other (Table 2-16). The proportion of districts with split results reached a peak in 1972 when Richard Nixon received 60.8 percent of the presidential vote while his party's candidates won only 46.4 percent of the congressional vote leaving the Democrats with a solid majority in the House. In 1992 the percentage of districts with split ticket results fell to its lowest level since 1952.

A president's ability to claim long coattails depends on both the size of his victory and the number of seats his party gains in Congress. Presidents John F. Kennedy and Jimmy Carter lost on both counts: the Republicans actually gained twenty-two House seats in 1960 and held their ground in 1976, while both victorious Democratic presidents ran ahead of Democratic representatives in only twenty-two districts (Table 2-17). In 1972 Richard Nixon ran ahead of a majority of the Republicans elected to the House, but this was small consolation in view of his failure to pull a sizable bloc of new Republicans into the House. In contrast, Lyndon Johnson could claim credit for dramatically increasing his party's margin in Congress. His reward was the Great Society legislation of 1965 and 1966.

In 1980 Ronald Reagan's presidential victory was accompanied by impressive Republican gains in the House, but fell short of the number needed to take control. Moreover, Reagan ran behind most of his party colleagues in the House. The more important manifestation of a Reagan tide was thought to be in the Senate, where a total of 50,000 votes accounted for seven Republican victories and, as a consequence, majority status. Reagan's 1984 landslide in the presidential sweepstakes, however, left barely a trace in the Senate and House elections. In 1988 George Bush saw his party lose seats in the House, underscoring the absence of presidential coattails. The Democrats suffered a similar fate in 1992, losing seats in the House while winning back the presidency after twelve years of Republican rule.

The past two decades have witnessed a substantial increase in the impact of local forces in congressional elections. Although the United States has never had a uniform swing across constituencies as Britain has, the figures in Table 2-18 illustrate how difficult it is to make national interpretations of the results of U.S. congressional elections. Election returns at the district level increasingly diverge from the national returns. These figures suggest an electoral base for the increasingly individualized behavior in the House of Representatives. The range in the swing across districts has increased markedly since the 1950s, and the variance, which measures the extent to which changes in local returns differ from the change in national returns, has more than doubled. Even the dramatic 1994 midterm elections, widely considered the most nationalized elections in decades, featured divergent swings across districts.

Table 2-19 presents data that confirm the basis in individual voting behavior for many of the electoral patterns reported in this chapter. The decline in the proportion of party-line voters in House elections since the 1960s is consistent with the view that voting is increasingly candidate centered. Yet the resurgence of party-line voting in the 1982 and 1994 midterm elections suggests that the electorate retains the capacity to respond to national political events in highly partisan ways.

NOTE

1. The growing number of and support for third party candidates has led to a gap between the number of members who captured 60 percent of the major party vote (recorded in Table 2-12) and 60 percent of the total vote. The 1994 difference was just under two percentage points.

Table 2-1   Turnout in Presidential and House Elections, 1930-1994
(percentage of voting age population)

Year	Presidential elections	House elections
1930	—	33.7
1932	52.4	49.7
1934	—	41.4
1936	56.9	53.5
1938	—	44.0
1940	58.9	55.4
1942	.—	32.5
1944	56.0	52.7
1946	—	37.1
1948	51.1	48.1
1950	—	41.1
1952	61.6	57.6
1954	—	41.7
1956	59.3	55.9
1958	—	43.0
1960	62.6	58.5
1962	—	45.4
1964	61.9	57.8
1966	—	45.4
1968	60.9	55.1
1970	—	43.5
1972	55.4	50.9
1974	—	36.1
1976	54.4	49.5
1978	—	35.1
1980	53.4	48.1
1982	—	37.7
1984	53.3	47.4
1986	—	33.4
1988	50.1	44.7
1990	—	33.0
1992	55.2	50.8
1994	—	36.0

Sources: U.S. Bureau of the Census, *Statistical Abstract of the United States* (Washington, D.C.: U.S. Government Printing Office, 1930 through 1976); U.S. Bureau of the Census, *Current Population Reports*, ser. P-25, no. 948 (Washington, D.C.: U.S. Government Printing Office); Clerk of the House of Representatives, *Statistics of the Presidential and Congressional Elections of November 6, 1984* (Washington, D.C.: U.S. Government Printing Office, 1985); *Congressional Quarterly Weekly Report*, March 31, 1979, 571; April 25, 1981, 716; February 17, 1983, 389; March 14, 1987, 485; January 21, 1989, 135; February 23, 1991, 484; April 17, 1993, 965-968; April 15, 1995, 1078.

Table 2-2 Popular Vote and House Seats Won by Party, 1946-1994

	Democratic candidates		Republican candidates		Change from last election[a]		Difference between Democratic percentage of seats and votes won
Year	Percentage of all votes[b]	Percentage of seats won	Percentage of all votes[b]	Percentage of seats won	Percentage of major party votes	Percentage of seats won	
1946	44.3	43.3	53.5	56.7	6.4R	12.8R	−1.0
1948	51.6	60.6	45.4	39.4	7.9D	17.3D	9.0
1950	48.9	54.0	48.9	46.0	3.2R	6.6R	5.1
1952	49.2	49.1	49.3	50.9	0.1R	4.9R	−0.1
1954	52.1	53.3	47.0	46.7	2.6D	4.2D	1.2
1956	50.7	53.8	48.7	46.2	1.5R	0.5D	3.1
1958	55.5	64.9	43.6	35.1	5.0D	11.1D	9.4
1960	54.4	60.0	44.8	40.0	1.2R	4.9R	5.6
1962	52.1	59.4	47.1	40.6	2.3R	0.6R	7.3
1964	56.9	67.8	42.4	32.2	4.8D	8.4D	10.9
1966	50.5	57.0	48.0	43.0	6.0R	10.8R	6.5
1968	50.0	55.9	48.2	44.1	0.3R	1.1R	5.9
1970	53.0	58.6	44.5	41.4	3.4D	2.7D	5.6
1972	51.7	55.8	46.4	44.2	1.7R	2.8R	4.1
1974	57.1	66.9	40.5	33.1	5.8D	11.1D	9.8
1976	56.2	67.1	42.1	32.9	1.3R	0.2D	10.9

(Table continues)

Table 2-2 (continued)

Year	Democratic candidates		Republican candidates		Change from last election[a]		Difference between Democratic percentage of seats and votes won
	Percentage of all votes[b]	Percentage of seats won	Percentage of all votes[b]	Percentage of seats won	Percentage of major party votes	Percentage of seats won	
1978	53.4	63.7	44.7	36.3	2.8R	3.4R	10.3
1980	50.4	55.9	48.0	44.1	3.2R	7.8R	5.5
1982	55.2	61.8	43.3	38.2	5.2D	5.9D	6.6
1984	52.1	58.2	47.0	41.8	4.1R	3.6R	6.1
1986	54.5	59.3	44.6	40.7	2.4D	1.2D	4.8
1988	53.3	59.8	45.5	40.2	1.1R	0.5D	6.5
1990	52.9	61.4	45.0	38.4[c]	0.1D	1.6D	8.5
1992	50.8	59.3	45.6	40.5[c]	1.4R	2.1R	8.5
1994	45.4	46.9	52.4	52.9[c]	6.3R	12.4R	1.5

[a] Data show percentage-point increase over previous election in votes or seats won by Republicans (R) or Democrats (D).

[b] Republican and Democratic percentages of all votes excludes districts in which candidates ran unopposed and no vote was recorded: for 1978, 8 districts from Arkansas, Florida, and Oklahoma; for 1980, 12 districts from Arkansas, Florida, Louisiana, and Oklahoma; for 1982, 11 districts from Florida and Louisiana; for 1984, 16 districts from Arkansas, Florida, and Louisiana; for 1986, 14 districts from Florida, Louisiana, and Oklahoma; for 1988, 16 districts from Florida and Louisiana; for 1990, 12 districts from Florida and Louisiana; for 1994, 13 districts from Florida and Louisiana.

For 1990-1994, total percentage of seats won—Democratic and Republican—does not equal one hundred due to the election of Bernard Sanders (I-Vt.).

[c] For 1990-1994, total percentage of seats won—Democratic and Republican—does not equal one hundred due to the election of Bernard Sanders (I-Vt.).

Sources: Congressional Quarterly Weekly Report, June 11, 1977, 1141; March 31, 1979, 571; April 25, 1981, 713; November 11, 1982, 2817-2825; February 19, 1983, 387; April 15, 1985, 687; March 14, 1987, 484; May 6, 1989, 1063; February 23, 1991, 487; April 17, 1993, 965-968; April 15, 1995, 1076-1079. Thomas E. Mann and Norman J. Ornstein, eds., The American Elections of 1982 (Washington, D.C.: American Enterprise Institute, 1983).

Table 2-3   Net Party Gains in House and Senate Seats, General and Special Elections, 1946-1994

Year	General elections[a]		Special elections[b]	
	House	Senate	House	Senate
1946	56R	13R	1R (8)	3R (8)
1948	75D	9D	0 (4)	0 (3)
1950	28R	5R	0 (10)	2R (6)
1952	22R	1R	2R (10)	2R (4)
1954	19D	2D	2D (8)	0 (9)
1956	2D	1D	0 (3)	2R (3)
1958	49D	15D	0 (10)	1D (4)
1960	22R	2R	1R (8)	1D (3)
1962	1R	3D	0 (12)	0 (6)
1964	37D	1D	2R (12)	0 (2)
1966	47R	4R	1D (10)	1R (3)
1968	5R	6R	1R (6)	0 (0)
1970	12D	2R	2D (14)	0 (2)
1972	12R	2D	0 (10)	0 (2)
1974	49D	4D	4D (10)	0 (0)
1976	1D	0	0 (7)	1D (1)
1978	15R	3R	4R (6)	1R (2)
1980	34R	12R	1R (7)	0 (0)
1982	26D	1R	0 (3)[c]	0 (0)
1984	14R	2D	1R (9)	1R (1)
1986	5D	8D	0 (5)[d]	1D (1)
1988	2D	0	1R (7)	0 (0)
1990	9D	1D	1D (12)[e]	0 (1)
1992	10R	0	1D (6)	2D (3)[f]
1994	52R	8R[g]	2R (7)	1R (2)

(Notes continue)

Note: D indicates Democrats; R indicates Republicans.

[a] The general election figure is the difference between the number of seats won by the party gaining seats in that election and the number of seats won by that party in the preceding general election.

[b] The special election figure is the net shift in seats held by the major parties as a result of special elections held between the two general elections. The number of special elections is given in parentheses.

[c] The voting for the House officially ended when elections were held in two Georgia districts, November 30, 1982. The balloting in the two Atlanta-area constituencies was postponed because of redistricting problems. In Indiana, Katie Hall won a special election to fill a seat vacated by the death of Rep. Adam Benjamin (D); the election was held November 2, 1982.

[d] Only four of the five House members elected in special elections actually served during the 99th Congress. The fifth, Cass Ballenger (R-N.C.), on November 4, 1986, won both the general election for the 100th Congress and the special election to serve out the remainder of the term of James Broyhill (R-N.C.), who had resigned his house seat when he was appointed to finish the term of the late Sen. James East (R-N.C.). However, since the House had adjourned the second session of the 99th Congress on October 18, 1986, Ballenger was not sworn in as a member until the 100th Congress.

[e] The total number of special elections (12) includes the special election in New Jersey's First District to fill the seat vacated by James Florio who was elected governor. The special election was held at the same time as the general election (November 6, 1990).

[f] The total number of special elections (3) includes the special election of Dianne Feinstein (D-Calif.) to fill the seat to which John Seymour was temporarily appointed. The special election was held at the same time as the general election (November 3, 1992).

[g] Sen. Richard Shelby (Ala.) switched from the Democratic to the Republican Party the day after the election, bringing the total Republican gain to nine.

Sources: Statistics of the Congressional Election of November 7, 1978 (Washington, D.C.: U.S. Government Printing Office, 1979), 45; *Congressional Quarterly Almanac*, vols. 2-40 (Washington, D.C.: Congressional Quarterly, 1946-1985); *Congressional Quarterly's Guide to U.S. Elections* (Washington, D.C.: Congressional Quarterly, 1975); *Congressional Quarterly Weekly Report*, November 8, 1986; November 12, 1988; and conversations with the Federal Election Commission. For 1992: *National Journal*, November 7, 1992, 2555; *Congressional Quarterly Almanac 1991*. For 1993-1994: *Congressional Quarterly Almanac 1993*; *Congressional Quarterly Weekly Report*, various issues, 1994. Congressional Quarterly Research Service.

Table 2-4   Losses by President's Party in Midterm Elections, 1862-1994

Year	Party holding presidency	President's party gain/loss of seats in House	President's party gain/loss of seats in Senate
1862	R	−3	8
1866	R	−2	0
1870	R	−31	−4
1874	R	−96	−8
1878	R	−9	−6
1882	R	−33	3
1886	D	−12	3
1890	R	−85	0
1894	D	−116	−5
1898	R	−21	7
1902	R	9[a]	2
1906	R	−28	3
1910	R	−57	−10
1914	D	−59	5
1918	D	−19	−6
1922	R	−75	−8
1926	R	−10	−6
1930	R	−49	−8
1934	D	9	10
1938	D	−71	−6
1942	D	−55	−9
1946	D	−45	−12
1950	D	−29	−6
1954	R	−18	−1
1958	R	−48	−13
1962	D	−4	3
1966	D	−47	−4
1970	R	−12	2
1974	R	−48	−5
1978	D	−15	−3
1982	R	−26	1
1986	R	−5	−8
1990	R	−8	−1
1994	D	−52	−8[b]

Note: Each entry is the difference between the number of seats won by the president's party in that midterm election and the number of seats won by that party in the preceding general election. Because of changes in the overall number of seats in the Senate and House, in the number of seats won by third parties, and in the number of vacancies, a Republican loss is not always matched precisely by a Democratic gain, or vice versa.

[a] Although the Republicans gained nine seats in the 1902 elections, they actually lost ground to the Democrats, who gained twenty-five seats after the increase in the overall number of representatives after the 1900 census.

[b] Sen. Richard Shelby (Ala.) switched from the Democratic to the Republican Party the day following the election for a total loss of nine seats.

Sources: Statistics of the Congressional Election of November 7, 1978, 44-45; Thomas Mann and Norman Ornstein, "The 1982 Election: What Will It Mean?" *Public Opinion,* June/July 1981, 49; *Congressional Quarterly Almanac,* vols. 10-40; *Congressional Quarterly Weekly Report,* November 8, 1986; November 10, 1990; *National Journal,* November 12, 1994.

Table 2-5   House Seats That Changed Party, 1954-1994

Year	Total changes	Incumbent defeated		Open seat	
		D→R	R→D	D→R	R→D
1954	26	3	18	2	3
1956	20	7	7	2	4
1958	50	1	35	0	14
1960	37	23	2	6	6
1962	19	9	5	2	3
1964	57	5	39	5	8
1966	47	39	1	4	3
1968	11	5	0	2	4
1970	25	2	9	6	8
1972	23	6	3	9	5
1974	55	4	36	2	13
1976	22	7	5	3	7
1978	33	14	5	8	6
1980	41	27	3	10	1
1982	31	1	22	3	5
1984	22	13	3	5	1
1986	21	1	5	7	8
1988	9	2	4	1	2
1990	21	6	9	0	6
1992	43	16	8	11	8
1994	60	34	0	22	4

Note: D indicates Democrat; R indicates Republican. This table reflects shifts in party control of seats from immediately before to immediately after the November elections. It does not include party gains resulting from the creation of new districts and does not account for situations in which two districts were reduced to one, thus forcing incumbents to run against each other.

Sources: Congressional Quarterly Almanac, vols. 10-40; *Congressional Quarterly Weekly Report,* November 10, 1984, 2900; November 8, 1986, 2844; November 12, 1988, 3270; November 10, 1990, 3801; *National Journal,* November 7, 1992, 2555; November 12, 1994, 2652.

Figure 2-1   House Seats that Changed Party, 1954–1994

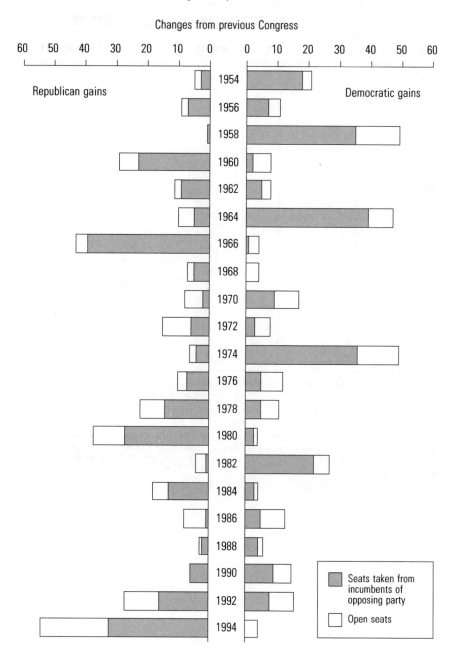

Changes from previous Congress

Source: Table 2-5.

Table 2-6   Senate Seats That Changed Party, 1954-1994

		Incumbent defeated		Open seat	
Year	Total changes	D$\gg$R	R$\gg$D	D$\gg$R	R$\gg$D
1954	8	2	4	1	1
1956	8	1	3	3	1
1958	13	0	.11	0	2
1960	2	1	0	1	0
1962	8	2	3	0	3
1964	4	1	3	0	0
1966	3	1	0	2	0
1968	9	4	0	3	2
1970	6	3	2	1	0
1972	10	1	4	3	2
1974	6	0	2	1	3
1976	14	5	4	2	3
1978	13	5	2	3	3
1980	12	9	0	3	0
1982	4	1	1	1	1
1984	4	1	2	0	1
1986	10	0	7	1	2
1988	7	1	3	2	1
1990	1	0	1	0	0
1992	4	2	2	0	0
1994	8[a]	2	0	6	0

Note: D indicates Democrat; R indicates Republican. This table reflects shifts in party control of seats from immediately before to immediately after the November election.

[a] Sen. Richard Shelby (Ala.) switched from the Democratic to the Republican Party the day after the election, bringing the total change to nine.

Sources: Congressional Quarterly Almanac, vols. 10-40; *National Journal,* November 10, 1984, 2137, 2147; *Congressional Quarterly Weekly Report,* November 8, 1986, 2813; November 12, 1988, 3264; November 10, 1990, 3825; *National Journal,* November 7, 1992, 2555; November 12, 1994, 2635.

Figure 2-2   Senate Seats that Changed Party, 1954–1994

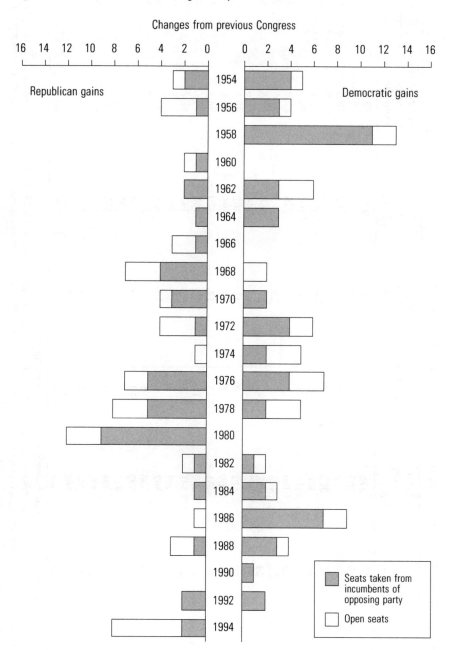

Table 2-7   House Incumbents Retired, Defeated, or Reelected, 1946-1994

Year	Retired[a]	Total seeking reelection	Defeated in primaries	Defeated in general election	Total reelected	Percentage of those seeking reelection	Reelected as percentage of House membership
1946	32	398	18	52	328	82.4	75.4
1948	29	400	15	68	317	79.3	72.9
1950	29	400	6	32	362	90.5	83.2
1952	42	389	9	26	354	91.0	81.4
1954	24	407	6	22	379	93.1	87.1
1956	21	411	6	16	389	94.6	89.4
1958	33	396	3	37	356	89.9	81.8
1960	26	405	5	25	375	92.6	86.2
1962	24	402	12	22	368	91.5	84.6
1964	33	397	8	45	344	86.6	79.1
1966	22	411	8	41	362	88.1	83.2
1968	23	409	4	9	396	96.8	91.0
1970	29	401	10	12	379	94.5	87.1
1972	40	390	12	13	365	93.6	83.9
1974	43	391	8	40	343	87.7	78.9
1976	47	384	3	13	368	95.8	84.6
1978	49	382	5	19	358	93.7	82.3
1980	34	398	6	31	361	90.7	83.0
1982	40	393	10	29	354	90.1	81.4
1984	22	411	3	16	392	95.4	90.1
1986	40	394	3	6	385	97.7	88.5
1988	23	409	1	6	402	98.3	92.4
1990	27	406	1	15	390	96.0	89.7
1992	65	368	19	24	325	88.3	74.7
1994	48	387	4	34	349	90.2	80.0

[a] Does not include persons who died or resigned before the election.

Sources: Congressional Quarterly Weekly Report, January 12, 1980, 81; April 5, 1980, 908; November 8, 1980, 3320-3321; November 10, 1984, 2900; October 11, 1986, 2398; November 8, 1986, 2844; November 12, 1988, 3270; November 7, 1992, 3579; National Journal, November 6, 1982, 1881; November 10, 1984, 2147; November 10, 1990, 2719; November 12, 1994, 2650-2651.

Table 2-8   Senate Incumbents Retired, Defeated, or Reelected,
            1946-1994

Year	Retired[a]	Total seeking reelection	Defeated in primaries	Defeated in general election	Total reelected	Reelected as percentage of those seeking reelection
1946	9	30	6	7	17	56.7
1948	8	25	2	8	15	60.0
1950	4	32	5	5	22	68.8
1952	4	31	2	9	20	64.5
1954	6	32	2	6	24	75.0
1956	6	29	0	4	25	86.2
1958	6	28	0	10	18	64.3
1960	5	29	0	1	28	96.6
1962	4	35	1	5	29	82.9
1964	2	33	1	4	28	84.8
1966	3	32	3	1	28	87.5
1968	6	28	4	4	20	71.4
1970	4	31	1	6	24	77.4
1972	6	27	2	5	20	74.1
1974	7	27	2	2	23	85.2
1976	8	25	0	9	16	64.0
1978	10	25	3	7	15	60.0
1980	5	29	4	9	16	55.2
1982	3	30	0	2	28	93.3
1984	4	29	0	3	26	89.6
1986	6	28	0	7	21	75.0
1988	6	27	0	4	23	85.2
1990	3	32	0	1	31	96.9
1992	7	28	1	4	23	82.1
1994	9	26	0	2	24	92.3

[a] Does not include persons who died or resigned before the election.

Sources: Congressional Quarterly Weekly Report, January 12, 1980, 81; April 5, 1980, 908; November 8, 1980, 3302; November 6, 1982, 2791; November 10, 1984, 2905; October 11, 1986, 2398; November 8, 1986, 2813; November 12, 1988; November 10, 1990; November 7, 1992, 3557; *National Journal,* November 12, 1994.

Table 2-9   House and Senate Retirements by Party, 1930-1994

Year	House		Senate	
	D	R	D	R
1930	8	15	2	5
1932	16	23	1	1
1934	29	9	3	1
1936	29	3	4	2
1938	21	5	3	1
1940	16	6	1	2
1942	20	12	0	0
1944	17	5	3	2
1946	17	15	4	3
1948	17	12	3	4
1950	12	17	3	1
1952	25	17	2	1
1954	11	13	1	1
1956	7	13	4	1
1958	6	27	0	6
1960	11	15	3	1
1962	10	14	2	2
1964	17	16	1	1
1966	14	8	1	2
1968	13	10	4	3
1970	11	19	3	1
1972	20	20	3	3
1974	23	21	3	4
1976	31	16	4	4
1978	31	18	4	5
1980	21	13	2	3
1982	19	21	1	2
1984	9	13	2	2
1986	20	20	3	3
1988	10	13	3	3
1990	10	17	0	3
1992	41	24	4	3
1994	28	20	6	3

Note: These figures include members who did not run again for the office they held and members who sought other offices; they do not include members who died or resigned before the end of the Congress.

Sources: Mildred L. Amer, "Information on the Number of House Retirees, 1930-1992," Congressional Research Service, Staff Report, Washington, D.C., May 19, 1992. *Congressional Quarterly Weekly Report,* November 8, 1980, 3320-3321; October 11, 1986, 2398; November 12, 1988; November 10, 1990; *National Journal,* November 6, 1982, 1881; November 11, 1984, 2147; November 10, 1990; November 7, 1992; November 12, 1994.

Table 2-10 Defeated House Incumbents, 1946-1994

Election	Party	Incumbents lost	Average terms	Consecutive terms served						
				1	2	3	1-3	4-6	7-9	10+
1946	Democrat	62	2.7	35	5	4	44	11	5	2
	Republican	7	3.6	2	0	1	3	3	1	0
	Total	69	2.8	37	5	5	47	14	6	2
1948	Democrat[a]	9	2.7	4	1	1	6	3	0	0
	Republican	73	2.2	41	3	12	56	14	2	1
	Total	82	2.2	45	4	13	62	17	2	1
1958	Democrat[b]	6	5.0	1	1	0	2	2	1	1
	Republican	34	4.3	9	0	4	13	14	6	1
	Total	40	4.4	10	1	4	15	16	7	2
1966	Democrat	43	3.3	26	6	0	32	4	1	6
	Republican	2	11.0	1	0	0	1	0	0	1
	Total	45	3.7	27	6	0	33	4	1	7
1974	Democrat	9	4.7	1	1	1	3	3	2	1
	Republican	39	3.8	11	2	6	19	15	2	3
	Total	48	3.9	12	3	7	22	18	4	4
1978	Democrat	19	4.0	3	8	2	13	2	1	3
	Republican	5	5.4	2	0	0	2	2	0	1
	Total	24	4.2	5	8	2	15	4	1	4
1980	Democrat	32	5.2	5	2	10	17	5	4	6
	Republican	5	5.3	1	0	1	2	1	1	1
	Total	37	5.2	6	2	11	19	6	5	7
1982	Democrat	4	2.9	1	0	1	2	2	0	0
	Republican[c]	23	3.0	12	3	2	17	2	2	2
	Total	27	3.0	13	3	3	19	4	2	2

(Table continues)

Table 2-10 (continued)

Election	Party	Incumbents lost	Average terms	Consecutive terms served						
				1	2	3	1-3	4-6	7-9	10+
1984	Democrat	16	4.1	6	1	2	9	4	1	2
	Republican	3	3.7	0	0	2	2	1	0	0
	Total	19	4.1	6	1	4	11	5	1	2
1986	Democrat	3	1.8	2	0	0	2	1	0	0
	Republican	6	1.5	4	1	1	6	0	0	0
	Total	9	1.6	6	1	1	8	1	0	0
1988	Democrat	2	12.0	0	0	0	0	0	0	2
	Republican	5	1.6	2	3	0	5	0	0	0
	Total	7	4.6	2	3	0	5	0	0	2
1990	Democrat	6	6.3	0	1	0	1	3	1	1
	Republican[d]	10	3.6	2	3	0	5	4	1	0
	Total	16	4.6	2	4	0	6	7	2	1
1992	Democrat	30	5.6	2	1	4	7	12	10	1
	Republican	13	6.8	2	0	2	4	1	6	2
	Total	43	6.0	4	1	6	11	13	16	3
1994	Democrat	37	4.2	16	3	5	24	7	2	4
	Republican	1	1.0	1	0	0	1	0	0	0
	Total	38	4.1	17	3	5	25	7	2	4

Note: The 1966 and 1982 numbers do not include races where incumbents ran against incumbents due to redistricting. And, incumbents who lost in the primary as their party's incumbent but then ran in the general election as a write-in or third party candidate were counted as an incumbent loss.

[a] Includes Leo Isacson (N.Y.) who was a member of the American Labor Party.

[b] Includes Vincent Dellay (N.J.) who was elected as a Republican but switched to a Democrat. He ran for reelection as an Independent.

[c] Includes Eugene Atkinson (Pa.) who began his House service January 3, 1979, as a Democrat. He became a Republican on October 14, 1981.

[d] Includes Bill Grant (Fla.) who began his House service January 6, 1987, as a Democrat, but later switched parties. The Republican Conference let his seniority count from 1987, and includes Donald Lukens (Ohio) who was defeated in the primary, then resigned October 24, 1990.

Sources: 1946, 1948, 1958, 1966, 1974, 1977–1993, *Congressional Quarterly Almanac*; *National Journal*, November 12, 1994; *Biographical Directory of the United States Congress 1774–1989.*

Table 2-11 Defeated Senate Incumbents, 1946-1994

Election	Party	Incumbents lost	Average terms	Consecutive terms served					
				1	2	3	4	5	6+
1946	Democrat	11	1.6	7	2	1	1	0	0
	Republican	2	4.0	0	0	0	2	0	0
	Total	13	2.0	7	2	1	3	0	0
1948	Democrat	2	1.5	1	1	0	0	0	0
	Republican	8	1.0	8	0	0	0	0	0
	Total	10	1.1	9	1	0	0	0	0
1958	Republican	10	1.4	6	4	0	0	0	0
	Total	10	1.4	6	4	0	0	0	0
1966	Democrat	4	2.0	2	0	2	0	0	0
	Total	4	2.0	2	0	2	0	0	0
1974	Democrat	2	3.0	1	0	0	0	1	0
	Republican	2	1.5	1	1	0	0	0	0
	Total	4	2.2	2	1	0	0	1	0
1978	Democrat	7	0.9	6	0	1	0	0	0
	Republican	3	2.7	0	2	0	1	0	0
	Total	10	1.4	6	2	1	1	0	0
1980	Democrat	12	2.4	5	1	3	2	0	1
	Republican	1	4.0	0	0	0	1	0	0
	Total	13	2.6	5	1	3	3	0	1
1982	Democrat	1	4.0	0	0	0	1	0	0
	Republican	1	1.0	1	0	0	0	0	0
	Total	2	2.5	1	0	0	1	0	0

(Table continues)

Table 2-11 (continued)

Election	Party	Incumbents lost	Average terms	Consecutive terms served					
				1	2	3	4	5	6+
1984	Democrat	1	2.0	0	1	0	0	0	0
	Republican	2	2.0	1	0	1	0	0	0
	Total	3	2.0	1	1	1	0	0	0
1986	Republican[a]	7	0.9	7	0	0	0	0	0
	Total	7	0.9	7	0	0	0	0	0
1988	Democrat	1	2.0	0	1	0	0	0	0
	Republican	3	1.4	2	0	1	0	0	0
	Total	4	1.6	2	1	1	0	0	0
1990	Republican	1	2.0	0	1	0	0	0	0
	Total	1	2.0	0	1	0	0	0	0
1992	Democrat	3	1.3	2	1	0	0	0	0
	Republican	2	1.2	1	1	0	0	0	0
	Total	5	1.3	3	2	0	0	0	0
1994	Democrat	2	1.8	1	0	1	0	0	0
	Total	2	1.8	1	0	1	1	0	0

[a] Includes James Broyhill (N.C.) who was appointed July 14, 1986, until November 4, 1986. He lost to Terry Sanford who took over the seat on November 5, 1986.

Source: 1946, 1948, 1958, 1966, 1974, 1977-1993, Congressional Quarterly Almanac; National Journal, November 12, 1994; Biographical Directory of the United States Congress 1774-1989.

Table 2-12   House Elections Won with 60 Percent of Major Party Vote,
1956-1994

Year	Number of incumbents running in general election	Percentage of incumbents reelected with at least 60 percent of the major party vote
1956	403	59.1
1958	390	63.1
1960	400	58.9
1962	376	63.6
1964	388	58.5
1966	401	67.7
1968	397	72.2
1970	389	77.3
1972	373	77.8
1974	383	66.4
1976	381	71.9
1978	377	78.0
1980	392	72.9
1982	383	68.9
1984	406	74.6
1986	391	86.4
1988	407	88.5
1990	406	76.4
1992	349	65.6
1994	383	64.5

Sources: Albert D. Cover and David R. Mayhew, "Congressional Dynamics and the Decline of Competitive Congressional Elections," in *Congress Reconsidered,* 2d ed., ed. Lawrence C. Dodd and Bruce I. Oppenheimer (Washington, D.C.: CQ Press, 1981); *Congressional Quarterly Weekly Report,* April 25, 1981, 717-725; February 19, 1983, 386-394; April 13, 1985, 689-695; March 14, 1987, 486-493; November 12, 1988; February 23, 1991, 493-500; Mann and Ornstein, *The American Elections of 1982; Congressional Quarterly Weekly Report,* April 17, 1993, 973-980; April 15, 1995, 1090-1097.

Table 2-13   Senate Elections Won with 60 Percent of Major Party Vote, 1944-1994

Election period	Number of incumbents running in general election	Percentage of incumbents reelected with at least 60 percent of the major party vote[a]		
		South	North	Total U.S.
1944-1948	61	100.0	22.9	39.3
1950-1954	76	100.0	18.3	35.5
1956-1960	84	95.5	24.2	42.9
1962-1966	86	70.0	36.4	44.2
1968-1972	74	71.4	38.3	44.6
1974-1978	70	57.1	37.5	41.4
1980-1984[b]	84	63.3	51.9	54.1
1986-1990	87	68.2	53.9	57.5
1992-1994	53	66.7	34.2	43.4

[a] For the purposes of this table, senators appointed to the Senate are not considered incumbents in the elections just after appointment.
[b] Includes two Democratic incumbents from Louisiana, who, by winning more than 50 percent of the vote in that state's all-party primary, avoided a general election contest. In 1980 Russell Long won 59.8 percent of the vote, and in 1984 J. Bennett Johnston won 86 percent of the vote.

Sources: Cover and Mayhew, "Congressional Dynamics"; *Congressional Quarterly Weekly Report,* April 25, 1981, 717-725; February 19, 1983, 386-394; April 13, 1985, 689-695; March 14, 1987, 484-493; November 12, 1988; February 23, 1991, 493-500; April 17, 1993, 973-980; April 15, 1995, 1090-1097.

Table 2-14   Marginal Races Among Members of the 104th Congress, 1995

Chamber	Members who ever won a congressional election by 60 percent or less		Members who ever won a congressional election by 55 percent or less	
	Number	Percentage	Number	Percentage
House	318	73.1	232	53.3
Senate	90	90.0	68	68.0

Sources: Congressional Quarterly's Guide to U.S. Elections; Richard M. Scammon and Alice V. McGillivray, eds., *America Votes 20* (Congressional Quarterly, 1991); *Congressional Quarterly Weekly Report,* April 15, 1995, 1090-1097; *Politics in America 1994* (Congressional Quarterly, 1995).

Table 2-15 Conditions of Initial Election for Members of the 104th Congress, 1995

| | House | | | | Senate | | |
Condition	Democrats	Republicans	Total	%	Democrats	Republicans	Total
Defeated incumbent							
In primary	17	6	23	5.3	6	0	6
In general election	30	68	98	22.6	19	13	32
Succeeded retiring incumbent							
Of same party	94	71	165	38.0	14	21	35
Of other party	24	50	74	17.0	6	15	21
Succeeded deceased incumbent							
Of same party	12	11	23	5.3	1	1	2
Of other party	3	4	7	1.6	0	1	1
Defeated candidate in general election who had earlier defeated incumbent in primary	2	5	7	1.6	1	2	3
New districts	22	15	37	8.5	0	0	0
Total	204	230	434[a]	100.0	47	53	100

Note: Percentages do not add to 100.0 because of rounding.

[a] Total does not include Bernard Sanders (I-Vt.).

Sources: Congressional Quarterly Almanac, vols. 11-39; *Congressional Directory* (Washington, D.C.: U.S. Government Printing Office, 1981, 1983, 1985); Alan Ehrenhalt, ed., *Politics in America* (Washington, D.C.: Congressional Quarterly, various years); Michael Barone and Grant Ujifusa, *The Almanac of American Politics* (Washington, D.C.: National Journal, various years); *Congressional Quarterly Weekly Report,* various issues.

Table 2-16   Ticket Splitting between Presidential and House
Candidates, 1900-1992

Year	Districts[a]	Districts with split results[b]	
		Number	Percentage
1900	295	10	3.4
1904	310	5	1.6
1908	314	21	6.7
1912	333	84	25.2
1916	333	35	10.5
1920	344	11	3.2
1924	356	42	11.8
1928	359	68	18.9
1932	355	50	14.1
1936	361	51	14.1
1940	362	53	14.6
1944	367	41	11.2
1948	422	90	21.3
1952	435	84	19.3
1956	435	130	29.9
1960	437	114	26.1
1964	435	145	33.3
1968	435	139	32.0
1972	435	192	44.1
1976	435	124	28.5
1980	435	143	32.8
1984	435	190	43.7
1988	435	148	34.0
1992	435	100	23.0

[a] Before 1952 complete data are not available on every congressional district.
[b] Congressional districts carried by a presidential candidate of one party and a House candidate of another party.

Sources: Congressional Quarterly Weekly Report, April 22, 1978, 972; Walter Dean Burnham, *Critical Elections* (New York: Norton, 1970), 109; Michael Barone and Grant Ujifusa, *The Almanac of American Politics 1982* (Washington: Barone and Co., 1981); Barone and Ujifusa, *The Almanac of American Politics 1985; National Journal,* April 29, 1989, 1048-1054; May 29, 1993, 1285-1291.

Table 2-17   District Voting for President and Representative, 1952-1992

Year	Number of districts carried by president[a]	President's vote compared with vote for his party's successful House candidates	
		President ran ahead	President ran behind
1952	297	n.a.	n.a.
1956	329	155	43
1960	204	22	243
1964	375	134[b]	158[b]
1972	377	104	88
1976	220	22	270
1980	309	38[c]	150[c]
1984	372	59	123
1988	299	26	149
1992	257	4[b,d]	247[b,d]

n.a. = not available

[a] Refers to the winning presidential candidate in each election.

[b] Does not include districts where the percentage of the total district vote won by House members equaled the percentage of the total district vote won by the president.

[c] Computed on the basis of the actual presidential vote with John Anderson and others included. If recomputed on the basis of Reagan's percentage of the major party vote, the president ran ahead in 59 districts and behind in 129 districts.

[d] Computed on the basis of the actual presidential vote with Ross Perot included. If recomputed on the basis of Clinton's percentage of the major party vote, the president ran ahead in 72 districts and behind in 179 districts.

Sources: Compiled from information in the *Congressional Quarterly Weekly Report*, April 22, 1978, 972; *Congressional Quarterly Almanac*, vol. 22; Barone and Ujifusa, *Almanac of American Politics 1982*, and *Almanac of American Politics 1986*; *National Journal*, April 29, 1989, 1048-1054; May 29, 1993, 1285-1291.

Table 2-18   Shifts in Democratic Major Party Vote in Congressional
Districts, 1956-1994

Period	Change in democratic percentage nationally	Change in Democratic percentage in congressional districts		
		Greatest loss	Greatest gain	Variance[a]
1956-1958	5.0	−9.5	27.3	30.3
1958-1960	−1.2	−22.1	14.4	31.4
1972-1974	5.8	−18.8	36.2	92.2
1974-1976	−1.3	−30.7	31.6	81.0
1976-1978	−2.8	−37.6	39.6	106.1
1978-1980	−3.2	−27.8	37.0	85.0
1982-1984	−4.1	−40.6	16.5	68.8
1984-1986	2.4	−46.1	22.5	63.6
1986-1988	−1.1	−23.5	36.1	65.9
1988-1990	0.1	−29.1	36.4	92.6
1992-1994	−6.3	−38.0	28.0	67.2

Note: Includes only those districts in which two major party candidates competed in both elections and in which the boundaries remained unchanged for both elections. Because of massive redrawing of district lines after each decennial census, no figures are computed for 1970-1972, 1980-1982, and 1990-1992.

[a] Variance, the square of the standard deviation, measures the extent to which the changes in local returns differ from the change in national returns.

Sources: Information for 1956-1976 from Thomas E. Mann, *Unsafe at Any Margin* (Washington, D.C.: American Enterprise Institute, 1978); for 1978-1980, computed by Larry Bartels, University of California, Berkeley; for 1982-1994, computed from official election returns.

Table 2-19 Party-Line Voting in Presidential and Congressional Elections, 1956-1994 (as a percentage of all voters)

Year	Presidential election			Senate elections			House elections		
	Party-line voters[a]	Defectors[b]	Pure independents[c]	Party-line voters[a]	Defectors[b]	Pure independents[c]	Party-line voters[a]	Defectors[b]	Pure independents[c]
1956	76	15	9	79	12	9	82	9	9
1958				85	9	5	84	11	5
1960	79	13	8	77	15	8	80	12	8
1962				n.a.	n.a.	n.a.	83	12	6
1964	79	15	5	78	16	6	79	15	5
1966				n.a.	n.a.	n.a.	76	16	8
1968	69	23	9	74	19	7	74	19	7
1970				78	12	10	76	16	8
1972	67	25	8	69	22	9	75	17	8
1974				73	19	8	74	18	8
1976	74	15	11	70	19	11	72	19	9
1978				71	20	9	69	22	9
1980	70	22	8	71	21	8	69	23	8
1982				77	17	6	76	17	6
1984	81	12	7	72	19	8	70	23	7

(Table continues)

Table 2-19 (continued)

Year	Presidential election			Senate elections			House elections		
	Party-line voters[a]	Defectors[b]	Pure independents[c]	Party-line voters[a]	Defectors[b]	Pure independents[c]	Party-line voters[a]	Defectors[b]	Pure independents[c]
1986				76	20	4	72	22	6
1988	81	12	7	72	20	7	74	20	7
1990				75	20	5	72	22	5
1992	68	24	9	73	20	7	70	22	8
1994				76	18	5	77	17	6

Note: Percentages may not add to 100 because of rounding.   n.a. = not available.

[a] Party identifiers who vote for the candidate of their party.

[b] Party identifiers who vote for the candidate of the other party.

[c] The SRC/CPS National Election Surveys use a seven-point scale to define party identification, including three categories of Independents—those who "lean" to one or the other party and those who are "pure" Independents. The "leaners" are included here among the party-line voters. Party identification here means self-identification as determined by surveys.

Sources: SRC/CPS National Election Studies, 1956-1986; calculations for 1956-1978 from Thomas E. Mann and Raymond E. Wolfinger, "Candidates and Parties in Congressional Elections," American Political Science Review (September 1980); calculations for 1980, Gary C. Jacobson, The Politics of Congressional Elections (Boston: Little, Brown, 1982); calculations for 1982-1986, Peverill Squire and Michael Hagen, University of California State Data Program; calculations for 1988, Jon Krasno, The Brookings Institution; calculations for 1990 by Benjamin Highton, University of California State Data Program; calculations for 1992 by Herb Asher, Ohio State University; calculations for 1994 by Thomas Mann, The Brookings Institution.

Campaign Finance 3

The 1994 congressional elections turned out to be of historic importance. Thus it was natural in the weeks after election day for commentators to write about what had changed. And while we need to recognize change when it occurs, we also should be disciplined enough to see when there are underlying consistencies that can help us make sense of what is new. The importance of this should become clear as we look at the role of money in the 1994 elections.

For years, if you wanted to make a prediction in the month or two before election day about whether a particular incumbent was facing a serious contest, the best single piece of financial information was the amount of money raised by the challenger. Some of the most common proposals to reform campaign finance have been based on the assumption that mandated spending limits, to equalize spending between challengers and incumbents, are needed to make elections more competitive. But it turns out that challengers do not have to spend as much as incumbents to win. They only have to spend enough to become known; to bring their cases to the voters so the voters can make informed choices.

From 1984 through 1990, House challengers were severely underfunded—and almost all challengers lost. The picture began to reverse in 1992. During that year of redistricting—when incumbents were unsettled by the need to introduce themselves to new constituents, by Ross Perot's antipolitician presidential campaign, and by fourteen successful

---

* The introductory essay for Chapter 3 has been adapted with permission from Michael J. Malbin, "The Money Story," in *America at the Polls 1994*, Everett Carll Ladd (Storrs, Conn.: The Roper Center, University of Connecticut, 1995), 127-129.

state initiatives on term limits—funding for congressional challengers climbed back to 1984 levels, and nineteen challengers defeated incumbents in the general election. (Compare with fourteen successful challengers in 1990, five in 1988, and six in 1986.) '

If 1992 was a financial turning point for challengers, 1994 was at least a temporary breakthrough. The average House challenger spent $240,000 in 1994. That was 43 percent more than the average challenger spent in 1992, 78 percent more than in 1990, and double the average of 1988. However, there was a partisan tilt to the 1994 increase: the average Republican challenger's receipts increased by 52 percent between 1992 and 1994, but the average Democrat's went up only 22 percent. Thirty-four Republican challengers were successful; none of the Democrats were. (See Table 3-1 for the challenger numbers, Table 3-3 for the increased number of challengers raising $200,000 and $500,000, and Table 3-5 for the increase in challenger/incumbent spending ratios.)

Let's look at successful House challengers. The thirty-four Republican challengers who defeated Democratic incumbents spent an average of almost $700,000 each in 1994. That is much more than successful challengers have spent in the past (except for a tiny handful who won in 1988). However, these successful 1994 challengers spent 30 percent *less* than the incumbents they beat. (The *average* defeated incumbent spent almost $1 million in 1994.) (See Table 3-6.)

This confirms that money, or having the ability to communicate, is essential to campaigning in contemporary congressional politics; but that money is not enough by itself to win. Having money means having the ability to be heard; it does not mean the voters will like what they hear. Incumbents who had worn out their welcome were heard, and rejected. So too were some challengers. Frederick Overby of Georgia was the only Democratic challenger to spend more than $1 million in 1994. Of the $1.25 million his campaign reported spending through November, more than $800,000 was his own money. That turned out to be enough to earn him 34 percent of the two-party vote against incumbent Republican Michael Collins.

In some respects, this House race was a smaller version of the most-expensive-ever race for the U.S. Senate: the contest between incumbent Dianne Feinstein and challenger Michael Huffington. Huffington spent more than $28 million of his own money on an election in which he outspent the incumbent by more than two-to-one, only to lose by a narrow two percent margin. In the end, however, more spending did no more for him than it does for an embattled incumbent. The voters felt they knew enough to make a decision and decided against him.

The same thing happened to Oliver North in Virginia. North outspent incumbent Charles Robb by almost four-to-one and still lost by four percentage points to a senator who proved to be only slightly less unpopular than he was. But the North campaign is also a lesson in how not to misread financial records. The Federal Election Commission (FEC) reports that Oliver North spent $21 million on his campaign. But a closer look at his itemized records makes it clear that a lot of that money was spent on direct mail to raise funds in small individual contributions. (North raised a total of $20.8 million; all but $200,000 were contributions from individuals.) There is a world of difference between this kind of fundraising—in which it often costs a dollar to raise one—and writing a check to yourself. (For Senate data, see Tables 3-4, 3-8, and 3-9.)

Using direct mail is a course that is open only to a candidate who is already a celebrity, or who has the sponsorship of an organization that can use hot issues to keep the small checks flowing. Neither comes easily. The uncertainty of direct mail combined with the low contribution limits that make it so hard to raise seed money helps to explain why almost one-fifth of the money raised by House challengers, and almost two-fifths of the money for Senate challengers, came from the candidates themselves. Huffington strongly influenced the Senate numbers. Even without him, it is clear that self-funding has been playing an important role for nonincumbent House and Senate candidates since 1984. (See Table 3-10.)

Overall there does not appear to have been major changes in the sources of funds for congressional candidates in 1994. (See Table 3-10.) After some years of steady increase, the proportional role of political action committee (PAC) contributions for both House and Senate candidates has steadied since the mid-1980s. In general, incumbents have relied more on PACs than challengers, House candidates more than Senate candidates, and Democrats more than Republicans. Putting all three of these factors together, House Democratic incumbents received 50 percent of their money from PACs in 1994, compared with only 3 percent for Senate Republican challengers, and 10 percent for House Republican challengers.

The Senate numbers for 1994 challengers and open-seat candidates in Table 3-10 may be somewhat misleading. As that table shows, the proportional importance of PACs and party organizations declined in 1994. However, that does not represent a decrease in their organizational effort. In fact, the absolute amount of money from these sources was more or less unchanged from 1992. (See Table 3-13.) The proportional shifts are explained by the substantial increases in candidate self-funding and in money from individual contributors.

One important shift may get lost in the midst of the 1994 GOP victory. In 1994, for the first time since disclosure, Democratic congressional candidates received more from their party than did Republicans.

(See Table 3-11.) With a majority in both chambers, however, the Republicans are likely to see their contributions increase in 1995 and 1996.

Political action committee contributions (especially the contributions from corporate and trade association PACs), were still directed primarily toward incumbents in 1994. In 1978-1982, nonincumbents received almost 40 percent of the money given by PACs to House and Senate candidates. By the late 1980s the number had dropped to about 25 percent. (See Table 3-14.) Some commentators trumpeted a shift by business toward GOP challengers late in the 1994 campaign, but the data do not support such a conclusion. Corporate PACs gave 78 percent of their money to incumbents in 1992 and 77 percent in 1994. For trade/membership/health association PACs, the figures actually increased from 73 percent in 1992 to 77 percent in 1994—most likely a reflection of the health care debate. (See Table 3-14.)

Finally we should examine the sources of funds that are outside the direct control of the candidates. The most obvious of these are independent expenditures—spending that directly advocates the election or defeat of a candidate and that legally must occur without consultation or coordination with the candidate. The Supreme Court has ruled that these expenditures are constitutionally protected against federal spending limits, but that reporting and disclosure may be required by law.

After any major election victory, it is normal to see supporters lining up to claim credit for having helped make the difference for the winner's success. This year, one of the most vocal interest groups on the day after the 1994 elections was the National Rifle Association, which put more than $1.5 million into independent spending in 1994. The NRA spent almost $1 million (or two-thirds of its total) on behalf of just nine Senate Republicans during the final month of the campaign—an average of more than $100,000 per race. That figure represents three-quarters of the total independent spending from all sources on behalf of all Senate Republicans in 1993-1994. The NRA's full spending budget also represents almost one-third of the entire nation's independent spending on all congressional races in 1994.

Contributions by the NRA were proportionally a much larger piece of the independent spending picture in 1994 than in the past. However, this was not because the NRA changed its own spending patterns. Rather, the NRA's proportion grew as independent spending from other sources dropped. In 1992, there was $6.3 million in independent spending for Congress. In 1994, there was only $4.6 million (Table 3-15). Two associations account for almost all of the decrease. The National Association of Realtors and the American Medical Association decided for tactical reasons to rely on direct contributions in 1994, rather than to use independent expenditures. The two groups each spent about

$1 million in 1988, 1990, and 1992. (The second largest independent spending organization was the National Right to Life Committee, which spent about $800,000 this year and $865,000 in 1992 on congressional candidates in addition to the $800,000 it spent on behalf of President Bush).

Yet this does not complete the financial picture. Independent spending is fully disclosed. Less well known are the undisclosed millions that influence elections in a more indirect way. Who knows, for example, how much was spent in 1994 on get-out-the-vote drives sponsored by labor unions and dozens of other kinds of organizations; the Christian Coalition's "report cards" that tell whether a candidate's issue positions agree with the organization's; or television and other advertising bought by U.S. Term Limits to persuade voters to write to former House Speaker Thomas Foley to urge him to drop his lawsuit against the state's term limits?

One lesson from these activities is that large, politically sophisticated interest groups are resilient organizations, fully able to adapt to complex regulatory environments. But that is old news. We could have said the same thing about every election since 1974, when the FEC was established. What made the 1994 election new was the return of the challenger as well as the potential resurgence of partisanship. It will be interesting to see whether these two phenomena continue to be linked in the future.

NOTE: Except where specifically indicated, the data in this chapter come from the Federal Election Commission. The entries for the recent years in several tables (3-1 through 3-9 and 3-14) are based on computer data downloaded from the FEC's Direct Access Program. The numbers in Tables 3-10 through 3-13 and 3-15 are either available in, or can be calculated from, the FEC's published *Reports on Financial Activity*. These reports are published about a year after each election. For the most recent cycle, we have relied on FEC press releases based on year-end reports. All of the numbers for the most recent cycle are subject to revision in the FEC's final reports.

Finally, we need to clarify a difference between our definition of "challenger" and "open seat candidate" and the FEC's. If an incumbent runs and is defeated in a primary election, the FEC will treat all of the nonincumbent candidates in the congressional district as challengers. Because our own candidate-centered tables (3-1 through 3-9) only include candidates who run in the general election, we have defined a candidate as a challenger only if that person is running against an incumbent in the general election. If the incumbent was defeated in a primary, the general election candidates are treated as if they are running for an open seat. For the tables we calculated directly from computer data, our definitions apply. For Tables 3-10 through 3-13 that are based on FEC press releases, the FEC's calculations are based on the FEC's definitions.

Table 3-1 House Campaign Expenditures, 1978-1994 (net dollars)

	1978	1980	1982	1984	1986	1988	1990	1992	1994
All candidates									
Total expenditures	86,129,169	115,222,222	174,921,844	176,882,849	217,562,967	222,258,024	237,680,795[a]	331,899,054	347,375,296
Mean expenditure	109,440 (N = 787)	153,221 (N = 752)	228,060 (N = 767)	241,313 (N = 733)	295,602 (N = 736)	273,380 (N = 813)	325,145[a] (N = 731)	408,240[a] (N = 813)	440,832[a] (N = 788)
Mean, Democrats	108,986 (N = 416)	143,277 (N = 396)	213,369 (N = 411)	237,732 (N = 399)	301,955 (N = 397)	286,851 (N = 429)	355,862 (N = 381)	462,897 (N = 409)	485,921 (N = 387)
Mean, Republicans	109,995 (N = 371)	164,282 (N = 356)	245,020 (N = 356)	245,591 (N = 334)	290,092 (N = 340)	258,330 (N = 384)	290,910 (N = 349)	352,351 (N = 403)	396,754 (N = 400)
Incumbents									
Mean, all incumbents	111,159 (N = 377)	165,081 (N = 391)	265,001 (N = 383)	279,044 (N = 408)	362,103 (N = 389)	378,544 (N = 412)	422,124 (N = 405)	594,699[a] (N = 349)	559,929[a] (N = 383)
Mean, Democrats	103,519 (N = 249)	158,010 (N = 248)	247,573 (N = 216)	279,203 (N = 254)	349,918 (N = 231)	358,260 (N = 248)	427,178 (N = 247)	621,890 (N = 211)	620,214 (N = 225)
Mean, Republicans	126,022 (N = 128)	177,345 (N = 143)	287,543 (N = 167)	278,781 (N = 154)	379,917 (N = 158)	409,217 (N = 164)	414,222 (N = 158)	552,952 (N = 137)	473,135 (N = 157)
Challengers									
Mean, all challengers	74,802 (N = 299)	121,751 (N = 277)	151,717 (N = 270)	161,994 (N = 273)	155,607 (N = 262)	119,621 (N = 348)	134,465[a] (N = 270)	167,411 (N = 290)	239,352 (N = 302)
Mean, Democrats	70,948 (N = 109)	93,313 (N = 105)	141,390 (N = 137)	124,508 (N = 119)	170,562 (N = 123)	143,785 (N = 154)	131,194 (N = 104)	143,935 (N = 110)	175,616 (N = 110)

(Table continues)

Table 3-1 (continued)

	1978	1980	1982	1984	1986	1988	1990	1992	1994
Mean, Republicans	77,012 (N = 190)	139,111 (N = 172)	162,354 (N = 133)	190,960 (N = 154)	141,356 (N = 139)	100,440 (N = 194)	133,889 (N = 165)	181,757 (N = 180)	275,867 (N = 192)
Open seats									
Mean, all open-seat candidates	201,049 (N = 111)	201,790 (N = 84)	284,476 (N = 114)	361,696 (N = 52)	430,484 (N = 86)	465,466 (N = 53)	543,129 (N = 56)	435,631 (N = 174)	588,722 (N = 103)
Mean, Democrats	211,871 (N = 58)	180,312 (N = 43)	256,004 (N = 58)	350,804 (N = 26)	420,138 (N = 43)	446,959 (N = 27)	547,541 (N = 30)	480,375 (N = 88)	561,258 (N = 52)
Mean, Republicans	189,205 (N = 53)	224,116 (N = 41)	314,547 (N = 56)	372,589 (N = 26)	440,830 (N = 43)	484,684 (N = 26)	538,037 (N = 26)	389,847 (N = 86)	616,724 (N = 51)

Note: Includes primary and general election expenditures for general election candidates who filed reports with the Federal Election Commission. The 1979 amendments to the Federal Election Campaign Act exempted low-budget (under $5,000) campaigns from reporting requirements. Low-budget candidates who did file reports are included in the table.

[a] Includes Bernard Sanders (I-Vt.).

Table 3-2   House Candidates Who Spent $200,000 or $500,000,
             1974-1994

Election	$200,000 or more	$500,000 or more
1974	10	0
1976	31	0
1978	128	7
1980	205	28
1982	353	67
1984	354	77
1986	399	119
1988	414	149
1990	430	170
1992	552	250
1994	559	282

Sources: For 1974, Common Cause; for 1976-1994, Federal Election Commission.

Table 3-3   House Incumbents, Challengers, and Open-Seat Candidates
             Who Spent $200,000 or $500,000, 1988, 1990, 1992, and 1994

	Incumbents		Challengers		Open Seat		Total
	D	R	D	R	D	R	
1988							
$200,000+	171	132	37	31	22	21	414
$500,000+	65	43	10	7	12	12	149
1990							
$200,000+	195	124	24	36	26	24	430[a]
$500,000+	76	48	5	12	15	13	170[a]
1992							
$200,000+	194	129	31	60	83	54	552[a]
$500,000+	116	65	4	11	32	21	250[a]
1994							
$200,000+	205	136	35	87	47	48	559[a]
$500,000+	116	61	8	37	26	33	282[a]

[a] Includes Bernard Sanders (I-Vt.).

Figure 3-1   House Candidates Who Spent $500,000, 1974–1994

Number of candidates

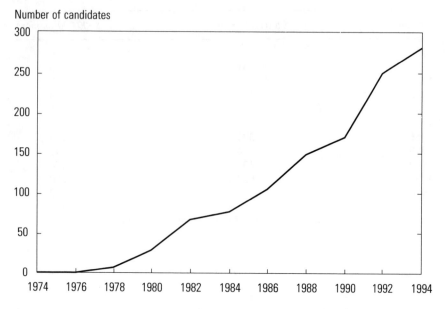

Source: Table 3-2.

Table 3-4 Senate Campaign Expenditures, 1978-1994 (net dollars)

	1978	1980	1982	1984	1986	1988	1990	1992	1994
All candidates									
Total expenditures	64,695,510	74,163,669	114,036,379	141,962,276	183,432,489	184,977,565	173,674,925	198,487,310	279,826,576
Mean expenditure	951,405 (N = 68)	1,106,920 (N = 67)	1,781,815 (N = 64)	2,327,250 (N = 61)	2,737,798 (N = 67)	2,802,690 (N = 66)	2,592,163 (N = 67)	2,876,627 (N = 69)	3,997,523 (N = 70)
Mean, Democrats	762,831 (N = 35)	1,170,580 (N = 34)	1,881,379 (N = 32)	2,160,637 (N = 31)	2,260,415 (N = 33)	2,938,533 (N = 33)	2,468,527 (N = 34)	2,815,826 (N = 35)	3,392,631 (N = 35)
Mean, Republicans	1,151,407 (N = 33)	1,041,332 (N = 33)	1,682,252 (N = 32)	2,499,417 (N = 30)	3,201,141 (N = 34)	2,666,848 (N = 33)	2,719,546 (N = 33)	2,939,218 (N = 34)	4,602,414 (N = 35)
Incumbents									
Mean, all incumbents	1,341,942 (N = 22)	1,301,692 (N = 25)	1,858,140 (N = 29)	2,539,929 (N = 28)	3,374,602 (N = 28)	3,748,126 (N = 27)	3,582,136 (N = 32)	3,852,428 (N = 27)	4,685,444 (N = 26)
Mean, Democrats	618,211 (N = 11)	1,355,660 (N = 19)	1,696,226 (N = 18)	1,755,004 (N = 12)	2,712,796 (N = 9)	3,457,145 (N = 15)	3,618,244 (N = 17)	2,851,102 (N = 15)	5,154,597 (N = 16)
Mean, Republicans	2,065,674 (N = 11)	1,130,792 (N = 6)	2,123,089 (N = 11)	3,128,622 (N = 16)	3,688,089 (N = 19)	4,111,852 (N = 12)	3,541,212 (N = 15)	5,104,086 (N = 12)	3,934,799 (N = 10)
Challengers									
Mean, all challengers	697,766 (N = 21)	842,547 (N = 24)	1,217,034 (N = 29)	1,241,434 (N = 25)	1,899,417 (N = 27)	1,820,058 (N = 17)	1,705,098 (N = 29)	1,824,993 (N = 26)	3,999,492 (N = 26)
Mean, Democrats	830,282 (N = 11)	557,006 (N = 6)	1,516,015 (N = 11)	1,515,412 (N = 15)	1,911,693 (N = 18)	2,160,770 (N = 12)	1,401,259 (N = 14)	2,551,654 (N = 12)	1,265,090 (N = 10)
Mean, Republicans	551,999 (N = 10)	937,727 (N = 18)	1,034,324 (N = 18)	830,466 (N = 10)	1,874,864 (N = 9)	1,547,489 (N = 15)	1,988,680 (N = 15)	1,202,141 (N = 14)	5,708,494 (N = 16)

(Table continues)

Table 3-4 (continued)

	1978	1980	1982	1984	1986	1988	1990	1992	1974
Open seats									
Mean, all open-seat candidates	820,787 (N = 25)	1,132,560 (N = 18)	4,142,687 (N = 6)	4,976,051 (N = 8)	3,138,282 (N = 12)	2,886,383 (N = 12)	1,599,792 (N = 6)	2,938,871 (N = 16)	3,001,013 (N = 18)
Mean, Democrats	828,127 (N = 13)	1,188,903 (N = 9)	4,331,959 (N = 3)	5,797,131 (N = 4)	2,628,009 (N = 6)	3,197,528 (N = 6)	934,046 (N = 3)	3,145,940 (N = 8)	2,624,182 (N = 9)
Mean, Republicans	812,835 (N = 12)	1,076,218 (N = 9)	3,953,415 (N = 3)	4,154,971 (N = 4)	3,648,555 (N = 6)	2,575,237 (N = 6)	2,265,538 (N = 3)	2,731,801 (N = 8)	3,377,844 (N = 9)

Note: Includes primary and general election expenditures for general election candidates only.

Table 3-5 Challenger-Incumbent Spending Ratios, 1976-1994
          (in percentages)

	1976	1978	1980	1982	1984	1986	1988	1990	1992	1994
House	64	67	74	57	48	43	32	32	28	43
Senate	73	52	65	65	49	56	49	48	47	85

Note: The above figures were obtained by dividing expenditures made by the average challenger who filed reports with the FEC by the expenditures made by the average incumbent.
Sources: Tables 3-1 and 3-4.

Figure 3-2   Expenditures of House Challengers Who Beat Incumbents, 1976–1994

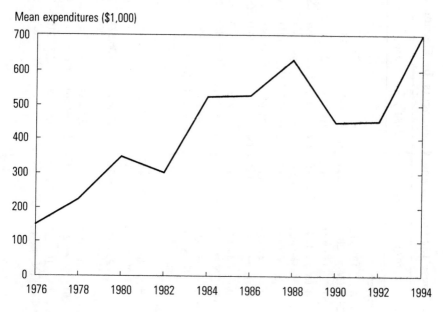

Mean expenditures ($1,000)

Source: Table 3-6.

Table 3-6 Expenditures of House Incumbents and Challengers, by Election Outcome, 1978-1994 (mean net dollars)

	1978	1980	1982	1984	1986	1988	1990	1992	1994
Incumbent won with 60% or more[a]									
Incumbents	92,696 (N = 287)	125,912 (N = 284)	200,170 (N = 264)	232,853 (N = 318)	291,591 (N = 331)	349,380 (N = 359)	362,563 (N = 313)	491,345 (N = 234)	452,360 (N = 264)
Democrats	85,424 (N = 184)	117,773 (N = 170)	206,670 (N = 178)	219,506 (N = 183)	293,026 (N = 210)	342,862 (N = 220)	374,552 (N = 197)	496,288 (N = 138)	451,565 (N = 121)
Republicans	105,687 (N = 103)	138,050 (N = 114)	186,717 (N = 86)	250,945 (N = 135)	289,099 (N = 121)	359,697 (N = 139)	342,200 (N = 116)	483,265 (N = 95)	453,033 (N = 143)
Challengers	34,132 (N = 209)	47,525 (N = 170)	82,373 (N = 163)	71,922 (N = 184)	94,461 (N = 204)	79,110 (N = 234)	60,352 (N = 180)	87,728 (N = 187)	113,030 (N = 183)
Democrats	36,040 (N = 84)	44,120 (N = 75)	36,628 (N = 62)	73,835 (N = 99)	75,893 (N = 86)	87,597 (N = 102)	43,088 (N = 65)	76,024 (N = 74)	131,256 (N = 96)
Republicans	32,850 (N = 125)	50,213 (N = 95)	110,454 (N = 101)	69,693 (N = 85)	107,994 (N = 118)	75,553 (N = 132)	70,109 (N = 115)	94,055 (N = 111)	92,936 (N = 87)
Incumbent won with less than 60%									
Incumbents	161,865 (N = 71)	261,901 (N = 76)	394,447 (N = 90)	437,752 (N = 74)	785,493 (N = 52)	701,406 (N = 44)	614,856 (N = 77)	782,328 (N = 91)	721,613 (N = 85)
Democrats	145,065 (N = 51)	223,345 (N = 50)	446,542 (N = 35)	421,834 (N = 58)	938,374 (N = 20)	691,035 (N = 23)	640,623 (N = 44)	833,388 (N = 57)	731,661 (N = 70)
Republicans	204,674 (N = 20)	336,046 (N = 26)	361,295[b] (N = 55)	495,455 (N = 16)	689,943 (N = 32)	712,765 (N = 21)	580,499 (N = 33)	696,727 (N = 34)	678,463 (N = 14)
Challengers	156,444 (N = 71)	197,499 (N = 76)	234,790 (N = 84)	307,938 (N = 72)	350,210 (N = 52)	391,549 (N = 44)	248,714 (N = 75)	281,211 (N = 84)	721,613 (N = 85)

Democrats	187,290 (N = 20)	195,135 (N = 26)	182,232[b] (N = 53)	386,819 (N = 16)	363,503 (N = 32)	445,871 (N = 21)	213,907 (N = 31)	274,047 (N = 29)	479,795 (N = 14)
Republicans	144,347 (N = 51)	198,728 (N = 50)	324,647 (N = 31)	285,401 (N = 56)	328,942 (N = 20)	341,951 (N = 23)	273,237 (N = 44)	283,801 (N = 56)	298,182 (N = 71)
Incumbent was defeated									
Incumbents	200,606 (N = 19)	286,559 (N = 31)	453,459 (N = 29)	463,070 (N = 16)	582,647 (N = 6)	956,081 (N = 5)	675,605 (N = 15)	890,975 (N = 24)	990,959 (N = 34)
Democrats	189,994 (N = 14)	285,636 (N = 28)	353,201[b] (N = 3)	483,204 (N = 13)	528,101 (N = 1)	935,494 (N = 2)	589,795 (N = 6)	951,743 (N = 16)	990,959 (N = 34)
Republicans	230,323 (N = 5)	295,170 (N = 3)	465,027 (N = 26)	375,824 (N = 3)	593,556 (N = 5)	969,806 (N = 3)	732,812[c] (N = 9)	796,437 (N = 8)	[d]
Challengers	217,083 (N = 19)	343,093 (N = 31)	296,273 (N = 23)	515,622 (N = 16)	542,442 (N = 6)	625,120 (N = 5)	452,582 (N = 15)	447,076 (N = 19)	697,358 (N = 34)
Democrats	192,037 (N = 5)	353,855 (N = 4)	292,781 (N = 22)	249,462[e] (N = 3)	564,055 (N = 5)	809,908 (N = 3)	526,537 (N = 8)	351,847 (N = 6)	[d]
Republicans	226,028 (N = 14)	341,499 (N = 27)	373,093 (N = 1)	577,044 (N = 13)	326,375 (N = 1)	349,438 (N = 2)	334,444 (N = 6)	491,028 (N = 13)	697,358 (N = 34)

Note: Includes primary and general election expenditures for general election candidates only.

[a] Percentage of the vote received by the two leading candidates.

[b] The number of challengers does not equal that of incumbents because of six incumbent-incumbent races in 1982 due to redistricting. The mean expenditure for Democrats in these races was $585,205; for Republicans, $592,080. The mean expenditure for winners (four Democrats, two Republicans) was $600,337; for losers, $583,824.

[c] One Republican incumbent was defeated by Bernard Sanders (I-Vt.), who spent $569,772.

[d] There were no defeated Republican incumbents in the 1994 elections.

[e] Includes Albert G. Bustamante who defeated Democratic incumbent Abraham Kazen, Jr. (33-Texas) in a primary.

Table 3-7 Expenditures for Open House Seats, by Election Outcome, 1984-1994 (mean net dollars)

	1984	1986	1988	1990	1992	1994
All winners	440,912 (N = 26)	523,759 (N = 46)	615,339 (N = 27)	625,760 (N = 30)	538,959 (N = 91)	605,804 (N = 52)
Democrats	428,416 (N = 8)	515,570 (N = 22)	555,499 (N = 13)	593,699 (N = 18)	508,167 (N = 57)	677,812 (N = 14)
Republicans	446,467 (N = 18)	531,266 (N = 24)	671,832 (N = 14)	673,851 (N = 12)	590,581 (N = 34)	579,169 (N = 38)
Winners with 60% or more	372,989 (N = 8)	543,382 (N = 9)	555,759 (N = 11)	632,189 (N = 14)	517,909 (N = 44)	613,120 (N = 21)
Democrats	290,693 (N = 3)	537,552 (N = 7)	397,458 (N = 7)	534,671 (N = 9)	397,636 (N = 33)	517,617 (N = 3)
Republicans	422,366 (N = 5)	546,783 (N = 12)	832,787 (N = 4)	807,721 (N = 5)	878,725 (N = 11)	619,037 (N = 18)
Winners with < 60%	471,100 (N = 18)	509,950 (N = 27)	656,299 (N = 16)	620,135 (N = 16)	558,666 (N = 47)	600,848 (N = 31)
Democrats	511,049 (N = 5)	505,312 (N = 15)	737,714 (N = 6)	652,727 (N = 9)	660,147 (N = 24)	705,138 (N = 11)
Republicans	455,736 (N = 13)	515,749 (N = 12)	607,450 (N = 10)	578,230 (N = 7)	452,773 (N = 23)	543,288 (N = 20)

All losers	282,480 (N = 26)	323,218 (N = 40)	444,707 (N = 23)	447,785 (N = 26)	322,344 (N = 83)	571,305 (N = 51)
Democrats	316,309 (N = 18)	320,161 (N = 21)	436,127 (N = 13)	290,911 (N = 12)	429,273 (N = 31)	518,317 (N = 38)
Republicans	206,363 (N = 8)	326,596 (N = 19)	455,860 (N = 10)	421,625 (N = 14)	258,597 (N = 52)	726,192 (N = 13)
Losers with > 40%	352,961 (N = 18)	400,872 (N = 25)	581,180 (N = 15)	472,178 (N = 18)	451,892 (N = 47)	686,012 (N = 31)
Democrats	393,262 (N = 13)	388,578 (N = 12)	506,283 (N = 9)	436,366 (N = 8)	476,578 (N = 23)	597,094 (N = 20)
Republicans	248,180 (N = 5)	412,220 (N = 13)	693,525 (N = 6)	507,989 (N = 8)	428,234 (N = 24)	847,680 (N = 11)
Losers with 40% or less	123,896 (N = 8)	193,794 (N = 15)	188,819 (N = 8)	408,756 (N = 10)	153,212 (N = 36)	393,509 (N = 20)
Democrats	116,232 (N = 5)	228,938 (N = 9)	278,276 (N = 4)	562,183 (N = 4)	293,272 (N = 8)	430,787 (N = 18)
Republicans	136,668 (N = 3)	141,077 (N = 6)	99,363 (N = 4)	306,472 (N = 6)	113,194 (N = 28)	58,005 (N = 2)

Table 3-8 Expenditures of Senate Incumbents and Challengers, by Election Outcome, 1978-1994 (mean net dollars)

	1978	1980	1982	1984	1986	1988	1990	1992	1994
Incumbent won with 60% or more[a]									
Incumbents	456,062 (N = 7)	1,162,385 (N = 10)	1,494,578 (N = 13)	376,867 (N = 77)	1,963,140 (N = 14)	2,777,202 (N = 15)	2,318,076 (N = 19)	2,698,728 (N = 13)	3,648,802 (N = 10)
Democrats	559,046 (N = 4)	1,220,616 (N = 6)	1,401,794 (N = 12)	1,620,869 (N = 7)	1,672,182 (N = 8)	2,355,863 (N = 10)	2,441,681 (N = 10)	2,661,953 (N = 9)	1,736,604 (N = 3)
Republicans	318,749 (N = 3)	1,075,038 (N = 4)	2,607,983 (N = 1)	1,606,604 (N = 11)	2,351,083 (N = 6)	3,619,881 (N = 5)	2,180,738 (N = 9)	2,781,472 (N = 4)	4,468,316 (N = 7)
Challengers	47,346 (N = 6)	302,812 (N = 9)	777,830 (N = 13)	384,263 (N = 15)	451,671 (N = 13)	591,566 (N = 15)	853,376 (N = 16)	701,442 (N = 12)	1,002,019 (N = 10)
Democrats	38,458 (N = 3)	265,822 (N =4)	424,507 (N = 1)	322,263[f] (N = 10)	155,853 (N = 5)	835,294 (N = 5)	449,666 (N = 8)	595,192 (N = 4)	1,365,381 (N = 7)
Republicans	56,233 (N = 3)	332,404 (N = 5)	807,276 (N = 12)	508,264 (N = 5)	636,557 (N = 8)	469,702 (N = 10)	1,253,086 (N = 8)	754,568 (N = 8)	154,174 (N = 3)
Incumbent won with less than 60%									
Incumbents	2,496,484 (N = 8)	945,423 (N = 6)	2,224,235 (N = 14)	4,505,574 (N = 7)	5,213,789 (N = 7)	6,235,410 (N = 8)	5,279,645 (N = 12)	4,922,413 (N = 10)	5,308,272 (N = 14)
Democrats	586,055 (N = 2)	796,984 (N = 4)	2,417,100 (N =5)	1,833,432 (N = 4)	11,037,707 (N = 1)	6,829,053 (N = 4)	5,299,049 (N = 7)	2,844,490 (N = 4)	6,022,367 (N = 11)
Republicans	3,133,293 (N = 6)	1,242,300 (N = 2)	2,117,088 (N = 9)	8,068,429 (N = 3)	4,243,136 (N = 6)	5,641,766 (N = 4)	5,252,478 (N = 5)	6,307,696 (N = 6)	2,689,926 (N = 3)

Challengers	735,956 (N = 4)	864,870 (N = 6)	1,615,338 (N = 14)	2,296,194 (N = 7)	3,389,477 (N = 7)	3,784,772 (N = 8)	2,870,438 (N = 12)	2,283,708 (N = 10)	5,551,166 (N = 14)
Democrats	1,212,929 (N = 6)	1,139,376 (N = 2)	1,629,490 (N = 9)	4,028,715 (N = 3)	1,990,836 (N = 6)	3,209,075 (N = 4)	2,927,948 (N = 5)	3,032,533 (N = 6)	1,031,077 (N = 3)
Republicans	332,537 (N = 2)	727,617 (N = 4)	1,589,864 (N = 5)	996,804 (N = 4)	11,781,316 (N = 1)	4,360,469 (N = 4)	2,829,360 (N = 7)	1,160,471 (N = 4)	6,783,918 (N = 11)
Incumbent was defeated									
Incumbents	908,348 (N = 7)	1,693,991 (N = 9)	1,658,623 (N = 2)	2,078,184 (N = 2)	4,358,340 (N = 7)	2,579,437 (N = 4)	7,229,154 (N = 1)	4,926,992 (N = 4)	5,508,854 (N = 2)
Democrats	678,406 (N = 5)	1,693,991 (N = 9)	1,625,042 (N = 1)	2,380,239 (N = 1)	—	1,338,622 (N = 1)	—	3,751,500 (N = 2)	5,508,854 (N = 2)
Republicans	1,483,203 (N = 2)	—	1,692,204 (N = 1)	4,090,013 (N = 2)	4,358,340 (N = 7)	2,993,042 (N = 3)	7,229,154 (N = 1)	6,138,484 (N = 2)	—
Challengers	918,054 (N = 7)	1,367,400 (N = 9)	793,123 (N = 2)	3,900,606 (N = 4)	3,098,027 (N = 7)	2,516,337 (N = 4)	1,380,560 (N = 1)	4,048,857 (N = 4)	8,125,137 (N = 2)
Democrats	870,079 (N =2)	—	1,586,245 (N = 1)	3,711,199 (N = 2)	3,098,027 (N = 7)	2,996,572 (N = 3)	1,380,560 (N = 1)	5,021,938 (N = 2)	—
Republicans	937,244 (N = 5)	1,367,400 (N = 9)	981,197 (N = 1)	1,776,128 (N = 1)	—	1,075,631 (N = 1)	—	3,075,776 (N = 2)	8,125,137 (N = 2)

Note: The Federal Election Commission included the following disclaimer along with its 1986 data, and *Vital Statistics* considers it appropriate for all years: "The small N's and unique nature of some Senate campaigns make all measures of central tendency like averages or medians problematic and, as a result, the Commission would not include tables such as these in its regular release of information."

a Percentage of the vote received by the two leading candidates.

Table 3-9 Expenditures for Open Senate Seats, by Election Outcome, 1984-1994 (mean net dollars)

	1984	1986	1988	1990	1992	1994
All winners	6,704,434 (N = 4)	3,258,889 (N = 7)	3,781,436 (N = 6)	2,265,538 (N = 3)	3,371,677 (N = 8)	3,377,844 (N = 9)
Democrats	3,180,975 (N = 1)	3,005,440 (N = 5)	5,186,633 (N = 2)	—	4,186,216 (N = 5)	—
Republicans	7,878,921 (N = 3)	3,892,511 (N = 2)	3,078,837 (N = 4)	2,265,538 (N = 3)	2,014,111 (N = 3)	3,377,844 (N = 9)
Winners with 60% or more	5,769,338 (N = 3)	2,233,094 (N = 2)	1,879,272 (N = 2)	1,536,352 (N = 2)	1,191,005 (N = 1)	2,754,477 (N = 4)
Democrats	3,180,975 (N = 1)	2,057,422 (N = 1)	2,881,666 (N = 1)	—	1,191,005 (N = 1)	—
Republicans	7,063,519 (N = 2)	2,375,402 (N = 1)	876,877 (N = 1)	1,536,352 (N = 2)	—	2,754,477 (N = 4)
Winners with < 60%	9,509,724 (N = 1)	3,669,207 (N = 5)	4,732,518 (N = 4)	3,723,911 (N = 1)	3,683,201 (N = 7)	3,876,538 (N = 5)
Democrats	—	2,933,757 (N = 3)	7,491,600 (N = 1)	—	4,935,019 (N = 4)	—
Republicans	9,509,724 (N = 1)	5,396,255 (N = 1)	3,812,824 (N = 3)	3,723,911 (N = 1)	2,014,111 (N = 3)	3,876,538 (N = 5)

All losers	3,247,669 (N = 4)	2,418,888 (N = 7)	2,000,372 (N = 6)	934,046 (N = 3)	2,506,064 (N = 8)	2,624,182 (N = 9)
Democrats	3,737,698 (N = 3)	2,454,680 (N = 2)	2,202,976 (N = 4)	934,046 (N = 3)	1,412,146 (N = 3)	2,624,182 (N = 9)
Republicans	1,777,581 (N = 1)	2,404,572 (N = 5)	1,595,165 (N = 2)	—	3,162,415 (N = 5)	—
Losers with > 40%	5,880,512 (N = 1)	2,940,269 (N = 5)	2,792,524 (N = 4)	1,936,914 (N = 1)	2,792,915 (N = 7)	2,784,692 (N = 5)
Democrats	5,880,512 (N = 1)	4,377,661 (N = 1)	2,753,999 (N = 3)	1,936,914 (N = 1)	1,412,146 (N = 3)	2,784,692 (N = 5)
Republicans	—	4,140,166 (N = 3)	2,908,101 (N = 1)	—	3,828,492 (N = 4)	—
Losers with 40% or less	2,370,054 (N = 3)	1,115,437 (N = 2)	416,069 (N = 2)	432,612 (N = 2)	498,107 (N = 1)	2,423,544 (N = 4)
Democrats	2,666,291 (N = 2)	531,698 (N = 1)	549,908 (N = 1)	432,613 (N = 2)	—	2,423,544 (N = 4)
Republicans	1,777,581 (N = 1)	1,699,175 (N = 1)	282,229 (N = 1)	—	498,107 (N = 1)	—

Note: The Federal Election Commission included the following disclaimer along with its 1986 data, and *Vital Statistics* considers it appropriate for all years: "The small *N*'s and unique nature of some Senate campaigns make all measures of central tendency like averages or medians problematic and, as a result, the Commission would not include tables such as these in its regular release of information."

Figure 3-3   Percentage of Incumbents' Campaign Funds that Came from PACs, House and Senate, 1984–1994

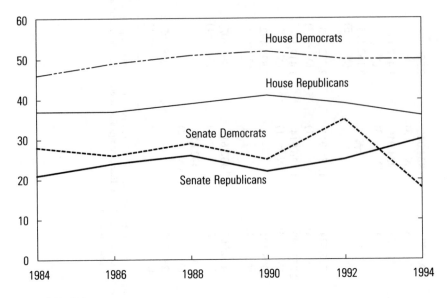

Source: Table 3-10.

Table 3-10 Campaign Funding Sources for House and Senate Candidates, 1984-1994

Party and candidate status	Number of candidates	Contributions plus party expenditures on behalf of candidates ($ millions)	Percentage coming from:				
			Individuals	PACs	Party (contributions plus expenditures)	Candidate to self (contributions plus loans)	Other
House, 1984							
All candidates[a]	816	$203.8	47	36	7	6	5
Democrats	434	107.2	44	41	3	6	6
Incumbents	258	81.8	39	46	2	2	11
Challengers	152	16.3	43	29	6	18	5
Open seats	24	9.1	45	22	6	24	3
Republicans	382	96.6	49	30	11	6	5
Incumbents	154	52.1	51	37	6	1	5
Challengers	204	33.8	48	18	17	13	4
Open seats	24	10.7	47	31	13	7	2
Senate, 1984							
All candidates[a]	68	$157.7	61	18	6	10	4
Democrats	33	73.1	56	18	6	16	4
Incumbents	12	22.8	61	28	3	< 1	8

(Table continues)

Table 3-10 (continued)

Party and candidate status	Number of candidates	Contributions plus party expenditures on behalf of candidates ($ millions)	Percentage coming from:				
			Individuals	PACs	Party (contributions plus expenditures)	Candidate to self (contributions plus loans)	Other
Challengers	17	25.5	69	17	9	2	3
Open seats	4	24.8	39	9	6	44	2
Republicans	35	84.6	65	18	6	5	4
Incumbents	17	55.7	68	21	6	1	5
Challengers	13	10.0	55	15	20	8	2
Open seats	5	19.0	60	10	9	17	8
House, 1986							
All candidates[a]	810	$234.2	48	36	4	6	6
Democrats	427	125.7	44	42	2	6	6
Incumbents	235	84.1	42	49	1	2	6
Challengers	147	22.1	49	29	6	13	3
Open seats	45	19.5	47	31	3	15	4
Republicans	383	108.5	53	29	6	7	5
Incumbents	160	67.3	53	37	4	1	5
Challengers	182	21.4	54	11	10	22	3
Open seats	41	19.8	53	24	10	10	3

Senate, 1986

All candidates[a]	68	208.6	60	21	9	6	4
Democrats	34	90.2	56	22	8	9	5
Incumbents	9	28.2	62	26	7	2	3
Challengers	18	40.3	51	19	9	16	5
Open seats	7	21.7	60	22	8	5	5
Republicans	34	118.5	63	21	9	2	5
Incumbents	18	68.9	63	24	8	< 1	5
Challengers	9	20.4	64	9	18	6	3
Open seats	7	29.1	61	22	6	2	9

House, 1988

All candidates[a]	813	$249.0	46	40	4	5	5
Democrats	429	140.0	40	47	3	5	5
Incumbents	238	103.8	39	51	2	1	7
Challengers	154	23.5	46	31	7	13	3
Open seats	27	12.7	39	36	7	14	4
Republicans	384	109.0	52	31	6	6	5
Incumbents	164	73.7	51	39	3	1	6
Challengers	194	21.6	55	10	13	19	3
Open seats	26	13.7	54	21	13	12	< 1

(Table continues)

Table 3-10 (continued)

Party and candidate status	Number of candidates	Contributions plus party expenditures) on behalf of candidates ($ millions)	Percentage coming from:				
			Individuals	PACs	Party (contributions plus expenditures)	Candidate to self (contributions plus loans)	Other
Senate, 1988							
All candidates[a]	66	199.4	59	22	9	5	5
Democrats	33	103.0	58	23	7	8	4
Incumbents	15	53.0	61	29	4	1	5
Challengers	12	29.1	66	16	11	3	4
Open seats	6	20.9	37	16	8	35	4
Republicans	33	96.3	61	22	11	2	4
Incumbents	12	50.8	62	26	8	<1	4
Challengers	15	27.7	63	11	18	6	2
Open seats	6	17.8	54	26	13	1	6
House, 1990							
All candidates[a]	807	$257.5	44	40	3	6	7
Democrats	413	146.5	39	47	3	5	6
Incumbents	249	113.2	37	52	1	2	8

Challengers	132	16.0	44	27	9	16	4
Open seats	32	17.3	42	33	4	17	4
Republicans	394	108.8	51	32	4	7	6
Incumbents	159	70.7	50	41	2	1	6
Challengers	206	23.9	54	10	7	24	5
Open seats	29	14.1	50	24	10	12	4

Senate, 1990

All candidates[a]	67	$191.0	61	21	7	5	6
Democrats	34	90.8	63	22	6	4	5
Incumbents	17	66.7	65	25	5	0	5
Challengers	14	21.0	58	12	9	15	6
Open seats	3	3.1	50	18	11	21	<1
Republicans	33	100.2	59	21	9	5	6
Incumbents	15	58.9	65	22	7	0	6
Challengers	15	33.4	51	16	12	15	6
Open seats	3	7.9	43	36	7	0	14

House, 1992

All candidates[a]	851	$331.5	47	36	5	9	3
Democrats	427	184.7	43	43	4	6	4
Incumbents	213	122.1	40	50	2	1	7
Challengers	140	25.1	48	26	10	13	3
Open seats	74	37.5	49	30	4	17	<1

(Table continues)

Table 3-10 (continued)

Party and candidate status	Number of candidates	Contributions plus party expenditures) on behalf of candidates ($ millions)	Percentage coming from:				
			Individuals	PACs	Party (contributions plus expenditures)	Candidate to self (contributions plus loans)	Other
Republicans	424	146.9	51	26	6	13	4
Incumbents	138	74.8	52	39	3	1	5
Challengers	216	44.5	47	9	10	22	12
Open seats	70	27.5	57	21	7	14	1
			Senate, 1992				
All candidates[a]	71	$214.2	58	21	13	5	3
Democrats	35	108.5	60	23	11	2	4
Incumbents	15	43.9	52	35	6	2	5
Challengers	13	43.1	68	12	14	3	3
Open seats	7	21.5	61	19	13	3	4
Republicans	36	106.9	55	19	15	7	4
Incumbents	12	59.4	58	25	13	<1	4
Challengers	17	24.0	55	9	20	14	2
Open seats	7	23.5	48	16	16	18	2

House, 1994

All candidates[a]	824	$371.3	49	34	5	8	4
Democrats	403	196.7	43	43	5	5	4
Incumbents	226	142.4	34	50	3	1	12
Challengers	130	23.6	45	23	11	17	4
Open seats	47	30.7	47	27	8	15	3
Republicans	421	174.6	56	24	6	11	3
Incumbents	157	82.9	58	36	2	1	3
Challengers	217	58.6	56	10	10	20	4
Open seats	47	33.1	50	19	8	19	4

Senate, 1994

All candidates[a]	70	$291.7	54	15	8	19	4
Democrats	35	124.9	55	18	10	12	5
Incumbents	16	86.4	54	18	8	14	6
Challengers	10	11.7	46	16	13	21	4
Open seats	9	26.9	60	16	14	3	7
Republicans	35	166.7	53	13	6	24	4
Incumbents	10	35.4	60	30	6	< 1	4
Challengers	16	96.1	47	3	5	41	4
Open seats	9	35.2	61	21	11	1	6

[a] Excludes minor-party candidates.

Source: Federal Election Commission.

Figure 3-4   Percentage of Nonincumbents' Campaign Funds that Came from Political Parties, House and Senate, 1984–1994

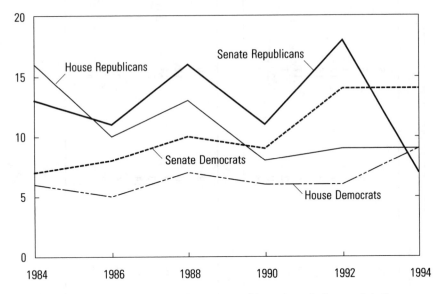

Note: Nonincumbents include challengers and open-seat candidates who ran in the general election.
Source: Table 3-10.

Figure 3-5   Political Party Contributions and Coordinated Expenditures for Congress, 1976–1994

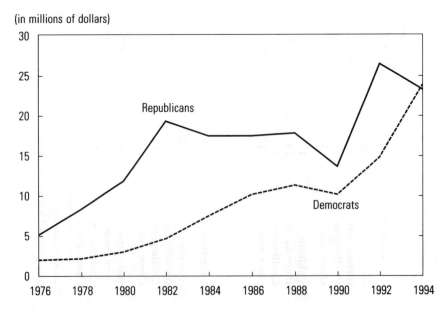

Source: Table 3-11.

Table 3-11 Political Party Contributions and Coordinated Expenditures for Congressional Candidates, 1976-1994 (in dollars)

	Senate		House		Total
	Contributions	Expenditures	Contributions	Expenditures	
1976					
Democrats	468,795	4,359	1,465,629	500	1,939,283
Republicans	930,034	113,976	3,658,310	329,583	5,031,903
1978					
Democrats	466,683	229,218	1,262,298	72,892	2,031,091
Republicans	703,204	2,723,880	3,621,104	1,297,079	8,345,267
1980					
Democrats	480,464	1,132,912	1,025,989	256,346	2,895,711
Republicans	677,004	5,434,758	3,498,323	2,203,748	11,813,833
1982					
Democrats	579,337	2,265,197	1,052,286	694,321	4,591,141
Republicans	600,221	8,715,761	4,720,959	5,293,260	19,330,201
1984					
Democrats	441,467	3,947,731	1,280,672	1,774,452	7,444,322
Republicans	590,922	6,518,415	4,060,120	6,190,309	17,359,766
1986					
Democrats	620,832	6,656,286	968,913	1,836,213	10,082,244
Republicans	729,522	10,077,902	2,520,278	4,111,474	17,439,176
1988					
Democrats	501,777	6,592,264	1,258,952	2,891,152	11,244,145
Republicans	719,006	10,260,600	2,657,069	4,162,207	17,798,882

(Table continues)

Table 3-11 (continued)

	Senate		House		
	Contributions	Expenditures	Contributions	Expenditures	Total
1990					
Democrats	515,332	5,210,002	943,135	3,401,579	10,070,048
Republicans	862,621	7,725,853	2,019,279	3,012,313	13,620,066
1992					
Democrats	689,953	11,915,878	1,234,553	5,883,678	19,724,102
Republicans	807,397	16,509,940	2,197,611	6,906,729	26,421,677
1994					
Democrats	638,618	13,204,309	1,501,220	8,455,070	23,799,217
Republicans	748,011	11,561,866	2,036,712	8,851,871	23,198,460

Note: The table includes direct contributions made by party committees to congressional candidates and coordinated expenditures made on their behalf, known as 441a(d) expenditures because the legal spending limits are contained in U. S. Code, Title 2, sec. 441a(d). Under this provision, party committees are allowed to spend money on behalf of federal candidates, in addition to the money they may contribute directly. Unlike "independent expenditures," which are prohibited to the parties (see Table 3-15 for a definition), this spending may be coordinated with a candidate.

House candidates may receive in direct contributions up to $10,000 each ($5,000 in the primary and $5,000 in the general election) from the national party, congressional campaign committee, Senate campaign committee, and state party. Senate candidates may receive in direct contributions a total of $17,500 from the national party and senatorial campaign committee and another $10,000 each from the congressional and state party. In addition, some state parties in 1989-1990 contributed to candidates from other states. Although the practice has been quite limited, the legal implications are very large: it opens up the theoretical possibility of an additional $490,000 (49 times $10,000) of party contributions per candidate.

The limits on 441a(d) expenditures are as follows: (a) for Senate candidates, two cents times the voting age population, or $20,000 in 1974 dollars adjusted for inflation, whichever is greater; (b) for House candidates from states with only one House district, $20,000 in 1974 dollars adjusted for inflation; and (c) for all other House candidates, $10,000 in 1974 dollars adjusted for inflation. State parties are allowed to spend equal amounts on behalf of congressional candidates, and court decisions permit state and local parties to designate a national party committee as its agent for these expenditures.

Combining the maximum national party contributions, home state party contributions, and 441a(d) expenditure limits would have given House candidates $99,600 in 1994. Senate limits ranged from a low of $157,700 in small states to a high of $2,688,325 in California.

Table 3-12 Number of Registered Political Action Committees, 1974-1994

Committee type	1974	1976	1978	1980	1984	1988	1990	1992	1994
Corporate	89	433	784	1,204	1,682	1,816	1,795	1,735	1,660
Labor	201	224	217	297	394	354	346	347	333
Trade/membership/health[a]	318	489	451	574	698	786	774	770	792
Nonconnected	—	—	165	378	1,053	1,115	1,062	1,145	980
Cooperative	—	—	12	42	52	59	59	56	53
Corporation without stock	—	—	24	56	130	138	136	142	136
Total	608	1,146	1,653	2,551	4,009	4,268	4,172	4,195	3,954

Note: Data as of December 31 for every year.

[a] Includes all noncorporate and nonlabor PACs through December 31, 1976.

Source: Federal Election Commission PAC count press release, issued annually.

Table 3-13 PAC Contributions to Congressional Candidates, 1978-1994 (in millions of dollars)[a]

Type of PAC	1978	1980	1982	1984	1986	1988	1990	1992	1994
Labor	9.9	13.2	20.3	24.8	29.9	33.9	33.6	39.7	40.7
Corporate	9.5	19.2	27.5	35.5	46.2	50.4	53.5	64.3	64.1
Trade/membership/health	11.2	15.9	21.9	26.7	32.9	38.9	42.5	51.4	50.1
Nonconnected	2.5	4.9	10.7	14.5	18.8	19.2	14.3	17.5	17.3
Other[b]	1.0	2.0	3.2	3.8	4.9	5.4	5.9	6.6	6.6
Total	34.1	55.2	83.6	105.3	132.7	147.8	149.7	179.4	178.8

[a] Contributions to all candidates for election in the year indicated, made during the two-year election cycle.
[b] Cooperatives and corporations without stock.

Table 3-14 How PACs Distributed Their Contributions to Congressional Candidates, 1978-1994

House

Percentage distribution

	Incumbent D	Incumbent R	Challenger D	Challenger R	Open seat D	Open seat R	Percent to chamber	Dollars to chamber (in millions)
House, 1978								
Corporate	22	18	1	10	4	8	63	6.2
Association	27	20	2	11	7	9	76	8.6
Labor	43	2	12	<1	14	<1	72	7.5
Nonconnected	9	10	3	29	4	18	74	2.1
Other PACs	49	12	2	1	8	5	77	0.8
All PACs	30	14	5	9	8	7	71	25.0
House, 1980								
Corporate	23	21	1	13	1	6	64	11.7
Association	29	24	1	13	2	6	75	11.2
Labor	50	3	12	<1	7	<1	72	8.9
Nonconnected	13	9	3	26	2	8	62	2.8
Other PACs	40	19	2	2	3	4	72	1.4
All PACs	31	17	3	10	3	5	69	36.0
House, 1982								
Corporate	22	31	1	6	2	6	69	18.1
Association	26	32	3	6	3	6	77	15.9
Labor	40	3	21	<1	11	1	75	14.6

Senate

Percentage distribution

	Incumbent D	Incumbent R	Challenger D	Challenger R	Open seat D	Open seat R	Percent to chamber	Dollars to chamber (in millions)	Total percent	Total dollars (in millions)
Senate, 1978										
Corporate	6	14	2	7	3	6	37	3.6	100	9.8
Association	5	8	2	4	2	3	24	2.8	100	11.3
Labor	10	2	9	<1	5	<1	28	2.8	100	10.3
Nonconnected	3	5	3	10	1	5	26	0.7	100	2.8
Other PACs	5	5	3	2	4	3	23	0.2	100	1.0
All PACs	6	8	4	4	3	3	29	10.2	100	35.2
Senate, 1980										
Corporate	9	5	<1	17	1	4	36	6.4	100	18.1
Association	9	4	1	8	1	2	25	3.8	100	15.0
Labor	18	3	4	<1	3	<1	28	3.4	100	12.3
Nonconnected	8	2	<1	20	<1	5	37	1.7	100	4.5
Other PACs	16	4	1	5	2	2	28	0.5	100	1.9
All PACs	11	4	1	10	2	2	31	15.9	100	51.9
Senate, 1982										
Corporate	8	13	<1	5	<1	4	31	8.3	100	26.4
Association	9	9	1	2	<1	2	23	4.9	100	20.8
Labor	14	2	7	<1	2	<1	25	4.8	100	19.4

Column headers for this table appear on the previous page. Columns are grouped as House (six detail columns, a subtotal, and dollars in millions), Senate (six detail columns, a subtotal, a "100" total, and dollars in millions), and Total ("100" total and dollars in millions).

Type of PAC	House								Senate									Total	
	1	2	3	4	5	6	Total	$	1	2	3	4	5	6	Total	100	$	100	$
(continued from previous page)																			
Nonconnected	20	13	11	12	5	7	69	6.9	9	6	5	7	2	2	31	100	3.2	100	10.0
Other PACs	40	25	3	1	4	3	78	2.4	11	5	2	<1	<1	2	22	100	0.7	100	3.1
All PACs	28	22	8	5	5	5	73	57.9	9	6	5	7	2	2	27	100	21.8	100	79.7
House, 1984 / Senate, 1984																			
Corporate	29	26	<1	7	<1	4	67	22.9	7	19	1	2	1	4	33	100	11.4	100	34.3
Association	36	28	2	5	2	4	77	19.8	6	11	2	1	1	1	23	100	6.0	100	25.8
Labor	57	4	14	<1	5	<1	80	18.7	6	1	9	<1	4	<1	20	100	4.6	100	23.3
Nonconnected	26	9	5	15	3	6	63	8.6	7	10	10	4	3	2	37	100	5.1	100	13.7
Other PACs	48	23	2	2	1	2	78	2.9	7	10	2	1	2	1	22	100	0.8	100	3.7
All PACs	38	18	4	6	2	3	72	72.9	6	11	4	2	2	2	28	100	27.9	100	100.8
House, 1986 / Senate, 1986																			
Corporate	26	24	1	2	2	4	58	26.4	5	20	3	3	2	9	42	100	19.0	100	45.3
Association	33	27	2	2	3	5	71	23.0	6	12	4	1	2	4	29	100	9.4	100	32.4
Labor	45	5	14	<1	10	<1	75	21.9	6	2	11	<1	6	<1	25	100	7.1	100	29.1
Nonconnected	21	12	8	5	7	6	59	10.7	6	11	10	2	7	5	41	100	7.5	100	18.2
Other PACs	36	23	1	2	2	2	67	3.2	6	15	6	1	2	3	33	100	1.6	100	4.8
All PACs	32	19	5	2	5	4	66	85.2	5	13	6	1	4	5	34	100	44.6	100	129.8
House, 1988 / Senate, 1988																			
Corporate	31	26	1	2	1	3	63	31.6	11	14	1	4	3	5	37	100	18.8	100	50.4
Association	37	26	2	1	3	4	73	28.6	9	9	1	2	2	3	27	100	10.4	100	38.9
Labor	50	6	15	<1	9	<1	79	26.8	9	1	6	<1	4	<1	21	100	7.1	100	33.9
Nonconnected	25	12	8	4	6	4	59	11.4	13	9	7	4	4	4	41	100	7.8	100	19.2
Other PACs	41	23	1	2	2	2	72	3.8	12	9	2	2	2	2	28	100	1.5	100	5.3
All PACs	36	19	6	1	4	3	69	102.2	10	9	3	2	2	3	31	100	45.7	100	147.8

(Table continues)

Table 3-14 (continued)

House

Percentage distribution

	Incumbent D	Incumbent R	Challenger D	Challenger R	Open seat D	Open seat R	Percent to chamber	Dollars to chamber (in millions)
House, 1990								
Corporate	32	25	1	2	2	4	66	35.4
Association	40	25	2	2	5	5	77	32.5
Labor	54	5	9	<1	13	<1	82	27.6
Nonconnected	26	13	4	4	8	5	60	8.5
Other PACs	46	21	1	2	2	2	74	4.3
All PACs	39	19	3	1	6	4	72	108.5
House, 1992								
Corporate	32	23	1	3	1	5	67	42.9
Association	35	22	3	3	7	6	76	38.7
Labor	48	3	11	<1	16	1	78	30.5
Nonconnected	25	11	5	5	9	1	60	10.3
Other PACs	43	19	1	2	4	3	72	4.2
All PACs	36	17	4	2	8	4	71	127.0
House, 1994								
Corporate	35	23	4	<1	2	4	70	44.3
Association	39	23	4	1	4	5	78	37.1
Labor	60	3	9	<1	12	<1	83	31.4

Senate

Percentage distribution

	Incumbent D	Incumbent R	Challenger D	Challenger R	Open seat D	Open seat R	Percent to chamber	Dollars to chamber (in millions)	Total percent	Total dollars (in millions)
Senate, 1990										
Corporate	13	11	6	<1	3	<1	34	18.0	100	53.5
Association	9	8	3	1	<1	1	23	10.0	100	42.5
Labor	11	1	5	<1	1	<1	18	6.0	100	33.6
Nonconnected	20	10	2	1	2	5	40	5.7	100	14.3
Other PACs	13	8	2	<1	2	2	26	1.5	100	5.8
All PACs	11	9	2	3	1	2	28	41.2	100	149.7
Senate, 1992										
Corporate	10	13	2	2	2	5	33	21.2	100	64.1
Association	8	8	2	1	2	2	24	12.4	100	51.1
Labor	9	1	7	<1	5	<1	22	8.6	100	39.1
Nonconnected	12	10	6	2	6	3	40	6.9	100	17.2
Other PACs	11	9	2	<1	4	1	28	1.6	100	5.7
All PACs	9	8	3	1	3	3	29	51.1	100	178.1
Senate, 1994										
Corporate	10	9	3	<1	2	7	30	18.7	100	63.0
Association	8	7	2	<1	2	5	22	10.7	100	47.9
Labor	9	<1	4	<1	4	<1	17	6.6	100	38.1

Nonconnected	33	12	3	7	7	6	68	11.1	12	7	1	3	4	4	32	5.3	100	16.4
Other PACs	45	19	1	3	3	3	75	4.7	11	6	<1	2	3	4	25	1.6	100	6.3
All PACs	42	18	3	3	5	4	75	126.6	9	6	1	2	2	4	25	43.0	100	169.6

Note: General election candidates only. D indicates Democrat; R indicates Republican. Percentages may not add to 100 because of rounding.

Source: Federal Election Commission.

Figure 3-6   Percentage of PAC Support for Nonincumbents, 1978–1994

Percent

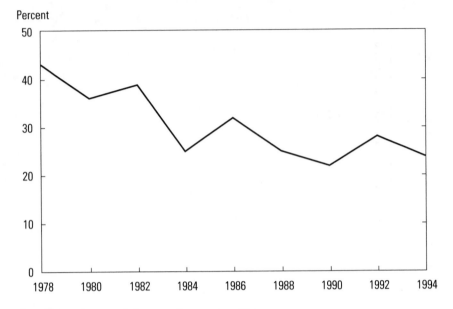

Note: Nonincumbents are challengers and open-seat candidates.
Source: Table 3-14.

Figure 3-7   Independent Expenditures in Senate and House Elections, 1978–1994

(in millions of dollars)

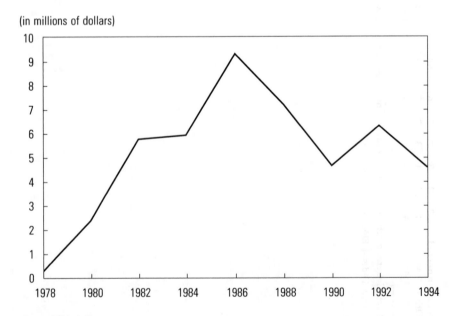

Source: Table 3-15.

Table 3-15   Independent Expenditures in House and Senate Elections, 1978-1994 (in dollars)

	For Democrats	Against Democrats	For Republicans	Against Republicans	Total
1978					
House	28,725	31,034	70,701	5,298	135,758
Senate	102,508	36,717	26,065	1,985	167,275
1980					
House	190,615	38,023	410,478	45,132	684,248
Senate	127,381	1,282,613	261,678	12,430	1,684,102
1982					
House	241,442	862,654	492,404	66,296	1,662,796
Senate	127,451	3,182,986	298,410	483,750	4,092,597
1984					
House	560,727	118,171	633,646	26,847	1,339,391
Senate	326,031	410,428	1,807,981	2,082,207	4,626,647
1986					
House	2,385,685	227,286	1,313,578	120,032	4,046,581
Senate	988,382	632,412	3,342,790	348,006	5,311,590
1988					
House	1,465,554	278,723	919,929	148,705	2,812,911
Senate	831,064	617,066	2,809,517	143,441	4,401,088
1990					
House	709,292	130,695	669,726	74,444	1,584,157
Senate	780,832	266,230	1,436,553	584,429	3,068,044
1992					
House	1,485,768	430,902	1,586,017	452,942	3,955,629
Senate	1,137,321	164,358	864,493	210,490	2,376,662
1994					
House	502,621	488,479	1,088,356	50,815	2,130,271
Senate	204,212	433,947	1,309,572	537,531	2,485,262

Note: An independent expenditure is defined as an "expenditure by a person for a communication expressly advocating the election or defeat of a clearly identified candidate that is not made with the cooperation or with the prior consent of, or in consultation with, or at the request or suggestion of, a candidate or any agent or authorized committee of such candidate" (11 C.F.R. 109.1[a]).

Committees 4

This chapter provides information on House and Senate committees and chairmanships from 1955 to 1995. Tables 4-1, 4-2, and 4-3 chart the ebb and flow in the number of committees and subcommittees in the House and Senate. It should be noted that the number of subcommittees in a given Congress is a particularly nebulous figure. During any Congress, subcommittees are added or dropped, and some ad hoc or special units may be listed or omitted from the various directories. At least two sources were consulted for each Congress to obtain the number of subcommittees.

Tables 4-1 and 4-2 show an erratic but persistent growth in the number of House panels from the 1950s through the Ninety-fourth Congress (1975-1976), with some stabilization and decline evident in the Ninety-sixth and Ninety-eighth Congresses. The numbers remained relatively stable until the 103d Congress, which saw a significant drop in the overall number of panels in the House. This decrease was due in part to rules changes that tightened restrictions on the number of subcommittees allowed each standing committee, as well as the elimination of the House's four select committees.

But these reforms were not considered substantial enough. The Joint Committee on the Organization of Congress was created to study the institution and introduce a comprehensive package of reforms. Unfortunately, when the particular recommendations for committee reforms were put before the full chamber, strong opposition and bickering among affected members prevented any significant reforms from being adopted. But at the outset of the 104th Congress, the new Republican majority approved a series of committee changes as part of their agenda to reform the way the House operates. The total number of House panels dropped by 25 percent. In addition to eliminating three committees—the first decline in the number of full committees since 1955—the new rules stipulated that, with the exception of three committees, no committee could have more than five subcommittees. This lowered the total number of subcommittees to just above the 1955 level.

A very different recent pattern for the Senate is revealed in Tables 4-1 and 4-3. As a result of that body's successful committee reorganization in 1977, the number of panels, particularly subcommittees, was cut dramatically—from an overall 205 in 1975-1976 to 130 in 1979-1980. Whereas the House and Senate had an equivalent number of panels in 1975, the House in 1980 had a clear numerical superiority. In the Ninety-seventh Senate—controlled by Republicans—the number of panels rose from its previous base, but quickly declined again. Similar to the House, the number of Senate committees for the 103d and 104th Congresses dropped, but not to the same extent.

Tables 4-4 and 4-5 display the average number of committee assignments of representatives and senators from 1955 to 1996. House committee and subcommittee assignments more than doubled from 1955 when representatives had an average of three assignments each to 1991 when that average had reached 6.8 assignments. The 1995 restructuring, including a limitation of two standing committee and four subcommittee assignments for most members, brought that average back down to under five assignments each. Senate assignments were cut back considerably with the 1977 reorganization, from an average of 17.6 in 1975 to 10.4 in 1980. The average rose slowly until hitting 11.8 in 1993 and then dropped slightly in 1995. But assignment inflation is a persistent phenomenon in the Senate; note that even with the dramatic decrease since 1975, senators are averaging more than twice as many assignments as their House counterparts.

Tables 4-6 and 4-7 examine chairmanships of committees and subcommittees in Congress. Table 4-6 shows that the proportions of majority party House members with chairmanships of one sort or another rose steadily in the 1960s and 1970s. This figure stabilized at about 50 percent in the 1980s and has fallen some since then. The rise in the 1960s was a direct result of the increase in the number of committees and subcommittees (see Table 4-1). Even though the number of panels declined between 1967 and 1971, the number and proportion of Democrats chairing them increased. This was the result of a 1971 Democratic reform that limited members to the chairmanship of only one subcommittee. The number of members with more than one chairmanship declined accordingly, and for the first time more than half of the majority party members held chairmanships of one kind or another.

The number holding multiple chairmanships of any sort fell somewhat through 1982, then rose substantially in 1983 and jumped again in 1985 and 1987. The norm against "stockpiling" chairmanships had apparently been relaxed, but in 1995 the direction shifted again. The total number of majority members serving as chairs decreased, though the smaller majority margin kept the percentage of majority members chairing panels from falling much at all. The impact of the new restriction on the number of subcommittees per committee may be best seen in this table with the sizable drop in the number of members chairing two or more committees. Only one member currently chairs more than two standing committees and subcommittees, versus twenty-five in 1991 and thirty-two in 1967.

The Senate has always been a different story when it comes to chairmanships (see Table 4-7). With the ratio of members to panels much smaller than in the House, few majority party senators have been denied a gavel of one sort or another since the 1950s; indeed, most majority senators have had at least two chairmanships. The average number of chairmanships rose to 2.9 in the mid-1970s, and then declined with the reorganization to 2.1 in 1979-1980.

Rather than diminishing leadership opportunities for junior senators, however, the reorganization expanded them by limiting the number of chairmanships each senator could hold. In 1979 every Democratic senator save one chaired at least one subcommittee or committee. The stunning arrival of a Republican majority did not change this pattern—every Republican senator except Majority Leader Howard Baker chaired at least one subcommittee in the 97th Congress, and all except Baker and one other held chairmanships in the 98th. Since the 100th Congress, the proportion of majority party senators holding chairmanships has remained below 90 percent. A Republican takeover in 1994 did not change the pattern.

Table 4-8 provides insights into the causes and consequences of seniority reforms of the 1970s, in the House of Representatives in particular. In the 1950s and early 1960s, Democrats from the Deep South constituted a near majority of their party (see Table 1-2 for a more detailed regional breakdown), and they held an even greater share of committee chairmanships. Their overall strength in numbers, however, discouraged any challenge to the system of selecting chairmen by nonsoutherners who opposed the system's unrepresentative results. By the late 1960s, the South's share of the Democratic Party in Congress was on the wane, but its hold on chairmanships of committees, especially the most powerful committees, was more tenacious. The declining number of southern members facilitated a change in the seniority pattern for the selection of chairmen in 1971. After this reform and the dramatic ouster of three southern chairmen in December 1974, the figures changed markedly. By 1979 southerners were underrepresented in committee chairmanships, and while they regained some power in the 1980s, southerners failed to regain the disproportionate share of House chair-manships they held in the 1950s and 1960s. One of the most significant results of the 1994 elections was the Republican takeover of the South. For the first time since Reconstruction, Republicans captured a majority of southern seats in the House and the Senate. Southerners now make up a smaller percentage of the majority and hold a smaller share of committee chairmanships than in the Democratic majority. But the gap is small—21 percent versus 27 percent in 1993—and two of the three exclusive committees in the House are chaired by southerners. If Republicans continue to gain seats in the South while holding onto their majority party status, southern Republicans will see their seniority strength rise. But newly-approved term limits on committee chairs will limit the ability of senior members to cash in.

Similar changes have occurred in the Senate. Through the departure from the Senate of senior southerners and their replacement at the top rungs of committee seniority by nonsouthern Democrats, a broader and more equal regional distribution of power and subcommittee chairman-ships, indicated in Table 4-8, was achieved by the mid-1970s. This meant that few senators felt so shortchanged of power that they would seek to accelerate these trends by a dramatic ouster of chairmen comparable to that in the House in 1974. The South was not disfranchised by the Republican takeover of the Senate in 1981; enough Republicans from the region had accumulated seniority, and enough southerners had been elected as Republicans, that the Senate numbers for 1981 were not dramatically different from those in the preceding Congress, when the Democrats were in the majority. In the meantime, a newer generation of southern Democrats has, almost unnoticed, moved up the seniority ladder. When the Democrats regained the majority in 1986, they were ready: Southerners, once again, had a disproportionately large share of committee chairmanships.

Their seniority strength remained fairly level for the next few years, but then in 1994 they were disfranchised by the Republican takeover. While their percentage of the majority party dropped only 1 percentage point, this was due mostly to a large number of freshman gains. Their seniority strength suffered, leaving them with only 12 percent of the chairmanships. Of course, as in the House, the new southern Republi-cans will gradually move up in seniority, but at a much slower pace in this chamber.

Table 4-1   Number of Committees in House and Senate, 84th-104th Congresses, 1955-1996

Congress	Senate	House	Total [a]
84th (1955-56)	133	130	242
90th (1967-68)	155	185	315
92d (1971-72)	181	175	333
94th (1975-76)	205	204	385
96th (1979-80)	130	193	314
97th (1981-82)	136	174	300
98th (1983-84)	137	172	299
99th (1985-86)	120	191	301
100th (1987-88)	118	192	298
101st (1989-90)	118	189	295
102d (1991-92)	119	185	284
103d (1993-94)	111	146	252
104th (1995-96)	92	110	198

Note: "Committees" include standing committees, subcommittees of standing committees, select and special committees, subcommittees of select and special committees, joint committees, and subcommittees of joint committees.

[a] Total is less than Senate and House combined because joint panels are counted only once.

Sources: Charles B. Brownson, *Congressional Staff Directory* (Washington, D.C.: Congressional Staff Directory, various years); *Congressional Quarterly Almanac* (Washington, D.C.: Congressional Quarterly, various years); *Congressional Yellow Book* (Washington, D.C.: Monitor Publishing Co., quarterly editions); *List of Standing Committees and Subcommittees and Select and Special Committees of the U.S. Senate,* Secretary of the Senate, March 25, 1991; *List of Standing Committees and Select Committees and Their Subcommittees of the House of Representatives,* Clerk of the House of Representatives, March 25, 1991; *Congressional Quarterly Committee Guide,* May 1, 1993; March 25, 1995.

Table 4-2   Number and Type of House Committees, 84th-104th Congresses, 1955-1996

Congress	Standing committees	Subcommittees of standing committees	Select and special committees	Subcommittees of select and special committees	Joint committees	Subcommittees of joint committees
84th (1955-56)	19	83	2	5	10	11
90th (1967-68)	20	133	1	6	10	15
92d (1971-72)	21	120	3	8	8	15
94th (1975-76)	22	151	3	4	7	17
96th (1979-80)	22	149[a]	5	8	4	5
97th (1981-82)	22	132	3	7	4	6
98th (1983-84)	22	130	3	7	4	6
99th (1985-86)	22	142	5	12	4	6
100th (1987-88)	22	140[b]	6	12	4	8
101st (1989-90)	22	138[b]	5	12	4	8
102d (1991-92)	22	135[b]	5	11	4	8
103d (1993-94)	22	115	1	3	5	0
104th (1995-96)	19	84	1	2	4	0

[a] Includes nine budget task forces and the Welfare and Pension Plans Task Force (of the Subcommittee on Labor Management Relations of the Education and Labor Committee).
[b] Includes panels and task forces only if committee has no subcommittees.

Sources: Brownson, Congressional Staff Directory; Congressional Quarterly Almanac; Congressional Yellow Book; Clerk of the House of Representatives; Congressional Quarterly Committee Guide, May 1, 1993; March 25, 1995.

Table 4-3 Number and Type of Senate Committees, 84th-104th Congresses, 1955-1996

Congress	Standing committees	Subcommittees of standing committees	Select and special committees	Subcommittees of select and special committees	Joint committees	Subcommittees of joint committees
84th (1955-56)	15	88	3	6	10	11
90th (1967-68)	16	99	3	12	10	15
92d (1971-72)	17	123	5	13	8	15
94th (1975-76)	18	140	6	17	7	17
96th (1979-80)	15	91	5	10	4	5
97th (1981-82)	15	94	5	12	4	6
98th (1983-84)	16	103	4	4	4	6
99th (1985-86)	16	90	4	0	4	6
100th (1987-88)	16	85	5	0	4	8
101st (1989-90)	16	86	4	0	4	8
102d (1991-92)	16	87	4	0	4	8
103d (1993-94)	17	86	3	0	5	0
104th (1995-96)	17	68	3	0	4	0

Sources: Brownson, *Congressional Staff Directory; Congressional Quarterly Almanac;* Walter Oleszek, "Overview of the Senate Committee System" (Paper prepared for the Commission on the Operation of the Senate, 1977); *Congressional Yellow Book;* Secretary of the Senate; *Congressional Quarterly Committee Guide,* May 1, 1993; March 25, 1995.

Table 4-4   Committee Assignments for Representatives, 84th-104th
Congresses, 1955-1996

Congress		Mean no. of standing committee assignments	Mean no. of subcommittees of standing committee assignments	Mean no. of other committee assignments[a]	Total
84th	(1955-56)	1.2	1.6	0.2	3.0
92d	(1971-72)	1.5	3.2	0.4	5.1
94th	(1975-76)	1.8	4.0	0.4	6.2
96th	(1979-80)	1.7	3.6	0.5	5.8
97th	(1981-82)	1.7	3.4	0.4	5.5
98th	(1983-84)	1.7	3.6	0.5	5.8
99th	(1985-86)	1.8	4.0	0.8	6.6
100th	(1987-88)	1.7	3.8	1.0[b]	6.5
101st	(1989-90)	1.8	3.9	1.1[b]	6.8
102d	(1991-92)	1.9	4.0	0.9[b]	6.8
103d	(1993-94)	2.0	3.7	0.2	5.9
104th	(1995-96)	1.8	2.9	0.1	4.8

[a] "Other" committees include select and special committees, subcommittees of select and special committees, joint committees, and subcommittees of joint committees.
[b] Includes task forces when committee has no other subcommittees.

Sources: Brownson, *Congressional Staff Directory; Congressional Quarterly Almanac; Congressional Yellow Book;* Clerk of the House of Representatives; *Congressional Quarterly Committee Guide,* May 1, 1993; March 25, 1995.

Table 4-5   Committee Assignments for Senators, 84th-104th Congresses, 1955-1996

Congress		Mean no. of standing committee assignments	Mean no. of subcommittees of standing committee assignments	Mean no. of other committee assignments[a]	Total
84th	(1955-56)	2.2	4.8	0.9	7.9
92d	(1971-72)	2.5	9.5	3.3	15.3
94th	(1975-76)	2.5	11.0	4.1	17.6
96th	(1979-80)	2.3	6.6	1.5	10.4
97th	(1981-82)	2.5	6.7	1.5	10.7
98th	(1983-84)	2.9	7.5	1.2	11.6
99th	(1985-86)	2.8	6.9	0.9	10.6
100th	(1987-88)	2.9	7.0	1.2	11.1
101st	(1989-90)	3.0	7.0	1.1	11.1
102d	(1991-92)	2.9	7.4	1.1	11.0
103d	(1993-94)	3.2	7.8	0.8	11.8
104th	(1995-96)	3.1	6.2	0.7	10.8

[a] "Other" committees include select and special committees, subcommittees of select and special committees, joint committees, and subcommittees of joint committees.

Sources: Brownson, *Congressional Staff Directory; Congressional Quarterly Almanac; Congressional Yellow Book;* Secretary of the Senate; *Congressional Quarterly Committee Guide,* May 1, 1993; March 25, 1995.

Table 4-6 Majority Party Chairmanships of House Committees and Subcommittees, 84th-104th Congresses, 1955-1996

Congress	Party in majority	No. of majority party members in House	No. chairing standing committees and sub-committees	No. with two or more chairman-ships	% chairing standing committees and sub-committees	No. chairing all committees and sub-committees[a]	No. with two or more chairman-ships	% chairing all committees and sub-committees[a]
84th (1955-56)	D	232	63	18	27.2	75	22	32.3
90th (1967-68)	D	247	111	32	44.9	117	38	47.4
92d (1971-72)	D	254	120	25	47.2	131	31	51.6
94th (1975-76)	D	289	142	24	49.1	150	28	51.9
96th (1979-80)	D	276	144	19	52.2	149	28	54.0
97th (1981-82)	D	243	121	16	49.8	125	26	51.4
98th (1983-84)	D	267	124	23	46.4	127	33	47.6
99th (1985-86)	D	253	129	27	51.0	131	37	51.8
100th (1987-88)	D	258	128	28	49.6	132[b]	42	51.2
101st (1989-90)	D	260	134	26	51.5	137	38	52.7
102d (1991-92)	D	267	130	25	48.7	135[b]	37	50.6
103d (1993-94)	D	258	113	19	43.8	116	22	45.0
104th (1995-96)	R	230	102	1	44.3	103	4	44.8

[a] Includes standing committees, subcommittees of standing committees, select and special committees, subcommittees of select and special committees, joint committees, and subcommittees of joint committees.

[b] Includes task forces when committee has no other subcommittees.

Sources: Brownson, *Congressional Staff Directory; Congressional Quarterly Almanac;* Clerk of the House of Representatives; *Congressional Quarterly Committee Guide,* May 1, 1993; March 25, 1995.

Table 4-7 Majority Party Chairmanships of Senate Committees and Subcommittees, 84th-104th Congresses, 1955-1996

Congress	Party in majority	No. of majority party in Senate	No. chairing standing committees and subcommittees	% chairing standing committees and subcommittees	Average no. of standing committees and subcommittees chaired by majority members	No. chairing all committees and subcommittees[a]	% chairing all committees and subcommittees[a]	Average no. of all committees and subcommittees chaired by majority members
84th (1955-56)	D	48	42	87.5	1.8	42	87.5	2.0
90th (1967-68)	D	64	55	85.9	1.8	58	90.6	2.1
92d (1971-72)	D	55[b]	51	92.7	2.6	52	94.5	2.9
94th (1975-76)	D	62[b]	57	91.9	2.4	57	91.9	2.9
96th (1979-80)	D	59[b]	58	98.3	1.8	58	98.3	2.1
97th (1981-82)	R	53	51	96.2	1.9	52	98.1	2.3
98th (1983-84)	R	54	52	96.3	1.9	52	96.3	2.5
99th (1985-86)	R	53	49	92.4	1.9	49	92.4	2.0
100th (1987-88)[c]	D	54	47	87.0	1.8	47	87.0	2.0
101st (1989-90)	D	55	46	83.6	1.9	46	83.6	1.9
102d (1991-92)	D	56	50	89.3	1.8	50	89.3	2.0
103d (1993-94)	D	57	46	80.7	1.8	46	80.7	1.9
104th (1995-96)	R	54	44	81.5	1.8	44	81.5	1.9

[a] Includes standing committees, subcommittees of standing committees, select and special committees, subcommittees of select and special committees, joint committees, and subcommittees of joint committees.

[b] Includes Harry Byrd, Jr., elected as an Independent.

[c] Figures for the 100th Congress were compiled after the death of Sen. Edward Zorinsky (D-Neb.) but before the appointment of his successor and the redistribution of his chairmanships.

Sources: Brownson, Congressional Staff Directory; Congressional Quarterly Almanac; Secretary of the Senate; Congressional Quarterly Committee Guide, May 1, 1993; March 25, 1995.

Table 4-8 Southern Chairmanships of House and Senate Standing Committees, 1955-1995

Year	House				Senate			
	Number of southern chairmen	% of chairmanships held by southerners	% of exclusive committees[a] chaired by southerners	% of majority party[b] from the South	Number of southern chairmen	% of chairmanships held by southerners	% of exclusive committees[a] chaired by southerners	% of majority party[b] from the South
1955	12	63	67	43	8	53	50	46
1967	10	50	100	35	9	56	100	28
1971	8	38	100	31	9	53	100	30
1975	9	41	33	28	6	33	100	27
1979	5	23	33	28	4	27	50	28
1981	6	27	33	29	3	20	25	19
1983	7	32	67	30	3	19	25	20
1985	8	36	67	29	2	13	0	19
1987	7	31	67	29	7	44	75	30
1989	8	36	67	29	6	38	50	27
1991	8	36	33	29	6	38	50	27
1993	6	27	33	33	6	35	25	26
1995	4	21	67	25	2	12	50	25

[a] In the House: Ways and Means, Rules, and Appropriations; in the Senate: Appropriations, Finance, Foreign Relations, and Armed Services.
[b] In 1981, 1983, 1985, and 1995, the Republicans were the majority party in the Senate; in 1995, they were also the majority party in the House. For all other years in the table, Democrats were the majority party in both the Senate and the House.

Sources: Congressional Directory (Washington, D.C.: U.S. Government Printing Office, various years); Congressional Yellow Book; Congressional Quarterly Committee Guide, May 1, 1993; March 25, 1995.

Table 4-9   Closed Committee Meetings, 1953-1975

Year	Total meetings	Number closed	% closed
1953	2,640	892	34
1954	3,002	1,243	41
1955	2,940	1,055	36
1956	3,120	1,130	36
1957	2,517	854	34
1958	3,472	1,167	34
1959	3,152	940	30
1960	2,424	840	35
1961	3,159	1,109	35
1962	2,929	991	34
1963	3,868	1,463	38
1964	2,393	763	32
1965	3,903	1,537	39
1966	3,869	1,626	42
1967	4,412	1,716	39
1968	3,080	1,328	43
1969	4,029	1,470	36
1970	4,506	1,865	41
1971	4,816	1,731	36
1972	4,073	1,648	40
1973	5,520	887	16
1974	4,731	707	15
1975[a]	6,325	449	7
Total	84,880	27,411	32

Note: Subcommittee meetings were included in the totals along with full committee sessions. Open meetings followed by closed meetings were counted twice, once in each category. Joint meetings of separate committees or subcommittees were counted as one meeting for each. The tabulations exclude meetings held when Congress was not in regular session, meetings held outside Washington, D.C., informal meetings without official status, and meetings of the House Rules Committee to consider sending legislation to the floor. Meetings of the House Appropriations Committee, all reported closed until 1971, were not included in the study until 1965.

[a] Figures have not been computed after 1975 because virtually all committee meetings have been open. At the start of the 104th Congress, House Republicans passed a rule that all committee and subcommittee meetings must be open unless it would pose a threat to national security.

Source: Congressional Quarterly's Guide to Congress, 2d ed. (Washington, D.C.: Congressional Quarterly, 1976), 370.

Congressional Staff   5
and Operating Expenses

Congress is made up of a great deal more than elected senators and representatives. With over 26,000 employees in 1993 (Table 5-1 and Figure 5-1), the legislative branch is larger than the departments of State, Labor, or Housing and Urban Development, making Congress by far the most heavily staffed legislative branch in the world.

In addition to the personal and committee staffs of representatives and senators, Congress also employs major research agencies, such as the Congressional Research Service (CRS) of the Library of Congress, and support personnel, such as mail carriers, police officers, television technicians, computer specialists, printers, carpenters, parking attendants, photographers, and laborers.

The development of this large congressional establishment is a twentieth-century phenomenon. At the turn of the century, representatives had no personal staff, and senators had a total of only thirty-nine personal assistants (see Table 5-2 and Figure 5-1). By contrast, 11,538 persons served on the personal staffs of representatives and senators in 1993, and more than 3,000 people were employed by congressional committees.

The enlargement of Congress's support staff reflects both the expanding role of the government in the United States and the changing role of the individual legislator. As government has done more, the congressional workload, in terms of both legislation and constituency service, has increased, and the staffing needs of Congress have expanded accordingly. The most dramatic staff growth took place in the years after World War II; the personal staffs of the House and Senate having increased more than fivefold and sixfold, respectively, since 1947. One reflection of the increased demands on legislators for constituency services and the members' encouragement of those demands for reelection purposes is the dramatic expansion of congressional staff working in constituency offices. More than 47 percent of the personal staffs of representatives and 35.7 percent of those of senators now work in district or state offices—a dramatic increase since the early 1970s (see Tables 5-3 and 5-4).

The explosion in congressional staffing is also evident on the standing committees: House committee staffs increased nearly twelvefold and Senate committee staffs more than fourfold between 1947 and 1989 (see Table 5-5). Committee staffing has grown steadily since the turn of the century, but the most dramatic increases occurred in the 1970s. House committee staffs were two and three-quarters times as large in 1979 as they were in 1970, and Senate committee staffs doubled over the same period. Staffs of both the House and Senate declined slightly in 1993, and Republicans opened the 104th Congress with a rule to cut committee staffs by one-third, and a stated commitment to cut other staffs, including those of the support agencies.

The enlargement of House committee staffs after 1970 is to a significant degree a result of the reform movement that swept the chamber. The sentiment for diluting the powers of committee chairmen extended to their nearly exclusive authority to hire and fire committee staff. Reforms allowed a much larger number of subcommittee chairmen and ranking members to hire their own staffs. The 1975 surge in committee staffing in the Senate reflects the passage of Senate Resolution 60, which authorized each senator to have a personal legislative assistant for each committee assignment. Another factor that has contributed to the growth of committee staffs is the increasing complexity of legislative and policy issues. Many committee staff members are considered to be experts in their field of policy analysis.

The modest reductions in Senate committee staffs in 1977 were caused by the committee reorganization that went into effect that year, which among other things reduced the number of Senate subcommittees and shifted employees hired under Senate Resolution 60 to personal staff payrolls.

Today congressional staffs have become the target for a good deal of the criticism aimed at Congress. Critics have portrayed congressional staffs as bloated and wasteful. While it is true that staffs have grown sharply since World War II, and particularly in the past quarter century, the majority of that growth occurred from the late 1960s through the mid-1970s. This growth coincided with the decentralization of Congress, noted above, as well as the growth of White House and executive branch staff. Staff growth has actually leveled off since the late 1970s. Today congressional staff sizes, personal and committee, are at approximately the same level they were ten years ago, with a slight decline in the past few years and projections for further cuts ahead.

Tables 5-6 and 5-7 rank the standing committees according to their current staff size. Each committee except the Senate Judiciary Committee had a significantly larger staff in 1993 than it had in 1960. Most committees employ well over fifty persons, a far cry from the post-World War II era of small, intimate, informal committee staffs. Still, reflecting the current negative attitude toward congressional staffs and the cost of employing them, all but six House committees saw their staffs decrease in 1993. The size of a committee staff does not appear to be related uniformly to the reported power or desirability of an assignment to that committee. The powerful Senate Finance Committee, for example, is modestly staffed compared with the less influential Labor and Human Resources and Governmental Affairs committees. Of course, some committees that are generally considered less desirable assignments may well have expanded their staffs to attract new members.

A significant part of the congressional staff works for Congress's four major research agencies (see Table 5-8). Two of these, the Congressional Budget Office (CBO) and the Office of Technology Assessment (OTA), were created in the mid-1970s, their creation reflecting a basic factor underlying the growth of congressional staff. The expanded role of the government in domestic and international affairs had made Congress increasingly dependent on the executive branch for information. A growing distrust of the executive branch, which festered during the Johnson and Nixon administrations, convinced Congress of the necessity for congressionally controlled sources of information. Congress thus authorized these new agencies and simultaneously expanded the roles of the Congressional Research Service (CRS) and the General Accounting Office (GAO). The GAO has multiple functions; its primary job is to review federal spending and management for Congress. In addition, the office offers legal opinions to government agencies, settles disputed claims by or against the United States, and prescribes accounting standards for government-wide use. While a majority of GAO's resources was devoted to these other functions during the 1970s, the balance has since shifted and today roughly 80 percent of GAO's work is directly related to Congress.

Although the numbers in these tables describe the growth of congressional staff, they do not reveal the many roles staff members play in the legislative process. The infinite variety of staffing arrangements that exists in members' offices and on committees and the influence exercised by various staff members become apparent only through close examination of individual offices and committees. The role played by staff within individual offices may also change over time with the ebb and flow of political tides. President Reagan's ability to make Congress focus on budget issues, for example, greatly reduced the number of bills Congress passed, as did the focus President Clinton placed on health care reform in 1993 (see Chapter 6). That meant less chance for members to use their staffs as policy entrepreneurs. Still, although the number of bills passed in 1993 declined, most committees claimed some jurisdiction over the health care reform issue and had their staffers working on it fervently. In short, it is difficult, if not impossible, to generalize about staffing roles and patterns solely on the basis of gross figures.

The costs of running Congress have grown along with the staff. Today's Congress is now more than a $2 billion enterprise. Although that may appear small when compared with the executive branch, it has grown at a dramatic pace from what it once was. In the years between 1946 and 1994, legislative branch appropriations increased 4,097.8 percent. Over the same period, the consumer price index went up "only" 659 percent (see Table 5-9). As recently as the mid-1960s, the cost of operating Congress was less than one-ninth of what it is today. Recent years have shown signs of more legislative self-control: in the years between FY1976, when Congress first approached the billion dollar threshold, and FY1994, legislative branch appropriations went up only 140 percent, while the consumer price index increased by 160 percent. In fact, the FY1994 overall budget reflects a $34.3 million decrease since 1992.

The figures summarizing legislative branch appropriations include much more than the cost of House and Senate operations. It also includes the expenses of such agencies as the Library of Congress, the Government Printing Office, the General Accounting Office, the Botanic Garden, and the Copyright Royalty Commission, which make up a large portion of the spending. In fact, actual House and Senate appropriations comprise under 50 percent of total legislative branch appropriations. And, while overall spending has fluctuated significantly through the years, figures within these other components have remained relatively stable over the last decade. (See Table 5-10.)

Table 5-11 traces one of the perquisites of office available to members of Congress—use of the frank to send materials pertaining to the official business of Congress through the U.S. mails. In 1993 the cost of the congressional franking privilege was $67.7 million. Until 1981, the main reasons for the growing use of the frank were a more liberal law, permitting members of Congress to send mail (including newsletters and questionnaires) addressed to "occupant," and the increased value that legislators attach to communications with their constituents. The explosive growth since 1981 is a reflection of grass-roots lobbying. In other words, the first wave of growth was stimulated by members, the second by constituents. The rules have now changed to limit use of the frank and to prevent members from using the frank as a campaign tool. And, the House Oversight Committee of the 104th Congress voted to cut franking authorization by one-third of the 1994 figures.

Tables 5-12 and 5-13 summarize the allowances available to representatives and senators for operating their offices and outline the changes in those allowances since 1977. In the past, expenses for such things as postage, stationery, office furnishings, equipment, and travel were governed by strict individual spending limits. The House in 1978 and the Senate in 1973 consolidated their office expense allowances into one account to give members greater flexibility in using their expense allowances. Because Congress is a labor intensive enterprise, however, the largest share of the congressional allowance is for staff.

NOTE: In the source notes to the tables in this chapter, two kinds of frequently cited legislative appropriations documents are abbreviated as follows: 1) *House LBA Hearings for 19xx* = U.S. Congress, House of Representatives, Committee on Appropriations, Subcommittee on Legislative Branch Appropriations, *Hearings on Legislative Branch Appropriations for 19xx*. 2) *Senate LBA Hearings for 19xx* = U.S. Congress, Senate, Committee on Appropriations, *Hearings on Legislative Branch Appropriations for 19xx*. The year in the citation is the fiscal year covered by the appropriation hearing, not the calendar year that may appear in the table.

Table 5-1 Congressional Staff, 1979-1993

	1979	1981	1983	1985	1987	1989	1991	1993
House								
Committee staff[a]	2,027	1,917	2,068	2,146	2,136	2,267	2,321	2,147[b]
Personal staff	7,067	7,487	7,606	7,528	7,584	7,569	7,278	7,400
Leadership staff[c]	162	127	135	144	138	133	149	137
Officers of the House, staff[d]	1,487	1,686	1,728	1,818	1,845	1,215	1,293	1,194
Subtotal, House	10,743	11,217	11,537	11,636	11,703	11,184	11,041	10,878
Senate								
Committee staff[a]	1,410	1,150	1,176	1,178	1,207	1,116	1,154	994
Personal staff	3,593	3,945	4,059	4,097	4,075	3,837	4,294	4,138
Leadership staff[c]	91	106	120	118	103	105	95	100
Officers of the Senate, staff[d]	828	878	948	976	904	926	1,092	1,165
Subtotal, Senate	5,922	6,079	6,303	6,369	6,289	5,984	6,635	6,397
Joint committee staffs	138	126	123	131	132	138	145	145
Support agencies[e]								
General Accounting Office	5,303	5,182	4,960	5,042	5,016	5,063	5,054	4,958
Congressional Research Service	847	849	853	860	860	860	831	814
Congressional Budget Office	207	218	211	222	226	226	226	230
Office of Technology Assessment	145	130	130	143	143	143	143	143
Subtotal, support agencies	6,502	6,379	6,154	6,267	6,245	6,292	6,254	6,145
Miscellaneous								
Architect	2,296	1,986	2,061	2,073	2,412	2,088	2,099	2,060

(Table continues)

132

Table 5-1 (continued)

	1979	1981	1983	1985	1987	1989	1991	1993
Capitol Police[f]	1,167	1,163	1,148	1,227	1,250	1,259	1,265	1,159
Subtotal	3,463	3,149	3,209	3,300	3,662	3,347	3,364	3,219
Total	26,768	26,950	27,326	27,703	28,031	26,945	27,439	26,784

Note: Totals for Tables 5-1 through 5-8 reflect number of full-time paid employees.

[a] Includes select and special committee staffs. Figures therefore do not agree with those in Table 5-5.

[b] In addition to the staffs (twenty-nine members) of the Permanent Select Committee on Intelligence and the Joint Committee on the Organization of Congress, which retained twenty-nine staff members, there were three other select committees in operation in 1993. These committees, the Select Committee on Aging, the Select Committee on Children, Youth, and Families, and the Special and Select Committee on Funerals, were not reauthorized by the 104th Congress. However, the committees stayed on for a few months to complete previous business. Although the committees did little business in 1993, it should be noted that they retained small staffs during this time.

[c] Includes legislative counsels' offices.

[d] Doorkeepers, parliamentarians, sergeants-at-arms, clerk of the House, Senate majority and minority secretaries, and postmasters.

[e] Adjustments were made in this edition to reflect the current division of labor among the various support agencies. Today approximately 80 percent of GAO's work is done directly for Congress; the Congressional Research Service is the branch of the Library of Congress that serves Congress most directly.

[f] Sworn officers only.

Sources: For 1979, *Report of the Clerk of the House,* July 1, 1979-September 30, 1979; *Report of the Secretary of the Senate,* April 1, 1979-September 30, 1979; U.S. Office of Personnel Management, Work Force Analysis and Statistics Branch, *Federal Civilian Workforce Statistics,* monthly release, October 31, 1979, 6. For 1981, U.S. Congress, House, Committee on Appropriations, Subcommittee on Legislative Branch Appropriations, *Hearings on Legislative Branch Appropriations for 1983,* pt. 1, 24-28; U.S. Congress, Senate, Committee on Appropriations, *Hearings on Legislative Branch Appropriations for 1982,* 117, 253, 266; Senate Committee on Rules and Administration, *Senate Committee Funding,* 97th Cong., 1st sess., 1981, Committee Print 2; *Report of the Secretary of the Senate,* October 1, 1981-March 31, 1982, 1-23. For 1983, *House LBA Hearings for 1985,* pt. 1, 23-27; Office of the Clerk of the House; Senate Committee on Rules and Administration, *Senate Committee Funding,* 98th Cong., 2d sess., 1984, Committee Print 3; *Senate LBA Hearings for 1984,* 47, 276; Office of the U.S. Capitol Police. For 1985, *House LBA Hearings for 1987,* pt. 1, 22-27; *Report of the Clerk of the House,* October 1, 1985-December 31, 1985; Senate Committee on Rules and Administration, *Senate Committee Funding,* 99th Cong., 2d sess., 1986, Committee Print 2; *Senate LBA Hearings for 1986; Report of the Secretary of the Senate,* October 1, 1985-March 31, 1986; Office of the U.S. Capitol Police. For 1987, *House LBA Hearings for 1989,* pt. 2; Office of the Clerk of the House; *Senate LBA Hearings for 1988; Report of the Secretary of the Senate,* October 1, 1987-March 31, 1988; Bureau of the Census, *Statistical Abstract of the United States 1989* (Washington, D.C.: U.S. Government Printing Office, 1989), 252; Office of the Architect of the Capitol; Office of the U.S. Capitol Police. For 1989, *House LBA Hearings for 1991,* pt. 1; Office of the Clerk of the House; *Senate LBA Hearings for 1990; Report of the Secretary of the Senate,* October 1, 1989-March 31, 1990. For 1991, *House LBA Hearings for 1993,* pt. 1; *Report of the Clerk of the House,* October 1, 1991-December 31, 1991; *Senate LBA Hearings for 1992; Report of the Secretary of the Senate,* October 1, 1991-March 31, 1992. For 1993, *House LBA Hearings for 1995,* pt. 1; *Report of the Clerk of the House,* October 1, 1993-December 31, 1993; House Office of Finance; *Senate LBA Hearings for 1994; Report of the Secretary of the Senate,* October 1, 1993-March 31, 1994.

Table 5-2   Staffs of Members of the House and the Senate, 1891-1993

Year	Employees in House	Employees in Senate	Year	Employees in House	Employees in Senate
1891	n.a.	39	1981	7,487	3,945
1914	n.a.	72	1982	7,511	4,041
1930	870	280	1983	7,606	4,059
1935	870	424	1984	7,385	3,949
1947	1,440	590	1985	7,528	4,097
1957	2,441	1,115	1986	7,920[a]	3,774[a]
1967	4,055	1,749	1987	7,584	4,075
1972	5,280	2,426	1988	7,564	3,977
1976	6,939	3,251	1989	7,569	3,837
1977	6,942	3,554	1990	7,496	4,162
1978	6,944	3,268	1991	7,278	4,294
1979	7,067	3,593	1992	7,597	4,249
1980	7,371	3,746	1993	7,400	4,138

n.a. = not available.

[a] Senate figures reflect the period immediately after Gramm-Rudman mandated staffing cuts. House figures are for the entire fiscal year, thus averaging post-Gramm-Rudman staffing levels with previous, higher levels.

Sources: For 1891 through 1976, Harrison W. Fox, Jr., and Susan W. Hammond, *Congressional Staffs: The Invisible Force in American Lawmaking* (New York: Free Press, 1977), 171. For 1977 and 1978, Judy Schneider, "Congressional Staffing, 1947-78," Congressional Research Service, Library of Congress, August 24, 1979, reprinted in U.S. Congress, House, Select Committee on Committees, *Final Report*, 96th Cong., 2d sess., 1980, 540. For 1977, 1978, and 1979 House, *Report of the Clerk of the House.* For 1979 Senate, *Report of the Secretary of the Senate.* For 1980, *House LBA Hearings for 1982*, pt. 1, 25; *Senate LBA Hearings for 1981*, pt. 1, 26. For 1981, *House LBA Hearings for 1983*, pt. 1, 24-28; *Report of the Secretary of the Senate*, October 1, 1981-March 31, 1982. For 1982, *House LBA Hearings for 1984*, pt. 1, 25; *Report of the Secretary of the Senate*, October 1, 1982-March 31, 1983. For 1983, *House LBA Hearings for 1985*, pt. 1, 24; *Report of the Secretary of the Senate*, October 1, 1983-March 31, 1984. For 1984, *House LBA Hearings for 1986*, pt. 1, 22; *Report of the Secretary of the Senate*, October 1, 1984-March 31, 1985. For 1985-1986, *House LBA Hearings for 1987*, pt. 1, 23; *Report of the Secretary of the Senate*, October 1, 1985-March 31, 1986. For 1987, *House LBA Hearings for 1989*, pt. 2; *Senate LBA Hearings for 1988*; *Report of the Secretary of the Senate*, October 1, 1987-March 31, 1988. For 1988, *House LBA Hearings for 1990*, pt. 2; *Report of the Secretary of the Senate*, April-September 1989, pt. 1. For 1989, *House LBA Hearings for 1991*, pt. 2; *Report of the Secretary of the Senate*, October 1, 1989-March 31, 1990. For 1990, *House LBA Hearings for 1992*, pt. 2; *Report of the Secretary of the Senate*, October 1, 1990-March 31, 1991. For 1991, *House LBA Hearings for 1993*, pt. 2; *Report of the Secretary of the Senate*, October 1, 1991-March 31, 1992. For 1992, House Appropriations Committee; *Report of the Secretary of the Senate*, October 1, 1992-March 31, 1993. For 1993, House Office of Finance; *Report of the Secretary of the Senate*, October 1, 1993-March 31, 1994.

Figure 5-1   Staff of Members and of Committees in Congress, 1891–1993

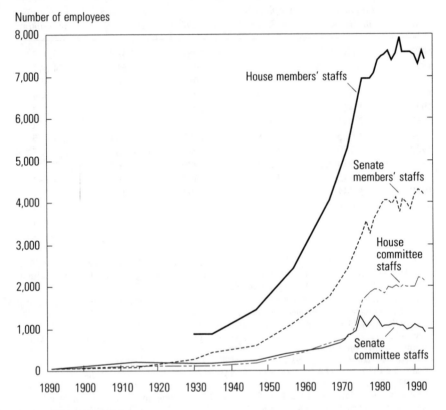

Number of employees

Sources: Tables 5-2 and 5-5.

Table 5-3   House Staff Based in District Offices, 1970-1994

Year	Employees	Percentage of total personal staffs in district offices
1970	1,035	n.a.
1971	1,121	n.a.
1972	1,189	22.5
1973	1,347	n.a.
1974	1,519	n.a.
1975	1,732	n.a.
1976	1,943	28.0
1977	2,058	29.6
1978	2,317	33.4
1979	2,445	34.6
1980	2,534	34.4
1981	2,702	36.1
1982	2,694	35.8
1983	2,785	36.6
1984	2,872	38.9
1985	2,871	38.1
1986	2,940	43.6
1987	2,503	33.0
1988	2,954	39.6
1989	2,916	38.5
1990	3,027	40.4
1991	3,022	41.5
1992	3,128	42.1
1993	3,130	46.5
1994	3,335	47.3

n.a. = not available.

Sources: For 1970-1978, Schneider, "Congressional Staffing, 1947-78." For 1979-1988, Charles B. Brownson, *Congressional Staff Directory* (Washington, D.C.: Congressional Staff Directory, annual editions). For 1989-1994, Ann Brownson, *Congressional Staff Directory.*

Table 5-4   Senate Staff Based in State Offices, 1972-1994

Year	Employees	Percentage of total personal staffs in state offices
1972	303	12.5
1978	816	25.0
1979	879	24.4
1980	953	25.4
1981	937	25.8
1982	1,053	26.1
1983	1,132	27.9
1984	1,140	28.9
1985	1,180	28.8
1986	1,249	33.1
1987	1,152	28.3
1988	1,217	30.6
1989	1,200	31.3
1990	1,293	31.1
1991	1,316	30.6
1992	1,368	31.6
1993	1,335	35.9
1994	1,345	35.7

Source: Brownson, *Congressional Staff Directory.*

Table 5-5   Staffs of House and Senate Standing Committees, 1891-1993

Year	Employees in House	Employees in Senate	Year	Employees in House	Employees in Senate
1891	62	41	1978	1,844	1,151
1914	105	198	1979	1,909	1,269
1930	112	163	1980	1,917	1,191
1935	122	172	1981	1,843	1,022
1947	167	232	1982	1,839	1,047
1950	246	300	1983	1,970	1,075
1955	329	386	1984	1,944	1,095
1960	440	470	1985	2,009	1,080
1965	571	509	1986	1,954	1,075
1970	702	635	1987	2,024	1,074
1971	729	711	1988	1,976	970
1972	817	844	1989	1,986	1,013
1973	878	873	1990	1,993	1,090
1974	1,107	948	1991	2,201	1,030
1975	1,460	1,277	1992	2,178	1,008
1976	1,680	1,201	1993	2,118	897
1977	1,776	1,028			

Note: Figures for 1947-1986 are for the statutory and investigative staffs of standing committees. They do not include select committee staffs, which varied between 31 and 238 in the House and between 62 and 172 in the Senate during the 1970s. For this reason, the numbers do not agree with those in Table 5-1. In an attempt to provide further accuracy, we have counted certain individuals as .5 of a staff member based on the length of employment and salary received. Rounding of these numbers then means that figures in this table do not necessarily equal those of the individual committees in Tables 5-6 and 5-7.

Sources: For 1891-1935, Fox and Hammond, *Congressional Staffs,* 171. For 1947-1978, Schneider, "Congressional Staffing, 1947-78." For 1979-1980 Senate, U.S. Congress, Senate, Committee on Rules and Administration, *Senate Inquiries and Investigations,* 96th Cong., 2d sess., 1980, Committee Print 2, March 5, 1980. For 1981-1986 Senate, U.S. Congress, Senate, Committee on Rules and Administration, *Senate Committee Funding,* annual committee prints. For 1981 House, *House LBA Hearings for 1983,* pt. 2, 107. For 1982 House, *House LBA Hearings for 1984,* pt. 2, 77. For 1983-1984 House, Office of the Clerk of the House. For 1985 House, *Report of the Clerk of the House,* October 1, 1985-December 31, 1985. For 1986 House, *Report of the Clerk of the House,* October 1, 1986-December 31, 1986. For 1987 House, *Report of the Clerk of the House,* October 1, 1987-December 31, 1987; Senate, Committee on Rules and Administration. For 1988 House, *Report of the Clerk of the House,* October 1, 1988-December 31, 1988; Senate, *Report of the Secretary of the Senate,* April-September 1989, pt. 1. For 1989 House, *Report of the Clerk of the House,* October 1, 1989-December 31, 1989; Senate, *Report of the Secretary of the Senate,* October 1, 1989-March 31, 1990, pt. 1. For 1990 House, *Report of the Clerk of the House,* October 1, 1990-December 31, 1990; Senate, *Report of the Secretary of the Senate,* October 1, 1990-March 31, 1991. For 1991 House, *Report of the Clerk of the House,* October 1, 1991-December 31, 1991; Senate, *Report of the Secretary of the Senate,* October 1, 1991-March 31, 1992. For 1992 House, *Report of the Clerk of the House,* October 1, 1992-December 31, 1992; Senate, *Report of the Secretary of the Senate,* October 1, 1992-March 31, 1993. For 1993 House, *Report of the Clerk of the House,* October 1, 1993-December 31, 1993; Senate, *Report of the Secretary of the Senate,* October 1, 1993-March 31, 1994.

Table 5-6 Staffs of House Standing Committees, 1947-1993

Committee	1947	1960	1970	1975	1979	1981	1983	1985	1987	1989	1991	1993
House Administration[a]	7	4	25	217	273	252	267	275	228	275	317	317
Appropriations	29	59	71	98	129	127	160	182	188	196	218	227
Ways and Means	12	22	24	63	99	91	94	99	108	94	94	142
Energy and Commerce	10	45	42	112	160	151	158	162	153	138	155	140
Education and Labor	10	25	77	114	121	121	121	119	127	114	117	112
Banking	4	14	50	85	97	87	93	90	99	108	112	100
Budget	b	b	b	67	86	93	97	109	124	96	101	98
Foreign Affairs	10	14	21	54	82	84	85	97	101	98	104	96
Public Works	6	32	40	88	81	86	84	84	83	83	97	89
Science and Technology	b	17	26	47	87	74	78	78	78	79	84	87
Government Operations	9	54	60	68	85	84	87	86	80	82	90	86
Armed Services	10	15	37	38	48	49	56	64	70	66	82	76
Post Office and Civil Service	6	9	46	61	66	74	87	83	85	83	87	76
Judiciary	7	27	35	69	80	75	82	81	81	80	71	75
Merchant Marine and Fisheries	6	9	21	28	91	82	81	79	77	74	76	75
Natural Resources	4	10	14	57	75	70	73	73	71	67	85[c]	71
Agriculture	9	10	17	48	66	62	70	67	69	69	69	70
Rules	4	2	7	18	47	43	47	45	43	41	49	48

Veterans' Affairs	7	18	18	26	34	34	32	32	44	41	44	46
Small Business	[b]	[b]	[b]	27	46	54	53	53	62	54	53	45
District of Columbia	7	8	15	43	41	41	46	42	42	39	40	34
Standards of Official Conduct	[b]	[b]	5	5	15	9	19	9	11	8	11	9

Note: Committees are ranked in order of their staff size in 1993. Through 1991, numbers ending in .5 are rounded up.

[a] After 1972, figures include employees of House Informations Systems, the House of Representatives' central computer facility.

[b] Not a standing committee.

[c] In 1993 the Natural Resources Committee was created out of the old Interior Committee. The staff figures for 1947-1991 are actually those of the Interior Committee.

Sources: For 1947-1975, Schneider, "Congressional Staffing, 1947-78." For 1979, *House LBA Hearings for 1983*, pt. 2, 107. For 1983, Office of the Clerk of the House. For 1985, *Report of the Clerk of the House*, October 1, 1985-December 31, 1985. For 1987, *Report of the Clerk of the House*, October 1, 1987-December 31, 1987. For 1989, *Report of the Clerk of the House*, October 1, 1989-December 31, 1989. For 1991, *Report of the Clerk of the House*, October 1, 1991-December 31, 1991. For 1993, *Report of the Clerk of the House*, October 1, 1993-December 31, 1993.

Table 5-7 Staffs of Senate Standing Committees, 1947-1993

Committee	1947	1960	1970	1975	1979	1981	1983	1985	1987	1989	1991	1993
Judiciary	19	137	190	251	223	134	141	141	138	127	139	108
Labor and Human Resources	9	28	69	150	155	119	125	127	127	122	122	108
Governmental Affairs	29	47	55	144	179	153	138	131	126	111	108	96
Appropriations	23	31	42	72	80	79	82	82	81	80	80	72
Commerce, Science, and Transportation	8	52	53	111	96	78	90	93	93	76	75	68
Budget	a	a	a	90	91	82	79	81	83	66	63	58
Foreign Relations	8	25	31	62	75	59	63	61	60	58	67	54
Banking, Housing, and Urban Affairs	9	22	23	55	48	39	39	38	39	51	57	51
Armed Services	10	23	19	30	31	36	41	48	49	51	50	50
Energy and Natural Resources (Interior)	7	26	22	53	55	50	56	57	57	50	49	46
Finance	6	6	16	26	67	50	53	54	54	55	58	46
Environment and Public Works	10	11	34	70	74	56	56	56	56	50	46	40
Agriculture	3	10	7	22	34	34	34	34	35	42	37	29
Rules and Administration	41	15	13	29	37	31	30	28	27	27	27	24

| Small Business | a | a | a | a | a | 26 | 24 | 26 | 22 | 21 | 24 |
| Veterans' Affairs | a | a | 32 | 24 | 22 | 22 | 25 | 23 | 25 | 25 | 24 |

Note: Committees are ranked in the order of their staff size in 1993. Through 1991, numbers ending in .5 are rounded up.

a Committee not in existence.

Sources: For 1947-1975, Schneider, "Congressional Staffing, 1947-78." For 1979-1987, U.S. Congress, Senate, Committee on Rules and Administration, *Senate Committee Funding* (this annual committee print lists the number of positions authorized for each committee; the number actually employed at any one time may be less). For 1989, *Report of the Secretary of the Senate, October 1, 1989-March 31, 1990,* pt. 1. For 1991, *Report of the Secretary of the Senate, October 1, 1991-March 31, 1992,* pt. 1. For 1993, *Report of the Secretary of the Senate, October 1, 1993-March 31, 1994,* pt. 1.

Table 5-8   Staffs of Congressional Support Agencies, FY1946-1993

Year	Library of Congress	Congres-sional Research Service only[a]	General Accounting Office[b]	Congres-sional Budget Office	Office of Technology Assessment
1946	—	—	14,219	—	—
1947	1,898	160	10,695	—	—
1950	1,973	161	7,876	—	—
1955	2,459	166	5,776	—	—
1960	2,779	183	5,074	—	—
1965	3,390	231	4,278	—	—
1970	3,848	332	4,704	—	—
1971	3,963	386	4,718	—	—
1972	4,135	479	4,742	—	—
1973	4,375	596	4,908	—	—
1974	4,504	687	5,270	—	10
1975	4,649	741	4,905	193	54
1976	4,880	806	5,391	203	103
1977	5,075	789	5,315	201	139
1978	5,231	818	5,476	203	164
1979	5,390	847	5,303	207	145
1980	5,047	868	5,196	218	122
1981	4,799	849	5,182	218	130
1982	4,803	849	5,027	218	130
1983	4,815	853	4,960	211	130
1984	4,802	858	4,985	210	139
1985	4,809	860	5,042	222	143
1986	4,806	860	5,019	222	143
1987	4,983	860	5,016	226	143
1988	4,874	825	5,042	211	143
1989	4,793	860	5,063	226	143
1990	4,659	797	5,066	226	143
1991	5,043	831	5,054	226	143
1992	5,050	838	5,062	218	143
1993	5,033	814	4,958	230	143

[a] Legislative Reference Service through 1970.
[b] Before 1950 the GAO was responsible for auditing all individual federal transactions and keeping a record of them. Legislation in 1950 transferred these responsibilities to the executive branch. The staff reductions through 1965 result from this 1950 change. *See* Frederich C. Mosher, *The GAO: The Quest for Accountability in American Government* (Boulder, Colo.: Westview Press, 1979), 124.

Sources: For Library of Congress and CRS 1946-1993, Library of Congress, *Annual Reports of the Librarian of Congress.* For GAO 1946-1965, *Annual Reports of the Comptroller General of the United States.* For CBO 1975, Joel Havemann, *Congress and the Budget* (Bloomington: Indiana University Press, 1978), 109. (Data are as of October 1975. The CBO's director took office on February 24, 1975.) For OTA 1974-1976, *Appendixes of the Budget of the United States,* fiscal 1976, 18; 1977, 18; 1978, 40. For GAO 1970-1978, CBO 1976-1978, and OTA 1977-1978, Schneider, "Congressional Staffing, 1947-78"; for 1979-1993 see sources in Table 5-1.

Table 5-9   Legislative Branch Appropriations and the Consumer Price
Index, 1946-1994

Year	Appropriation (dollars)	Increase (percent)	Consumer Price Index[a]	Increase (percent)
1946	54,065,614	—	58.5	—
1947	61,825,020	14.4	66.9	14.4
1948	62,119,714	0.5	72.1	7.8
1949	62,057,678	−0.1	71.4	−1.0
1950	64,313,460	3.6	72.1	1.0
1951	71,888,244	11.8	77.8	7.9
1952	75,673,896	5.3	79.5	2.2
1953	77,670,076	2.6	80.1	0.8
1954	70,925,361	−8.7	80.5	0.5
1955	86,304,923	21.7	80.2	−0.4
1956	94,827,986	9.9	81.4	1.5
1957	120,775,798	27.4	84.3	3.6
1958	107,785,560	−10.8	86.6	2.7
1959	136,153,580	26.3	87.3	0.8
1960	131,055,385	−3.7	88.7	1.6
1961	140,930,781	7.5	89.6	1.0
1962	136,686,715	−3.0	90.6	1.1
1963	150,426,185	10.1	91.7	1.2
1964	168,467,869	12.0	92.9	1.3
1965	221,904,318	31.7	94.5	1.7
1966	197,965,307	−10.8	97.2	2.9
1967	221,715,643	12.0	100.0	2.9
1968	282,003,322	27.2	104.2	4.2
1969	311,542,399	10.5	109.8	5.4
1970	361,024,327	15.9	116.3	5.9
1971	443,104,319	22.7	121.3	4.3
1972	564,107,992	27.3	125.3	3.3
1973	645,127,365	14.4	133.1	6.2
1974	662,180,668	2.6	147.7	11.0
1975	785,618,833	18.6	161.2	9.1
1976[b]	947,185,778	20.6	170.5	5.8
1977	963,921,185	1.8	181.5	6.5
1978	1,009,225,350	4.7	195.4	7.7
1979	1,124,766,400	11.4	217.4	11.3
1980	1,199,061,463	6.6	246.8	13.5
1981	1,285,943,826	7.2	272.4	10.4
1982	1,365,272,433	6.2	289.1	6.1
1983	1,467,318,263	7.5	298.4	3.2
1984	1,644,160,600	12.0	311.1	4.3

(Table continues)

Table 5-9   (continued)

Year	Appropriation (dollars)	Increase (percent)	Consumer Price Index[a]	Increase (percent)
1985	1,599,977,138	−2.7	322.2	3.6
1986	1,783,255,000	11.4	328.4	1.9
1987	1,635,190,214	−8.3	340.4	3.6
1988	1,745,201,500	6.7	354.3	4.1
1989	1,804,624,000	3.4	371.3	4.8
1990	1,968,441,000	9.1	391.4	5.4
1991	2,161,367,000	9.8	408.0	4.2
1992	2,303,844,000	6.6	420.3	3.0
1993	2,302,924,000	−0.1	432.7	3.0
1994	2,269,558,000	−1.4	444.0	2.6
1946-1994	—	4,097.8	—	659.0

Note: Appropriations include supplementals, except for 1986; appropriations are for fiscal years, but the consumer price index is the year average for calendar years.

[a] CPI base is 1967=100.

[b] From fiscal year 1946 through fiscal year 1976, the fiscal year began on July 1. Beginning with fiscal year 1977, the start of the fiscal year was shifted to October 1. During the transition quarter of July 1-September 30, 1976, the amount appropriated for legislative branch operations was $207,391,365. This amount is not included.

Sources: For 1946-1976, U.S. Congress, House, Committee on House Administration, *Studies Dealing with Budgetary, Staffing, and Administrative Activities of the U.S. House of Representatives, 1947-78*, 95th Cong., 2d sess., 1978. For 1977-1979, *Congressional Quarterly Almanac* (Washington, D.C.: Congressional Quarterly, 1977-1980). For 1980, *House LBA Hearings for 1981*, pt. 1, 10-11; *Senate LBA Hearings for 1981*, pt. 1, 15-23; Public Law 96-304 (July 8, 1980); Public Law 97-51 (October 1, 1981). For 1981, *House LBA Hearings for 1982*, pt. 1, 15-23; *Senate LBA Hearings for 1982*, 268; U.S. Congress, Senate, Committee on Appropriations, *Comparative Statement of New Budget Authority and Outlays—Fiscal Year 1983*, 97th Cong., 2d sess., 1982 (unpublished committee document), 3; Public Law 97-12 (June 5, 1981). For 1982-1986, House Committee on Appropriations, *Comparative Statement of New Budget Authority* (unpublished committee documents). For 1987-1994, *Congressional Quarterly Almanac*. For consumer price index, 1946-1986, *Economic Report of the President*, January 1989. For 1987-1994, U.S. Department of Labor, Bureau of Labor Statistics.

Table 5-10 Legislative Branch Appropriations, by Category, FY1982-1994 (in thousands of dollars)

	1982	*1983*	*1984*	*1985*	*1986*[a]
Senate	228,034	239,008	255,856	285,930	308,834
House of Representatives	380,386	367,871	419,784	439,398	455,431
Joint items[b]	84,472	102,448	128,933	96,415	155,804
Architect of the Capitol[c]	83,173	143,768	82,021	85,181	112,191
Botanic Garden	2,351	1,897	2,158	2,080	2,197
Congressional Budget Office	13,226	15,094	16,723	17,541	18,455
Congressional Research Service	31,605	33,851	36,700	39,833	38,963
Copyright Royalty Commission	487	469	210	217	227
General Accounting Office	236,000	252,665	271,710	299,704	339,639
Government Printing Office[c]	129,851	121,829	125,700	122,704	122,268
Library of Congress	195,123	209,185	228,715	228,242	242,829
Office of Technology Assessment	12,169	13,084	14,831	15,692	17,000

(Table continues)

Table 5-10   (continued)

1987	1988	1989	1990	1991	1992	1993	1994
307,658	337,314	340,677	373,761	437,223	449,568	451,451	443,315
463,907	513,786	506,068	537,207	647,675	693,970	699,109	684,696
103,136	94,981	120,983	170,454	114,187	80,716	80,476	78,750
101,633	107,306	103,640	116,221	139,806	151,633	149,613	150,223
2,062	2,221	2,521	2,638	3,519	2,862	4,906	3,008
17,251	17,886	18,361	19,580	21,183	22,542	22,542	22,317
39,602	43,022	44,684	46,895	52,743	56,583	57,291	56,718
123	129	123	101	127	130	130	128
304,910	329,847	347,339	364,720	419,130	442,647	435,167	430,815
94,956	89,521	85,731	98,018	79,615	91,591	89,591	29,082
183,670	191,998	199,650	211,100	239,924	248,308	252,808	250,813
15,532	16,901	17,937	18,900	19,557	21,025	21,025	21,315

Note: Includes supplemental appropriations, except for 1986.

[a] Figures for 1986 are prior to Gramm-Rudman-Hollings sequestration.

[b] Includes such items as joint committees and the Capitol Police. Prior to 1991, official mail costs were also included in this category.

[c] Figures for the Architect of the Capitol and Government Printing Office include appropriations for legislative activities only.

Sources: For 1982-1986, House Committee on Appropriations, *Comparative Statement of New Budget Authority.* For 1987, *Congressional Quarterly Almanac,* vol. 43 (1988). For 1988, *Congressional Quarterly Almanac,* vol. 44 (1989). For 1989, *Congressional Quarterly Almanac,* vol. 45 (1990). For 1990, *Congressional Quarterly Almanac,* vol. 46 (1991). For 1991, *Congressional Quarterly Almanac,* vol. 47 (1992). For 1992, *Congressional Quarterly Almanac,* vol. 48 (1993). For 1993, *Congressional Quarterly Almanac,* vol. 49 (1994). For 1994, *Congressional Quarterly Almanac,* vol. 50 (1995).

Table 5-11   Costs of Official Mail, 1971-1993

Year	Appropriations (dollars)	Average unit cost of franked mail (cents)
1971	11,244,000	8.0
1972	14,594,000	8.0
1972 supplement	18,400,000	
1973	21,226,480	9.0
1974	30,500,000	9.9
1975	38,756,015	11.4
1976	46,101,000	13.2
Transition period[a]	11,525,000	
1976 supplement	16,080,000	
1977	46,904,000	13.4
1978	48,926,000	11.4
1979	64,944,000	12.8
1980[b]	50,707,000	13.4
1981	52,033,000	12.4
1982	75,095,000	13.9
1983	93,161,000	13.1
1984	117,277,000	12.8
1985	85,797,000	12.6
1986	95,700,000	12.6
1987	91,423,000	18.4
1988	82,163,000	14.1
1989	85,262,000[c]	14.9
1990	99,016,000	15.3[d]
1991	88,834,000	15.7
1992	112,000,000	14.9
1993	67,700,000	15.5

Note: See Table 6-8 for number of pieces of franked mail.

[a] Reflects change in the fiscal year from July 1 to October 1.
[b] Lower figure reflects decrease in bulk mail rates.
[c] Adjusted to reflect FY89 shortfall in the mail account.
[d] In 1990 the U.S. Postal Service altered its method for calculating the average unit cost. Average figures prior to 1990 are combined House and Senate figures. Figures for 1990 and later are for the House only.

Sources: For 1971-1987, Office of the Clerk of the House. For 1988 and 1989, Congressional Research Service Report for Congress, "U.S. Congress Official Mail Costs: FY1972 to FY1991," July 20, 1990. For 1990 and 1991, Congressional Research Service. For 1992-1993, U.S. Postal Service.

Table 5-12   Allowances for Representatives, 1977-1995

Category	1977	1979	1981	1983
Clerk-hire	$238,580	$288,156	$336,384	$366,648
Postage	$211	b	b	b
Stationery	$6,500	b	b	b
Travel (round trips)	33	b	b	b
Telephone/telegraph	$5,200 for equipment; 15,000 long-distance minutes	b	b	b
District and state offices rental	2,500 sq. ft.	b	b	b
Furnishings (one-time)	$27,000	b	b	b
Official expenses	$7,000	$50,000– 130,000	$66,200– 248,601	$588,850– 279,470
Constituent communications (begun in 1975)	$5,000	b	b	b
Equipment lease	$9,000	b	b	b

[a] Each member entitled to an annual clerk-hire allowance of the designated amount for a staff not to exceed twenty-two employees, four of whom must fit into five categories: (1) shared payroll—employees, such as computer experts, who are shared by members; (2) interns; (3) employees on leave without pay; (4) part-time employees; (5) temporary employees—employees hired for a specific purpose for not more than ninety days.

[b] As of January 3, 1978, previous individual allowances for travel, office equipment lease, district office lease, stationery, telecommunications, mass mailings, postage, computer services, and other official expenses were consolidated in a single allowance category—the official expenses allowance. Members may budget funds for each category as they see fit. The average allowance for 1995 was $193,000.

[c] Each member is entitled to a base official expenses allowance of $122,500. In addition, there are three variables that determine the total amount allotted for official expenses: (1) transportation costs, (2) telecommunications costs, and (3) cost of office space. The amount allotted for travel is computed as follows: 64 multiplied by the rate per mile multiplied by the mileage between the District of Columbia and the farthest point in the member's district. The minimum amount allotted for travel in 1995 was $6,200 per member.

The amount allotted for telecommunications is computed as follows: 15,000 times the highest long-distance rate per minute from the District of Columbia to the member's district. The minimum amount allotted for telecommunications in 1995 was $6,000 per member. If the member has elected to use WATS or a similar service in his office, the 15,000-minute multiplier will be reduced by one-half.

The amount allotted for office space costs is computed as follows: 2,500 square feet multiplied by the highest applicable rate per square foot charged by the administrator of the General Services Administration to federal agencies in the district for rental of office space.

The official expenses allowance may not be used for:

1. expenses relating to the hiring and employment of individuals, including, but not limited to, employment service fees, transportation of interviewees to and from employment interviews, and cost of relocation upon acceptance or termination of employment

1985	1987	1989	1991	1993	1995
$394,680	$406,560	$431,760[a]	$475,000[a]	$557,400[a]	568,560[a]
b	b	b	b	b	b
b	b	b	b	b	b
b	b	b	b	b	b
b	b	b	b	b	b
b	b	b	b	b	b
b	b	b	b	b	b
$105,513−	$105,513−	$108,400−	$135,000−	$152,128−	152,128−
306,509	306,509[c]	306,500	317,000	302,008	334,629
b	b	b	b	b	b
b	b	b	b	b	b

2. items purchased from other than the House stationery store that have a useful life greater than the current term of the member and that would have a residual value of more than $25 upon the expiration of the current term of the member

3. holiday greeting cards, flowers, and trophies

4. personal advertisements (other than meeting or appearance notices)

5. donations of any type, except flags of the United States flown over the Capitol and items purchased for use as gifts when on official travel

6. dues other than to legislative support organizations as approved by the Committee on House Administration

7. educational expenses for courses of study or information or training programs unless the benefit accrues primarily to the House and the skill or knowledge is not commonly available

8. purchases of radio and television time

9. parking for member and employees at district offices, except when included as an integral part of the lease or occupancy agreement for the district office space.

Each member may allocate up to $40,000 from the clerk-hire allowance to supplement the official expenses allowance. A member also may allocate up to $40,000 from the official expenses allowance to supplement the clerk-hire allowance, provided that monthly clerk-hire disbursements not exceed 10 percent of the total clerk-hire allowance.

Sources: For 1977 and 1979, Committee on House Administration, *Studies Dealing with Budgetary, Staffing and Administrative Activities of the U.S. House of Representatives, 1946-1978.* For 1981, 1983, and 1985, U.S. House of Representatives, *Congressional Handbook.* For 1987, "Salaries and Allowances: The Congress," Congressional Research Service, Library of Congress, Washington, D.C., July 15, 1987, update. For 1989, Office of the Clerk of the House. For 1991 and 1993, Committee on House Administration. For 1995, House Oversight Committee.

Table 5-13   Allowances for Senators, 1977-1995

Category	1977	1979	1981	1983
Clerk-hire	$311,577-588,145[a]	$508,221-1,021,167[a]	$592,608-1,190,724[a]	$645,897-1,297,795[a]
Legislative assistance	n.a.	$157,626[b]	$183,801[b]	$200,328[b]
Postage	$1,215-1,520	[c]	[c]	[c]
Stationery	$3,600-5,000	[c]	[c]	[c]
Travel (round trips)	20-22	[c]	[c]	[c]
District and state offices rental	n.a.	4,800-8,000 sq. ft.[d]	4,800-8,000 sq. ft.[d]	4,800-8,000 sq. ft.[d]
Furnishings, state offices	n.a.	$22,550-31,350	$22,550-31,350	$22,550-31,350
Official office expense account	n.a.	$33,000-143,000[f]	$33,000-143,000[f]	$36,000-156,000[f]

n.a. = not applicable.

[a] There is no limit on the number of employees a senator may hire. He or she must, however, use only the clerk-hire or legislative assistance allowance to pay staff salaries. The clerk-hire allowance varies according to state population.

[b] In addition to clerk-hire, each senator has a legislative assistance allowance worth $377,000 in 1995. This allowance is reduced for any committee chairman or ranking minority member of a committee. It is also reduced for any other senator authorized by a committee chairman to recommend or approve any individuals for appointment to the committee staff who will assist that senator "solely and directly" in his duties as a member of the committee. The reduction requirements were waived for the 99th and 100th Congresses.

[c] This allowance is one of the allocations of the consolidated office expense allowance. Before January 1, 1973, senators were authorized individually controlled allowances for six expense categories as follows: transportation expenses for the senator and his staff; stationery; air mail and special delivery postage; long-distance telephone calls; telegram charges; and home state expenses, which include home state office expenses; telephone service charges incurred outside Washington, D.C.; subscriptions to newspapers, magazines, periodicals, and clipping or similar services; and home state office rent (repealed effective July 1, 1974).

Effective January 1, 1973, the Supplemental Appropriations Act, 1973, provided for the consolidation of these same allowances to provide flexibility to senators in the management of the same dollars provided for their expense allowances. No limit was imposed on any expense category by this authorization. The allowance was designated as the consolidated office expense allowance. Effective January 1, 1977, the Legislative Branch Appropriation Act redesignated the consolidated office expense allowance as the official office expense account.

[d] Effective July 1, 1974, the Legislative Branch Appropriations Act, 1975, provided a formula for the allowable aggregate square feet of office space in the home state of a senator. There is no limit on the number of offices that may be established by a senator in his home state, but the designated square footage may not be exceeded. The cost of office space in the home state is not chargeable to the official office expense account.

[e] An aggregate furniture and furnishings allowance is provided through the General Services Administration for one or more state offices in either federal or privately owned

1985	1987	1989	1991	1993	1995
$695,244-1,396,947[a]	$716,102-1,438,856[a]	$754,000-1,636,000[a]	$814,000-1,760,000[a]	$1,540,000-1,914,000[a]	1,660,000-1,935,000[a]
$215,634[b]	$243,543[b]	$248,000[b]	$269,000[b]	374,000[b]	377,400[b]
c	c	c	c	c	c
c	c	c	c	c	c
c	c	c	c	c	c
4,800-8,000 sq. ft.[d]	4,800-8,000 sq. ft.	4,800-8,000 sq. ft.[d]	4,800-8,000 sq. ft.[d]	4,800-8,000 sq. ft.[d]	4,800-8,000 sq. ft.[d]
$22,550-31,350	$30,000-41,744	$30,000-41,744[e]	$30,000-41,744[e]	$30,000-41,744[e]	30,000-41,744[e]
$36,000-156,000[f]	$36,000-156,000	$33,000-156,000[f]	$47,000-122,000[f]	$44,000-200,000[f]	90,000-250,000[f]

buildings. The $30,000 minimum allowance for office space not greater than 4,800 square feet is increased by $734 for each authorized increase of 200 square feet of space.

[f] The expense account may be used for the following expenses (2 U.S.C. 58[a], as amended):

1. official telegrams and long-distance phone calls and related services
2. stationery and other office supplies purchased through the stationery room for official business
3. costs incurred in the mailing or delivery of matters relating to official business
4. official office expenses in home state, other than equipment or furniture (purchase of office equipment beyond stated allocations may be made through 10 percent funds listed under item 9 below)
5. official telephone charges incurred outside Washington, D.C.
6. subscriptions to newspapers, magazines, periodicals, or clipping or similar services
7. travel expenses incurred by a senator or staff member, subject to certain limitations
8. expenses incurred by individuals selected by a senator to serve on panels or other bodies making recommendations for nominees to service academies or federal judgeships
9. other official expenses as the senator determines are necessary, including (a) additional office equipment for Washington, D.C., or state offices; (b) actual transportation expenses incurred by the senator and employees for official business in the Washington metropolitan area (this is also allowed to employees assigned to a state office for actual transportation expenses in the general vicinity of the office to which assigned but is not available for a change of assignment within the state or for commuting between home and office).

The total reimbursement expense for the calendar year may not exceed 10 percent of the total official office expense account.

Beginning with fiscal year 1981, each senator was also allowed to transfer funds from the administrative, clerical, and legislative assistance allowances to the official office expense account.

Sources: For 1972, *Senate LBA Hearings for 1980.* For 1979-1985, U.S. Senate, *Congressional Handbook.* For 1987, "Salaries and Allowances: The Congress." For 1989, Office of the Secretary of the Senate; Office of the Sergeant-at-Arms. For 1991 and 1993, Senate Disbursing Office. For 1995, Senate Disbursing Office and Sergeant-at-Arms.

Workload 6

The tables in this chapter provide a picture of an institution in which the workload increased dramatically in the 1970s, peaking in about 1976 or 1977, and then began to decline, although not back to its level in the 1950s. The overall number of bills, votes, hours in session, meetings, and hearings multiplied during the 1960s and 1970s (see Tables 6-1 and 6-2). Paradoxically, however, through much of the 1970s the number of bills passed by the House and the Senate and the number of bills enacted into law decreased. More and more activity was combined with fewer and fewer products. Since 1980 the workload—hearings, meetings, and so on—has slowed, while output has increased, yet there is still a decided gap between activity and output.

Bills Introduced

The number of bills introduced in the House has had several pronounced increases or decreases. From an average of about 10,000 per Congress in the 1940s and early 1950s, the number jumped to 13,169 in the Eighty-fourth Congress (1955-1956). It remained at approximately 14,000 until the Eighty-ninth Congress (1965-1966), when it jumped to nearly 20,000. In the 1970s bills introduced declined steadily, to 15,587 in the Ninety-fifth Congress, in part because of changes in the rules regarding cosponsorship, which reduced the need to introduce multiple numbers of an identical bill. The numbers dropped dramatically in the Ninety-sixth Congress—by 42 percent—and have continued to decline. The One-hundredth Congress had the lowest total in forty years; the average increased slightly for the 101st Congress, and by a larger margin for the 102d, but then declined again slightly in the 103d, all the while remaining well below 10,000 bills. The Senate has shown no such distinct ebbs and flows. While there was a real decline between the Ninety-fifth and the One-hundredth Congresses, the total number of bills introduced has risen steadily since then, though as in the House, the number declined in the 103d.

Bills Passed

An examination of bills passed in both houses shows a definite decline in the 1960s and again in the 1970s, though not in a uniform fashion, stabilizing in the 1980s at roughly half the total of the 1950s. Overall, bills passed in each house went from a rough average of 2,000 per Congress in the 1950s to 1,500 in the 1960s, to 1,000 in the 1970s, and to 950 or so in the 1980s and early 1990s. (The Ninety-seventh Congress, the first under Ronald Reagan and with a Republican Senate, had a distinctly lower total.) Tables 6-1 and 6-2 also examine the ratio of bills passed to bills introduced. Although the significance of these figures is limited because some bills are introduced by more than one member and some that are passed may originally have been introduced in the other body, the ratios can be used for comparisons over time. In both institutions, there has been a steady and marked decline since 1947 in the proportion of bills passed. A bill introduced now has less than half the chance of success that it would have had in the Eightieth Congress. While the batting averages were on the rise in the mid- to late-1980s, recent years have witnessed a decline.

At the heart of the decline in bills introduced and the more substantial decline in number of bills passed in the House and the Senate in the 103d Congress, is the overwhelming domination of one major piece of legislation each year—the Clinton economic package in 1993 and health care reform (which did not pass) in 1994.

Recorded Votes

The number of recorded votes remained quite low in the House through the 1940s and 1950s, increased somewhat in the mid-1960s, and jumped dramatically in the 1970s with each Congress from the Ninety-second (1971-1972) through the Ninety-fifth (1977-1978). A rules change in 1971, which permitted recorded teller votes and thereby expanded the opportunities for recorded votes on amendments, has clearly been a major factor in increasing the number of recorded votes in the House. The Senate also showed a marked though not as great increase in recorded votes beginning in 1971, even though no comparable procedural reform was introduced there. In the Ninety-fifth Congress the House for the first time had more recorded votes than the Senate. It appears that both procedural reforms and a decentralization of power and initiative in the House and Senate contributed to the trend toward increased numbers of recorded votes.

Table 6-3, which breaks down recorded votes by year, shows a small but relatively steady decline in the votes in the Senate since 1977, with steep decreases in the late 1970s and again in the 1980s. The House rates declined significantly in 1979 and 1980, dropped sharply in 1981 to levels of a decade earlier, then increased somewhat to a rough average of 450 per year. Although long-term future trends are difficult to discern, it seems likely that the number of recorded votes in both chambers will stabilize at levels below the peak years of the mid-1970s but above those of the 1960s. In the 104th Congress, the fast, early pace, crowded agenda, and use of more open rules in the House promised a jump in the number of recorded votes, which might prove a temporary phenomenon.

Time in Session

As Tables 6-1 and 6-2 indicate, there has been substantial fluctuation in the numbers of days in session per Congress, with no particular longitudinal pattern until recently; Congress has been in session fewer days, but distinctly longer hours. This pattern is true of both houses. The House went from an average of 4.2 hours per day in the 1950s to 4.4 in the 1960s and 5.3 in the 1970s, with an average of 5.8 hours per day in 1979-1980. But in the past three Congresses, the average has been just over 6.5 hours per day.

In the Senate, where floor procedures have always been looser and more informal and filibusters have periodically extended the time in session, sessions in the 1970s and 1980s have consistently been long, only once falling below 2,000 hours. In the earlier period they demonstrated considerably more fluctuation, with only five of the twelve sessions between 1947 and 1970 running over 2,000 hours. The average hours per day in session jumped in the Ninety-ninth Senate to 8.1 and reached its highest level in at least forty-six years (8.6 hours) in the 103d Senate.

Committee and Subcommittee Meetings

The number of committee and subcommittee meetings and hearings rose consistently in the House of Representatives beginning in 1965-1966, the most substantial increases occurring in the mid-to-late 1970s. The 1977-1978 figures for the House were more than double the average number per Congress in the 1950s and 1960s. The expansion of power and initiative of subcommittees and the wider distribution of chairmanships probably account for much of this change. The figures for the 1980s and early 1990s indicate a marked cutback in committee and subcommittee activity to levels of a decade or more earlier.

The Senate numbers also increased, but then peaked and declined earlier than in the House. The number of meetings and hearings jumped substantially in the late 1960s and early 1970s, beginning especially with the famous "Great Society" Eighty-ninth Congress (1965-1966) and reaching a peak a decade later in the Ninety-fourth Congress (1975-1976) of 4,265, some 70 percent higher than in the 1950s. Beginning in 1977, however—after the committee system re-organization that sharply cut back the number of subcommittees and assignments (see Chapter 4)—the number of meetings and hearings began to decline steadily, to 2,373 in the Ninety-ninth Congress, a number comparable to levels in the 1950s and 1960s. With the exception of the One-hundredth Congress, the number has continued to decline since then. As with recorded votes, the 104th Congress promises to be an exception to this trend.

Laws and Other Output

Table 6-4, focusing more directly on congressional output, shows the number of public and private bills enacted into law (that is, passed by both the House and the Senate and signed by the president) and the number of pages of enacted bills. There has been a decline from the Eighty-fourth through the 103d Congresses in the number of public bills enacted, combined with a striking increase in the average page length of the statutes since 1975-1976. From the 1950s through the mid-1960s, the average number of pages per statute was approximately 2.5. The average jumped to approximately 5 pages in the mid-1970s, reached 7 pages in the Ninety-fourth Congress, and jumped to between 8 and 9 pages in the Ninety-fifth through Ninety-eighth Congresses. The average reached a new high in the 103d Congress at 16.2 pages per statute. Divided government through the 102d Congress, when fewer bills had a chance of being enacted, often resulted in the inclusion of various issues and interests in a single piece of legislation that had a reasonable likelihood of becoming law. It is important to understand that a handful of these omnibus measures (megabills) account for a large proportion of total statute pages.

Actions of Congress, in votes and laws, affect the workload, job difficulty, and output of the federal executive as well. Table 6-5 shows the number of pages in the *Federal Register* per year since 1971, along with those of some earlier years for comparison. As the average length of statutes increased in Congress in the 1970s, the number of pages in the *Federal Register*—which among other things displays regulations mandated by these statutes—jumped correspondingly. In 1981, as de-regulation proceeded in the Reagan administration and the number of substantive bills declined, the total pages in the *Federal Register* dropped by 27 percent—to the level of 1977-1978, at the beginning of the Carter administration. The number of pages dropped further during the Reagan administration, reaching a level of 47,418 pages in 1986, the lowest in twelve years. The page count then rose during the Bush administration and has continued to rise. Although the number of bills enacted fell during the 103d Congress, the number of pages reached more than 68,000.

Table 6-6 describes the postwar record of presidential vetoes and veto overrides. President Truman exercised his veto power far more than any of his successors; the record shows a total of seventy-five vetoes in the so-called "Do-Nothing" Eightieth Congress. The number of presidential vetoes is generally higher when presidents face Congresses with opposition party majorities, as Truman did in the Eightieth Congress. With a split Congress during his first six years in office, President Reagan showed a much lower propensity to veto than his Republican predecessors. But even after Democrats took back the Senate in the One-hundredth Congress, Reagan vetoed fewer bills than he had in either of the two previous Congresses.

Presidents Nixon and Ford faced the greatest resistance from Congress. The Ninety-third and Ninety-fourth Congresses attempted a much higher number of veto overrides than any of the other Congresses in the previous thirty years, and a large number of their attempts were successful. The first three Congresses under Reagan did not show any particular inclination to override his vetoes, but the last picked up a bit overriding 37.5 percent of Reagan's vetoes. President Bush's use of the veto was comparable to his most recent predecessors in terms of numbers. However, Bush tended to reserve the veto for crucial pieces of legislation, such as the Civil Rights Act of 1990, and had impressive success sustaining them.

President Clinton, however, became the first president since 1853 not to veto a single bill during an entire Congress. Having a Democratic House and Senate certainly diminished his need or willingness to use the veto, yet zero vetoes is highly unusual. Clinton seems to be a president much more prone to compromise than to confrontation. But this will not last for long. The Republican takeover of Congress in 1994 has transformed executive-congressional relations, ensuring a substantial number of vetoes during the 104th Congress.

Table 6-7 examines the use of filibusters (measured by the number of cloture votes) in the Senate since the Sixty-sixth Congress (1919-1920). The table shows that the filibuster was a rarely exercised privilege until the 1960s, when the civil rights debates increased the average number of cloture votes from one or two to six or seven per Congress. The number of filibusters and cloture votes increased strikingly in the 1970s, after Majority Leader Mike Mansfield introduced a "two-track" system to enable the Senate to conduct other business as a filibuster proceeded. The increased use of filibusters on a wider variety of issues led the Senate to amend the rules in 1975, changing the number of votes required to invoke cloture from two-thirds of those present and voting to three-fifths of the total Senate. This did not reduce the number of filibusters or cloture votes, but the success rate for cloture votes appears to have increased. Note that, except for the Nixon-Ford years, filibusters are generally more prevalent in the second session of a Congress, when delaying tactics have a greater likelihood of succeeding. Republican filibusters were used routinely in the 103d Congress to frustrate President Clinton's agenda; Democrats appear to be returning the favor on the House-passed Contract With America.

Table 6-8 examines outgoing congressional mail. It shows that the amount of franked mail generated by Congress increased tremendously from the 1960s through the 1980s, averaging approximately 700 million pieces per year from 1984-1989. The record was 924.6 million pieces in the election year of 1984. In light of these escalating numbers, in 1990 Congress came under considerable pressure to adopt reforms in an attempt to curb the use of franked mail. The House imposed new restrictions on franked mailings including a requirement that each member adhere to an individual mail budget and that all expenditures be publicly disclosed. These restrictions have succeeded in not only lowering the overall cost of official mail, but also reducing the amount of mail being sent by members. These changes are reflected in the drastically reduced number of mailings for 1991—down 54 percent— from 1990's total. Despite these overall reductions, note that we still see increases in the amount of franked mail in election years and the decline in off years—despite House rules that limit newsletter production and distribution as the election nears. For example, after 1991's figure of 259.8 million pieces, it jumped by more than 76 percent to 458 million pieces in the 1992 election year and declined once again in 1993, to just over 200 million.

Over the years the system for counting incoming mail has been changed so much that reliable data cannot be compiled.

Table 6-1 House Workload, 80th-103d Congresses, 1947-1994

Congress	Bills introduced[a]	Average no. of bills introduced per member	Bills passed	Ratio of bills passed to bills introduced	Recorded votes[b]	Time in session		Hours per day in session	Committee, subcommittee meetings[c]
						Days	Hours		
80th (1947-48)	7,611	17.5	1,739	0.228	159	254	1,224	4.8	n.a.
81st (1949-50)	10,502	24.1	2,482	0.236	275	345	1,501	4.4	n.a.
82d (1951-52)	9,065	20.8	2,008	0.222	181	274	1,163	4.2	n.a.
83d (1953-54)	10,875	25.0	2,129	0.196	147	240	1,033	4.3	n.a.
84th (1955-56)	13,169	30.3	2,360	0.179	147	230	937	4.1	3,210
85th (1957-58)	14,580	33.5	2,064	0.142	193	276	1,147	4.2	3,750
86th (1959-60)	14,112	32.4	1,636	0.116	180	265	1,039	3.9	3,059
87th (1961-62)	14,328	32.9	1,927	0.134	240	304	1,227	4.0	3,402
88th (1963-64)	14,022	32.2	1,267	0.090	232	334	1,251	3.7	3,596
89th (1965-66)	19,874	45.7	1,565	0.079	394	336	1,547	4.6	4,367
90th (1967-68)	22,060	50.7	1,213	0.055	478	328	1,595	4.9	4,386
91st (1969-70)	21,436	49.3	1,130	0.053	443	350	1,613	4.6	5,066
92d (1971-72)	18,561	42.7	970	0.052	649	298	1,429	4.8	5,114
93d (1973-74)	18,872	43.4	923	0.049	1,078	318	1,487	4.7	5,888
94th (1975-76)	16,982	39.0	968	0.057	1,273	311	1,788	5.7	6,975
95th (1977-78)	15,587	35.8	1,027	0.066	1,540	323	1,898	5.9	7,896
96th (1979-80)	9,103	20.9	929	0.102	1,276	326	1,876	5.8	7,033
97th (1981-82)	8,094	18.6	704	0.087	812	303	1,420	4.7	6,078
98th (1983-84)	7,105	16.3	978	0.137	906	266	1,705	6.4	5,661

99th (1985-86)	6,499	14.9	973	0.150	890	281	1,794	6.4	5,272
100th (1987-88)	6,263	14.4	1,061	0.169	939	298	1,659	5.6	5,388
101st (1989-90)	6,683	15.4	968	0.145	915	281	1,688	6.0	5,305
102d (1991-92)	7,771	17.9	932	0.120	932	277	1,795	6.5	5,152
103d (1993-94)	6,647	15.3	749	0.113	1,122	265	1,887	7.1	4,304

Note: n.a. = not available.

[a] All bills and joint resolutions introduced.

[b] Includes all quorum calls, yea and nay votes, and recorded votes.

[c] Figures do not include the House Appropriations Committee for the Eighty-fourth to Eighty-eighth Congresses. House Appropriations included in subsequent Congresses numbered 584 in the Eighty-ninth Congress, 705 in the Ninetieth, 709 in the Ninety-first, 854 in the Ninety-second, and 892 in the Ninety-third.

Sources: Arthur G. Stevens, "Indicators of Congressional Workload and Activity," staff report, Congressional Research Service, Library of Congress, Washington, D.C., May 30, 1979; U.S. Congress, *Congressional Record—Daily Digest*, "Resume of Congressional Activity," vol. 126, no. 180, December 30, 1980; vol. 127, no. 188, pt. 3, December 16, 1981; vol. 130, no. 136, November 14, 1984; vol. 133, no. 1, January 6, 1987; vol. 134, no. 152, November 10, 1988; vol. 135, no. 165, pt. 4, November 21, 1989; vol. 136, no. 151, November 2, 1990; vol. 139, no. 1, January 5, 1993; vol. 140, no. 150, December 20, 1994. *Congressional Quarterly Almanac* (Washington, D.C.: Congressional Quarterly, various years); Roger H. Davidson and Carol Hardy, "Indicators of Congressional Workload and Activity," staff report, Congressional Research Service, Library of Congress, Washington, D.C., June 8, 1987; Office of the Official Reporters to House Committees, U.S. House of Representatives.

Table 6-2 Senate Workload, 80th-103d Congresses, 1947-1994

Congress	Bills introduced[a]	Average no. of bills introduced per member	Bills passed	Ratio of bills passed to bills introduced	Recorded votes[b]	Time in session		Hours per day in session	Committee, subcommittee meetings
						Days	Hours		
80th (1947-48)	3,186	33.2	1,670	0.524	248	257	1,462	5.7	n.a.
81st (1949-50)	4,486	46.7	2,362	0.527	455	389	2,410	6.2	n.a.
82d (1951-52)	3,665	38.2	1,849	0.505	331	287	1,648	5.7	n.a.
83d (1953-54)	4,077	42.5	2,231	0.547	270	294	1,962	6.7	n.a.
84th (1955-56)	4,518	47.1	2,550	0.564	224	224	1,362	6.1	2,607
85th (1957-58)	4,532	47.2	2,202	0.486	313	271	1,876	6.9	2,748
86th (1959-60)	4,149	42.3	1,680	0.405	422	280	2,199	7.9	2,271
87th (1961-62)	4,048	40.5	1,953	0.482	434	323	2,164	6.7	2,532
88th (1963-64)	3,457	34.6	1,341	0.388	541	375	2,395	6.4	2,493
89th (1965-66)	4,129	41.3	1,636	0.396	497	345	1,814	5.3	2,889
90th (1967-68)	4,400	44.0	1,376	0.313	595	358	1,961	5.5	2,892
91st (1969-70)	4,867	48.7	1,271	0.261	667	384	2,352	6.1	3,264
92d (1971-72)	4,408	44.1	1,035	0.235	955	348	2,294	6.6	3,559
93d (1973-74)	4,524	45.2	1,115	0.246	1,138	334	2,028	6.1	4,067
94th (1975-76)	4,114	41.1	1,038	0.252	1,290	320	2,210	6.9	4,265
95th (1977-78)	3,800	38.0	1,070	0.282	1,151	337	2,510	7.4	3,960
96th (1979-80)	3,480	34.8	977	0.281	1,028	333	2,324	7.0	3,790
97th (1981-82)	3,396	34.0	803	0.236	948	312	2,158	6.9	3,236
98th (1983-84)	3,454	34.5	936	0.271	673	281	1,951	6.9	2,471
99th (1985-86)	3,386	33.9	940	0.278	740	313	2,531	8.1	2,373

100th (1987-88)	3,325	33.3	1,002	0.301	799	307	2,342	7.6	2,493
101st (1989-90)	3,669	36.7	980	0.267	638	274	2,254	8.2	2,340[c]
102d (1991-92)	4,245	42.5	947	0.223	550	287	2,291	8.0	2,039
103d (1993-94)	3,177	31.8	682	0.215	724	291	2,513	8.6	2,043

Note: n.a. = not available.

[a] All bills and joint resolutions introduced.

[b] All yea and nay votes.

[c] Where final legislative calendars were not available, figures were compiled from *Congressional Information Service Abstracts* and the *Congressional Record*.

Sources: Davidson and Hardy, "Indicators of Congressional Workload and Activity," *Congressional Activity*," vol. 126, no. 180, December 30, 1980; vol. 127, no. 188, pt. 3, December 16, 1981; vol. 130, no. 136, November 14, 1984; vol. 133, no. 1, January 6, 1987; vol. 134, no. 152, November 10, 1988; vol. 135, no. 165, pt. 4, November 21, 1989; vol. 136, no. 151, November 2, 1990; vol. 139, no. 1, January 5, 1993; vol. 140, no. 150, December 20, 1994. *Congressional Quarterly Almanac*, various years; final legislative calendars for each committee, 100th and 101st Congresses.

Figure 6-1   Ratio of Bills Passed to Bills Introduced, 80th–103d Congresses, 1947–1994

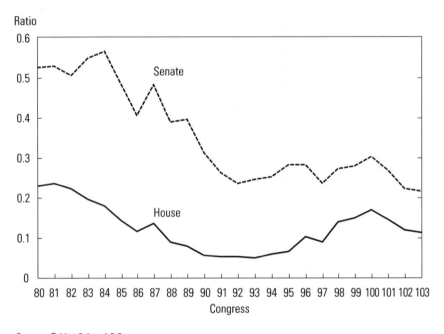

Sources: Tables 6-1 and 6-2.

Figure 6-2   Recorded Votes in the House and the Senate, 80th–103d Congresses, 1947–1994

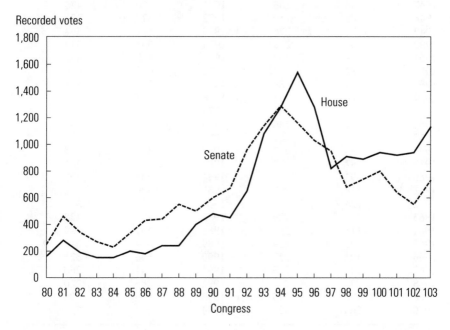

Sources: Tables 6-1 and 6-2.

Table 6-3   Recorded Votes in the House and the Senate, 1947-1994

Year	House	Senate	Year	House	Senate
1947	84	138	1971	320	423
1948	75	110	1972	329	532
1949	121	226	1973	541	594
1950	154	229	1974	537	544
1951	109	202	1975	612	602
1952	72	129	1976	661	688
1953	71	89	1977	706	635
1954	76	181	1978	834	516
1955	73	88	1979	672	497
1956	74	136	1980	604	531
1957	100	111	1981	353	483
1958	93	202	1982	459	465
1959	87	215	1983	498	381
1960	93	207	1984	408	292
1961	116	207	1985	439	381
1962	124	227	1986	451	359
1963	119	229	1987	488	420
1964	113	312	1988	451	379
1965	201	259	1989	379	312
1966	193	238	1990	536	326
1967	245	315	1991	444	280
1968	233	280[a]	1992	488	270
1969	177	245	1993	615	395
1970	266	422	1994	507	329

Note: House figures reflect the total number of quorum calls, yea and nay votes, and recorded votes, while Senate figures include only yea and nay votes.

[a] This figure does not include one yea and nay vote that was ruled invalid for lack of a quorum.

Sources: "Resume of Congressional Activity," vol. 130, no. 136, November 14, 1984; vol. 133, no. 1, January 6, 1987; vol. 134, no. 152, November 10, 1988; vol. 137, no. 1, January 3, 1991; vol. 139, no. 1, January 5, 1993; vol. 140, no. 150, December 20, 1994. *Congressional Quarterly Almanac,* various years.

Table 6-4   Congressional Workload, 80th-103d Congresses, 1947-1994

Congress	Public bills			Private bills		
	No. of bills enacted	Total pages of statutes	Average pages per statute	No. of bills enacted	Total pages of statutes	Average pages per statute
80th (1947-48)	906	2,236	2.5	458	182	0.40
81st (1949-50)	921	2,314	2.5	1,103	417	0.38
82d (1951-52)	594	1,585	2.7	1,023	360	0.35
83d (1953-54)	781	1,899	2.4	1,002	365	0.36
84th (1955-56)	1,028	1,848	1.8	893	364	0.41
85th (1957-58)	936	2,435	2.6	784	349	0.45
86th (1959-60)	800	1,774	2.2	492	201	0.41
87th (1961-62)	885	2,078	2.3	684	255	0.37
88th (1963-64)	666	1,975	3.0	360	144	0.40
89th (1965-66)	810	2,912	3.6	473	188	0.40
90th (1967-68)	640	2,304	3.6	362	128	0.35
91st (1969-70)	695	2,927	4.2	246	104	0.42
92d (1971-72)	607	2,330	3.8	161	67	0.42
93d (1973-74)	649	3,443	5.3	123	48	0.39
94th (1975-76)	588	4,121	7.0	141	75	0.53
95th (1977-78)	633	5,403	8.5	170	60	0.35
96th (1979-80)	613	4,947	8.1	123	63	0.51
97th (1981-82)	473	4,343	9.2	56	25	0.45
98th (1983-84)	623	4,893	7.8	54	26	0.48
99th (1985-86)	664	7,198	10.8	24	13	0.54
100th (1987-88)	713	4,839	6.8	48	29	0.60
101st (1989-90)	650	5,767	8.9	16	9	0.56
102d (1991-92)	590	7,544	12.8	20	11	0.55
103d (1993-94)	465	7,542	16.2	8	9	1.10

Sources: Stevens, "Indicators of Congressional Workload and Activity"; *U.S. Code Congressional and Administrative News,* volumes for 97th, 98th, 99th, and 100th Congresses; Office of the Law Revision Counsel, U.S. House of Representatives. For the 101st, 102d, and 103d Congresses, Office of the Law Revision Counsel; *Federal Register.*

Table 6-5   Pages in the *Federal Register,* 1936-1994

Year	Pages	Year	Pages	Year	Pages
1936	2,355	1976	57,072	1986	47,418
1946	14,736	1977	63,629	1987	49,654
1956	10,528	1978	61,261	1988	53,376
1966	16,850	1979	77,497	1989	53,821
1969	20,464	1980	87,012	1990	53,618
1971	25,442	1981	63,554	1991	67,715
1972	28,920	1982	58,493	1992	62,919
1973	35,586	1983	57,703	1993	68,869
1974	45,422	1984	50,997	1994	68,630
1975	60,221	1985	53,479		

Figure 6-3   Public Bills in the Congressional Workload, 80th–103d Congresses, 1947–1994

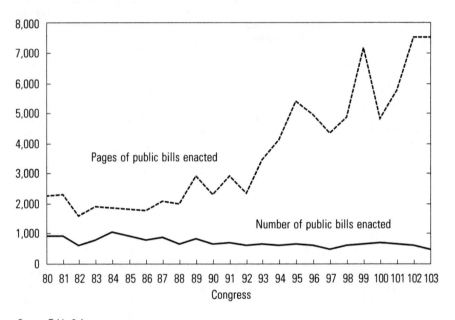

Source: Table 6-4.

Table 6-6 Vetoes and Overrides, 80th-103d Congresses, 1947-1994

Congress		Total no. of presidential vetoes	No. of regular vetoes	No. of pocket vetoes	Vetoes overridden		House attempts to override vetoes	Senate attempts to override vetoes
					Total	Percentage of regular vetoes		
80th	(1947-48)	75	42	33	6	14.3	8	8
81st	(1949-50)	79	70	9	3	4.3	5	5
82d	(1951-52)	22	14	8	3	21.4	4	4
83d	(1953-54)	52	21	31	0	—	0	0
84th	(1955-56)	34	12	22	0	—	1	1
85th	(1957-58)	51	18	33	0	—	1	1
86th	(1959-60)	44	22	22	2	9.1	5	6
87th	(1961-62)	20	11	9	0	—	0	0
88th	(1963-64)	9	5	4	0	—	0	0
89th	(1965-66)	14	10	4	0	—	0	0
90th	(1967-68)	8	2	6	0	—	0	0
91st	(1969-70)	11	7	4	2	28.6	4	4
92d	(1971-72)	20	6	14	2	33.3	3	4
93d	(1973-74)	39	27	12	5	18.5	12	10
94th	(1975-76)	37	32	5	8	25.0	17	15
95th	(1977-78)	19	6	13	0	—	2	0
96th	(1979-80)	12	7	5	2	28.6	2	2
97th	(1981-82)	15	9	6	2	22.2	4	3

(Table continues)

Table 6-6 (continued)

Congress	Total no. of presidential vetoes	No. of regular vetoes	No. of pocket vetoes	Vetoes overridden		House attempts to override vetoes	Senate attempts to override vetoes
				Total	Percentage of regular vetoes		
98th (1983-84)	24	9	15	2	22.2	2	2
99th (1985-86)	20	13	7	2	15.4	3	3
100th (1987-88)	19	8	11	3	37.5	5	4
101st (1989-90)	21	16	5	0	—	9	5
102d (1991-92)	25	15	10[a]	1	6.7	3	3
103d (1993-94)	0	0	0	0	—	0	0

[a] President Bush asserted that he had pocket-vetoed S1176, although some members in Congress dispute that on the grounds that bills can be pocket-vetoed only after Congress has adjourned, not during a recess.

Sources: Roger H. Davidson and Carol Hardy, "Indicators of Congressional Workload and Activity," staff report, Congressional Research Service, Library of Congress, Washington, D.C., 1989. For 1989-1990, Congressional Quarterly Research Query Service. For 1991-1992, Congressional Quarterly Weekly Report, December 19, 1992, 3925-3926. For 1993-1994, Congressional Quarterly Weekly Report, December 31, 1994, 3623.

Table 6-7   Attempted and Successful Cloture Votes in the Senate, 1919-1994

Congress	1st session attempted	1st session successful	2d session attempted	2d session successful	Total attempted	Total successful
66th (1919-20)	1	1	0	0	1	1
67th (1921-22)	1	0	1	0	2	0
68th (1923-24)	0	0	0	0	0	0
69th (1925-26)	0	0	2	1	2	1
70th (1927-28)	5	2	0	0	5	2
71st (1929-30)	0	0	0	0	0	0
72d (1931-32)	0	0	0	0	0	0
73d (1933-34)	1	0	0	0	1	0
74th (1935-36)	0	0	0	0	0	0
75th (1937-38)	0	0	2	0	2	0
76th (1939-40)	0	0	0	0	0	0
77th (1941-42)	0	0	1	1	1	1
78th (1943-44)	0	0	1	1	1	0
79th (1945-46)	0	0	4	0	4	0
80th (1947-48)	0	0	0	0	0	0
81st (1949-50)	0	0	2	0	2	0
82d (1951-52)	0	0	0	0	0	0
83d (1953-54)	0	0	1	0	1	0
84th (1955-56)	0	0	0	0	0	0
85th (1957-58)	0	0	0	0	0	0
86th (1959-60)	0	0	1	0	1	0
87th (1961-62)	1	0	3	1	4	1
88th (1963-64)	1	0	2	1	3	1
89th (1965-66)	2	1	5	0	7	1
90th (1967-68)	1	0	5	1	6	1
91st (1969-70)	2	0	4	0	6	0
92d (1971-72)	10	2	10	2	20	4
93d (1973-74)	10	2	21	7	31	9
94th (1975-76)	23	13	4	4	27	17
95th (1977-78)	5	1	8	2	13	3
96th (1979-80)	4	1	17	9	21	10
97th (1981-82)	7	2	20	7	27	9
98th (1983-84)	7	2	12	9	19	11
99th (1985-86)	9	1	14	9	23	10
100th (1987-88)	24	6	20	6	44	12
101st (1989-90)	9	6	15	5	24	11
102d (1991-92)	21	9	28	14	49	23
103d (1993-94)	20	4	22	10	42	14

Note: The number of votes required to invoke cloture was changed March 7, 1975, from two-thirds of those present and voting to three-fifths of the total Senate membership, as Rule XXII of the standing rules of the Senate was amended.

Source: Davidson and Hardy, "Indicators of Congressional Workload and Activity" (1989). For 1989-1992, Congressional Research Service, Library of Congress-Government Division. For 1993, *Congressional Quarterly Almanac* 1994, 14. For 1994, *Congressional Monitor,* October 11, 1994, 17.

Table 6-8   Congressional Mailings, 1954-1993

Fiscal year	Millions of pieces	Increase or decrease (%)
1954	43.5	—
1955	45.6	4.8
1956	58.2	27.6
1957	59.6	2.4
1958	65.4	9.7
1959	86.5	32.3
1960	108.0	24.9
1961	85.1	−21.2
1962	110.1	29.4
1963	94.7	−14.0
1964	110.5	16.7
1965	120.9	9.4
1966	197.5	63.4
1967	192.9	−2.3
1968	178.2	−7.6
1969	190.0	6.6
1970	201.0	5.8
1971	238.4	18.6
1972	308.9	29.6
1973	310.6	0.6
1974	321.0	3.3
1975	312.4	−2.7
1976	401.4	28.5
Transition quarter	159.9	—
1977	293.3	−26.9
1978	430.2	46.7
1979	409.9	−4.7
1980	511.3	24.7
1981	395.6	−22.6
1982	771.8	95.1
1983	556.8	−27.9
1984	924.6	60.3
1985	675.0	−27.9
1986	758.7	12.4
1987	494.7	−34.8
1988	804.9	62.7
1989	598.6	−25.6
1990	564.2	−5.7
1991	259.8	−54.0
1992	458.0	76.3
1993	200.7	−56.3

Sources: For 1954-1978, U.S. Congress, House, Committee on Appropriations, Subcommittee on Legislative Branch Appropriations, *Hearings on Legislative Branch Appropriations for 1980*, pt. 2; for 1979, *House LBA Hearings for 1981*, pt. 2; for 1980-1983, Office of the Clerk of the House; for 1984, *House LBA Hearings for 1986*, pt. 2; for 1985, *House LBA Hearings for 1987*, pt. 2; for 1986, *House LBA Hearings for 1988*, pt. 2; for 1987, *House LBA Hearings for 1989*, pt. 2; for 1988, *House LBA Hearings for 1990*, pt. 2; for 1989, Congressional Research Service Report for Congress, "U.S. Congress Official Mail Costs: FY1972 to FY1991"; for 1990-1991, Congressional Research Service, "U.S. Congress Official Mail Costs: FY1972 to FY1993 (Est.)"; for 1992-1993, U.S. Postal Service.

Budgeting 7

The Constitution gives Congress the power to levy taxes and to appropriate money. Accordingly, the executive branch can raise and spend money only to the extent and in the manner authorized by Congress. In addition to its taxing and appropriating power, Congress makes financial decisions through its authorizations and budget processes. The authorizations process is anchored in the rules of the House (and, to a lesser extent, those of the Senate), which require that agencies and programs be authorized in law before funds are appropriated for them. The budget process was established by the Congressional Budget Act of 1974, which provided that Congress adopt two budget resolutions each year to coordinate the numerous fiscal decisions made in separate revenue, spending, and debt legislation. In recent years, however, Congress has adopted only a single budget resolution. The process itself has been reformed numerous times and came under reexamination again in 1994 and 1995 with proposed legislation for biennial budgeting, a presidential line-item veto, and a constitutional amendment requiring a balanced budget—all changes that would greatly alter the current system and balance of power.

Budget Resolutions

Since the inception of the congressional budget process, voting on the resolutions has reflected a sharp split in the House between the Democratic and Republican parties. Table 7-1 shows remarkable Repub-

Allen Schick, professor of public policy at the University of Maryland, wrote and assembled the original version of Chapter 7 for *Vital Statistics in Congress 1980*. This is an updated version of Schick's essay.

lican cohesion until 1989, when more members began to break party ranks. During the 1976-1981 fiscal years, approximately 95 percent of House Republicans voted against adoption of the budget resolutions. For the fiscal 1982 and 1983 budgets, however, the Republicans (despite their minority status in the House) gained control of the budget process, and most of them voted in favor of budget resolutions supported by Republican president Ronald Reagan. When they lost control of the fiscal 1984 resolution, the Republicans reverted to opposition and persisted in opposing all budget resolutions until the 1989 agreement resulted in a GOP split and a wide margin of victory for the resolution. A similar pattern held in 1990; however, 1991 saw renewed opposition, which has endured. The Republicans were unanimously opposed to the 1993, 1994, and 1995 budgets.

Because House Democrats have not been as united as the Republicans, the latter have sometimes prevailed on budget resolutions. At various times Democrats from both the liberal and the conservative wings of the party have opposed the position taken by most of their colleagues. Nevertheless, during the 1976-1981 fiscal years, House Democrats supplied sufficient votes to pass the budget resolutions, although on two occasions (the first resolution for fiscal 1978 and the second resolution for fiscal 1980) only after the initial version was rejected. In voting on the 1982 and 1983 budget resolutions, most House Democrats opposed the president's position and, when their view was rejected, voted against adoption of the budget resolutions. But in subsequent years Democrats managed remarkable unity and passed resolutions without GOP help for each fiscal year from 1984 through 1988. In 1989, the split in the Republican vote resulted in a large, bipartisan margin of victory, breaking the previous vote mold. Democrats supported the resolutions of 1990 and 1991, but by smaller margins. Democratic defections combined with Republican solidarity nearly caused the majority to lose the vote on 1993's budget resolution. The Democrats squeezed out a narrow victory (209-207), in which the Speaker cast an extremely rare floor vote.

The 1994 and 1995 budgets were based on a budget request from a Democratic president for the first time in twelve years. Democrats demonstrated early support for Clinton by passing the 1994 resolution swiftly and by a wide margin (243-183). The much more difficult vote, a cliff-hanger in both the House and the Senate, was on the reconciliation package to implement the deficit reduction agreement. The FY1995 budget was routine, following the five-year plan approved the year before.

Until the 1982 fiscal year, the Senate displayed a different voting pattern, a bipartisan coalition of Republicans and Democrats ensuring passage of the resolutions by a wide margin (see Table 7-2). The two parties were polarized on the 1982 and 1983 budgets, and in both years a majority of Senate Democrats voted against approval of the budget resolution. Growing Democratic opposition was matched by increasing Republican support for the resolutions, a pattern that reversed when the Democrats regained control of the Senate before the 1988 fiscal year. As in the House, the 1989 resolution won a comfortable bipartisan majority, built on a unified Democratic vote and a split GOP. Democrats were much less unified in 1990 and 1991; Republicans remained split. The resolutions from 1992 through 1995 passed largely on the basis of unified Democratic support, with the majority of Republican senators opposing both of them.

In voting on the budget resolutions, Congress goes on record with respect to key budget aggregates (total revenues, budget authority, outlays, and deficit) and functional allocations. Table 7-3 compares congressional decisions on the aggregates with presidential budget recommendations and with the actual results for each fiscal year from 1976 through 1995. During the early years of the budget process, actual spending and the deficit tended to be below those set by Congress in its budget resolutions. In 1980, however, the final results began to consistently show higher spending. The level of disparity varied with the largest occurring with the 1991 deficit—projected at $64 billion in the budget resolution and actually totaling $268.7 billion. Working within the confines of the 1990 Budget Enforcement Act, budget writers were forced to make more realistic deficit projections in 1992 and 1993. In 1993 the actual deficit as well as all key budget aggregates were below that of Congress's resolution for the first time since the 1980 trend began. The actual deficit dropped again in 1994, once more falling below that set by Congress. Strong economic growth and smaller than expected increases in health outlays will likely produce a similar drop in the projected deficit in fiscal 1995.

Congressional Control of the Budget

Although Congress holds the power of the purse, its ability to effectively exercise this power has been hampered by the rise of uncontrollable spending. During fiscal years 1967-1992 "relatively uncontrollable" outlays soared from less than $100 billion to more than $1 trillion and from less than 60 percent of total outlays to nearly 80 percent (see Table 7-4). In 1993 and 1994, this proportion remained stable with the major increases in outlays once again occurring in Social Security, Medicare, and Medicaid.

Most uncontrollables are in the form of entitlements: provisions of law that mandate payments to eligible recipients. Most entitlements are open-ended and cannot be controlled through budgetary or appropriations actions. Moreover, many entitlements are indexed to the rate of inflation, so that payments are adjusted to increases in the cost of living without congressional action. Entitlements can only be controlled by changing the laws that mandate the payments. Congress developed the reconciliation process in 1980 as a means of reducing certain entitlements that would then, lawmakers hoped, bring expenditures for them in line with congressional budget decisions. But this method proved ineffective, and as deficit reduction became a greater national priority, the massive growth of entitlement spending, especially that of Social Security, Medicare, and Medicaid gained much attention.

In 1993 and 1994, Medicare and Medicaid spending came under intense scrutiny during the debate over health care reform. But when discussion of cuts began, legislators were quickly reminded of the wide public support of these programs. The future of Social Security expenditures brought much contention to the 1995 debate over an amendment requiring a balanced federal budget. Senate Democrats demanded that legislation proposed by Republicans include a measure protecting Social Security from budget cuts. Both of these measures failed, but major cuts in federal entitlements were included in the Republican budget proposals in 1995 and promise to be controversial.

The Appropriations Process

A budget resolution is advisory. No funds can be spent by government agencies pursuant to the amounts set in a resolution. The actual provision of funds occurs in appropriation bills, of which there are supposed to be thirteen regular bills and a number of supplemental measures each year.

The Appropriations committees see themselves as guardians of the Treasury, a role that is reflected in their determination to appropriate less money than has been requested by the president. Table 7-5, drawn from the official records of the House Appropriations Committee, shows that in almost every year the total amount appropriated is below the president's budget request. These figures do not include permanent appropriations (which are not reviewed by the Appropriations committees) or "backdoor" authority provided in other legislation.

Although the Appropriations committees provide less money than the president requests, they also enact sizable supplemental appropriations each year (see Table 7-6). Supplemental appropriations are made for a number of reasons: to provide for agencies not funded in the regular appropriation bills, to pay for the salary increases of federal employees, to supplement the funds for agencies facing a deficiency, to finance new or expanded programs, to pay for natural disasters like floods or hurricanes, and, as in 1991, to finance major military operations such as Desert Shield/Desert Storm for which an additional $42.6 billion was appropriated. The number of supplemental bills and their amounts rose after the congressional budget process was introduced, but both have declined in the past five fiscal years to where they cannot be considered ways to evade budget limits. Indeed, with the focus on deficit reduction, it has become increasingly difficult to pass supplemental spending. In FY1993 and FY1994, Republicans and conservative Democrats demanded that the bulk of the supplementals be offset by spending cuts elsewhere.

Historically, budget cutting has been concentrated in the House, which, under longstanding precedent, considers appropriation bills before they are taken up by the Senate. This role depends largely on the ability of the House Appropriations Committee to protect its bills against floor amendments to provide additional funds. But as Table 7-7 shows, from 1965 through 1980 there was a steady rise in the number of amendments proposed and the number agreed to by the House.

One important factor in this upward trend was the Legislative Reorganization Act of 1970, which provided for recorded votes in the Committee of the Whole, where most House action on appropriation bills (and other measures) takes place. Another reason for the increase in floor amendments has been the practice of attaching "limitations" to appropriation bills. Although the rules bar the insertion of legislation in such bills, limitations that restrict the use of appropriated funds are permissible. The House adopted three times as many limitation amendments in the 1970s as it did in the 1960s. Some of the most contentious issues of recent times, such as U.S. policy in Vietnam, school busing, aid to the Nicaraguan contras, and abortions, have been considered as limitations in appropriation bills.

Although the data in Table 7-7 do not show it, there appears to have been a downturn in the number of limiting amendments because of a change in rules adopted by the House at the start of the Ninety-eighth Congress in 1983. The new rule makes it easier for the House to avoid consideration of these amendments, but if a House majority wants to do so, it can still use appropriation bills as an effective means of controlling government policy by limiting the use of appropriated funds.

The Congressional Budget Act of 1974 established a timetable designed to ensure enactment of all regular appropriation bills by October 1, when the new fiscal year begins. Despite the legislative schedule, Congress has had difficulty in completing its work on regular appropriation bills by the start of the fiscal year. As a consequence, it has been compelled to provide stopgap funding through continuing appropriations (see Table 7-8). There have only been three fiscal years—1977, 1989, and 1995—when it has not been necessary to rely on continuing appropriations. Only three of the thirteen regular appropriation bills for fiscal 1980 were enacted by the start of the fiscal year; only one regular appropriation bill for fiscal 1981 was enacted on time; and none of these bills had been enacted into law when fiscal 1982 began. The record improved slightly in subsequent years, with one bill enacted by the start of fiscal 1983 and four bills by the start of fiscal 1984 and 1985, but then Congress failed to enact any regular appropriation bills at the start of fiscal 1986, 1987, 1988, 1990, and 1991. That record makes passage of all thirteen bills for 1989 all the more remarkable, reflecting a broad bipartisan agreement to get things done in the presidential election year, while putting off the hottest and most controversial budget issues to the next administration. Nevertheless, congressional activity quickly reverted back to normal, and no appropriation bills were passed by the start of FY1990 or FY1991. Yet, another surge came with the passage of all bills before FY1995 commenced. It remains to be seen whether this swiftness can last more than one year at a time. Prospects for FY1996 are not bright.

The Budgetary Work of Congress

To an extraordinary degree, the business of Congress is related to the budget. Tables 7-9 and 7-10 show a steep increase between 1955 and 1982 in the number of House and Senate roll calls dealing with budgetary issues. Budget-related votes include all roll calls on appropriation bills, tax legislation (other than tax treaties and tariffs), budget resolutions, and reconciliation bills, as well as votes pertaining to the level of authorizations. The number of budget-related votes has escalated in both chambers during the past quarter of a century, but the increase has been especially striking in the Senate. With the exception of 1988, consistently nearly 50 percent of House roll calls each year have been budget related, though it reached 60 percent in 1993. In the Senate, budget-related roll call votes hit 71 percent in 1981 and leveled off at 60 percent. They declined a bit from 1986 to 1992, but then climbed back to 62 percent in 1993.

One interesting pattern that emerges from the data in Tables 7-9 and 7-10 is that despite the establishment of the congressional budget process, Congress still gives a great deal of attention to authorizations, appropriations, and tax legislation. Congressional budget activity—especially in the Senate—was extraordinary during the 1981 session, which coincided with Ronald Reagan's first year in office. The new president organized his domestic agenda around the federal budget and called for major changes in economic policies and spending priorities. Inevitably, Congress increased its budget activity. In subsequent years, budget activity was more normal, though the increase that began in 1993 is likely to continue through at least the 104th Congress because the budget and the deficit have once again become a top priority.

Rescissions and Deferrals

One of the key purposes of the congressional budget process is to ensure that congressional spending priorities prevail when they are in conflict with those of the president. To achieve this end, the Impound-ment Control Act established procedures for congressional review of presidential proposals to defer or rescind funds provided by Congress. When a president proposes rescission, Congress has a forty-five-day period during which it can pass a bill rescinding the funds; if Congress fails to act during this period, the president is required to make the funds available for expenditure. The deficit control mentality of the 1990s led many members, mostly Republicans but also some Democrats, to call for passage of a presidential line-item veto. In the first part of the Republican-led 104th Congress, the House and Senate each passed different versions of this legislation. While a compromise bill must still be formed, each version would allow the president to veto specific sections of appropriations bills and require a two-thirds vote by Congress to overturn them.

Table 7-11 shows that the use of the rescission process varies sharply from year to year. In 1975 and 1976 President Gerald Ford proposed billions of dollars in rescissions, but Congress actually rescinded less than 10 percent of the amount. During Jimmy Carter's administration, rescissions dropped sharply. Reagan resorted to rescissions to implement his budget policy, however, and 90 percent of the amount he proposed to rescind in fiscal 1981 was approved by Congress. The approval rate and dollar amounts of Reagan's proposed rescissions dropped substantially in later years until fiscal 1986, when Reagan sharply increased his use of rescissions and deferrals. Congress also rescinded several billion dollars in 1986. In the last two years of the Reagan administration, however, the president found that Congress voted down all but 1 percent of his proposed rescissions, and in the last year, he did not propose any. President Bush proposed only seventeen rescissions in his first two years in office, with Congress rescinding less than 1 percent of the funds requested. Bush relied on rescissions to a much greater extent in 1991 and 1992. While he had little success in 1991, in 1992, 26 percent of the nearly $8 billion he proposed to rescind was approved by Congress. In 1993 and 1994 deficit cutting was such a top priority for most members that Congress went far beyond approving President Clinton's proposed rescissions. They initiated seventy-four of their own in 1993 and eighty-one in 1994. Then in 1995 the new Republican Congress forced the president to accept more than $16 billion in FY1995 rescissions.

When a president proposes deferrals, either the House or the Senate can approve an "impoundment resolution" compelling the release of the affected funds. The constitutional status of this procedure was questioned by the June 1983 decision of the Supreme Court that invalidated all legislative vetoes. Because the president now proposes only non-policy deferrals, Congress usually disapproves only a small portion of them. In fact, from 1988 through 1994, Congress accepted all of the president's proposed deferrals.

Table 7-1   House Votes on Adoption of Budget Resolutions, by Party, Fiscal Years, 1976-1995

Fiscal year	Resolution	Total Yes	Total No	Democrats Yes	Democrats No	Republicans Yes	Republicans No
1976	First	200	196	197	68	3	128
	Second	225	191	214	67	11	124
1977	First	221	155	208	44	13	111
	Second	227	151	215	38	12	113
	Third	239	169	225	50	14	119
1978	First (first round)	84	320	82	185	2	135
	First (second round)	213	179	206	58	7	121
	Second	199	188	195	59	4	129
1979	First	201	197	198	61	3	136
	Second	217	178	215	42	2	136
1980	First	220	184	211	50	9	134
	Second (first round)	192	213	188	67	4	146
	Second (second round)	212	206	212	52	0	154
	Third[a]	241	174	218	45	23	129
1981	First	225	193	203	62	22	131
	Second	203	191	201	45	2	146
1982	First	270	154	84	153	186	1
	Second	206	200	70	150	136	50
1983	First	219	206	63	174	156	32
1984	First	229	196	225	36	4	160
1985	First	250	168	229	29	21	139
1986	First	258	170	234	15	24	155
1987	First	245	179	228	19	17	160
1988	First	215	201	212	34	3	167
1989	First	319	102	227	24	92	78
1990	First	263	157	157	96	106	61
1991	First	218	208	218	34	0	174
1992	First	239	181[b]	231	25	8	155
1993	First	209	207[b]	209	47	0	159
1994	First	243[b]	183	242	11	0	172
1995	First	223[b]	175	222	11	0	164

Note: These votes are on passage of the resolutions in the House, not on adoption of the conference report. Beginning with the 1983 fiscal year, Congress has adopted only one budget resolution each year, rather than the two originally prescribed by the Congressional Budget Act.

[a] The third resolution for fiscal 1980 was part of the first resolution for the 1981 fiscal year, but it was voted on separately in the House.

[b] Total includes Bernard Sanders (I-Vt.).

Sources: Congressional Record; Congressional Quarterly Almanac (Washington, D.C.: Congressional Quarterly, various years); *Congressional Quarterly Weekly Report,* May 6, 1989, May 5, 1990, May 25, 1991, May 23, 1992, March 20, 1993, March 19, 1994.

Table 7-2   Senate Votes on Adoption of Budget Resolutions, by Party, Fiscal Years, 1976-1995

Fiscal year	Resolution	Total Yes	Total No	Democrats Yes	Democrats No	Republicans Yes	Republicans No
1976	First	69	22	50	4	19	18
	Second	69	23	50	8	19	15
1977	First	62	22	45	6	17	16
	Second	55	23	41	5	14	18
	Third	72	20	55	3	17	17
1978	First	56	31	41	14	15	17
	Second	63	21	46	8	17	13
1979	First	64	27	48	8	16	19
	Second	56	18	42	6	14	12
1980	First	64	20	44	5	20	15
	Second	62	36	45	14	17	22
1981	First	68	28	49	6	19	22
	Second	48	46	33	21	15	25
1982	First	78	20	28	18	50	2
	Second	49	48	2	44	47	4
1983	First	49	43	3	41	46	2
1984	First	50	49	29	17	21	32
1985	First	41	34	1	31	40	3
1986	First	50	49	1	45	49[a]	4
1987	First	70	25	38	6	32	19
1988	First	53	46	50	3	3	43
1989	First	69	26	44	6	25	20
1990	First	68	31	38	17	30	14
1991	First[b]	—	—	—	—	—	—
1992	First	57	41	49	7	8	34
1993	First	52	41	36	16	16	25
1994	First	54	45	54	2	0	43
1995	First	57	40	55	0	2	40

Note: These votes are on passage of the resolutions in the Senate, not on adoption of the conference report. Beginning with the 1983 fiscal year, Congress has adopted only one budget resolution each year, rather than the two originally prescribed by the Congres-·sional Budget Act.

[a] Vice President George Bush cast the deciding vote for the Republicans.

[b] The Senate Budget Resolution (S. Con. Res. 110) was approved by voice vote on June 14, 1990.

Sources: Congressional Record; Congressional Quarterly Almanac, various years; *Congressional Quarterly Weekly Report,* May 6, 1989, June 16, 1990, May 25, 1991, May 23, 1992, March 27, 1993, April 2, 1994.

Table 7-3 Budgeted and Actual Revenues, Budget Authority, Outlays, and Deficits, Fiscal Years, 1976-1995 (billions of dollars)

	Revenues	Budget authority	Budget outlays	Budget deficit
1976				
President's budget	297.7	385.8	349.4	51.7
First budget resolution	298.2	395.8	367.0	68.8
Second budget resolution	300.8	408.0	374.9	74.1
Actual	300.0	415.3	366.4	66.4
1977				
President's budget	351.3	433.4	394.2	42.9
First budget resolution	362.5	454.2	413.3	50.8
Second budget resolution	362.5	451.6	413.1	50.6
Third budget resolution	347.7	472.9	417.5	69.8
Fourth budget resolution	356.6	470.2	409.2	52.6
Actual	357.8	464.4	402.7	44.9
1978				
Ford budget	393.0	480.4	440.0	47.0
Carter budget	401.6	507.3	459.4	57.8
First budget resolution	396.3	503.5	461.0	64.7
Second budget resolution	397.0	500.1	458.3	61.3
Actual	402.0	500.4	450.8	48.8
1979				
President's budget	439.6	568.2	500.2	60.6
First budget resolution	447.9	568.9	498.8	50.9
Second budget resolution	448.7	555.7	487.5	38.8
Third budget resolution	461.0	559.2	494.5	33.5
Actual	465.9	556.7	493.6	27.7
1980				
President's budget	502.6	615.5	531.6	29.0
First budget resolution	509.0	604.4	532.0	23.0
Second budget resolution	517.8	638.0	547.6	29.8
Third budget resolution	525.7	658.9	572.7	47.0
Actual	520.0	658.8	579.6	59.6
1981				
President's budget	600.0	696.1	615.8	15.8
Revised budget	628.0	691.3	611.5	−16.5
First budget resolution	613.8	697.2	613.6	−0.2
Second budget resolution	605.0	694.6	632.4	27.4
Third budget resolution	603.3	717.5	661.4	58.1
Actual	599.3	718.4	657.2	57.9

(Table continues)

Table 7-3   (continued)

	Revenues	Budget authority	Budget outlays	Budget deficit
1982				
Carter budget	711.8	809.8	739.3	27.5
Reagan budget	650.3	772.4	695.3	45.0
Budget resolution	657.8	770.9	695.5	37.7
Revised resolution	628.4	777.7	734.1	105.7
Actual	617.8	779.9	728.4	110.6
1983				
President's budget	666.1	801.9	757.6	91.5
Budget resolution	665.9	822.4	769.8	103.9
Actual	600.6	866.7	796.0	195.4
1984				
President's budget	659.7	900.1	848.5	188.8
Budget resolution[a]	679.6	919.5	849.5	169.9
		928.7	858.9	179.3
Revised resolution	672.9	918.9	845.6	172.7
Actual	666.5	949.8	851.8	185.3
1985				
President's budget	745.1	1,006.5	925.5	180.4
Budget resolution	750.9	1,021.4	932.1	181.2
Actual	734.1	1,074.1	946.3	212.2
1986				
President's budget	793.7	1,060.0	973.7	180.0
Budget resolution	795.7	1,069.7	967.6	171.9
Actual	769.1	1,072.8	989.8	220.7
1987				
President's budget	850.4	1,102.0	994.0	143.6
Budget resolution	852.4	1,093.4	995.0	142.6
Actual	854.1	1,099.9	1,003.8	149.7
1988				
President's budget	916.6	1,142.2	1,024.4	107.8
Budget resolution	921.6	1,153.2	1,055.5	133.9
Actual	909.0	1,185.5	1,064.0	155.0
1989				
President's budget	964.7	1,222.1	1,094.2	129.5
Budget resolution	964.3	1,232.0	1,098.2	133.9
Actual	990.7	1,309.9	1,144.1	153.4
1990				
President's budget	1,059.3	1,331.2	1,151.8	92.5
Budget resolution	1,065.5	1,350.9	1,165.3	99.8
Actual	1,031.3	1,368.5	1,251.7	220.4

Table 7-3   (continued)

	Revenues	Budget authority	Budget outlays	Budget deficit
1991				
President's budget	1,170.2	1,396.5	1,233.3	63.1
Budget resolution	1,172.9	1,485.6	1,236.9	64.0
Actual	1,054.3	1,398.2	1,323.0	268.7
1992				
President's budget	1,172.2	1,579.3	1,442.2	270.0
Budget resolution	1,169.2	1,590.1	1,448.0	278.8
Actual	1,091.7	1,469.2	1,381.9	290.2
1993				
President's budget	1,171.2	1,516.8	1,503.0	331.8
Budget resolution	1,173.4	1,516.4	1,500.0	326.6
Actual	1,153.5	1,473.6	1,408.7	255.1
1994				
President's budget	1,242.1	1,512.6	1,500.6	258.5
Budget resolution	1,241.8	1,507.1	1,495.6	253.8
Actual	1,257.7	1,528.4	1,460.9	203.2
1995				
President's budget	1,353.8	1,537.0	1,518.9	165.1[b]
Budget resolution	1,338.2	1,540.7	1,513.6	175.4

[a] Larger figures for authority, outlays, and deficit assumed enactment of programs in a reserve fund.

[b] Assumed enactment of president's health care reforms.

Sources: Congressional Budget Office; *The Budget of the United States Government* for fiscal years 1984-1996; *Congressional Quarterly Almanac*, vols. 39-40; *Congressional Quarterly Weekly Report*, 1985-1987, and March 26, 1988; *Congressional Record*, vol. 136, no. 131, October 7, 1990. For 1992, *Congressional Quarterly Weekly Report*, May 25, 1991; for 1993, Congressional Budget Office; for 1994, *Congressional Quarterly Weekly Report*, April 3, 1993; for 1995, *Congressional Quarterly Weekly Report*, May 7, 1994.

184

Table 7-4 Relatively Uncontrollable Federal Outlays under Present Law, Fiscal Years, 1967-1995 (billions of dollars)

Fiscal year	Social Security and other retirement	Medical care	Other payments to individuals	Net interest	Outlays from prior obligations	Other uncontrollables	Total uncontrollables	Percent budget uncontrollable
1967	26.3	4.6	10.7	10.3	37.0	4.7	93.5	59.1
1968	29.1	7.2	11.4	11.1	42.3	6.2	107.3	60.0
1969	33.1	8.9	12.9	12.4	41.9	6.9	116.1	63.1
1970	36.9	9.9	15.4	14.4	41.5	7.6	125.7	64.0
1971	43.8	11.2	22.3	14.8	40.2	8.0	140.4	66.4
1972	49.2	13.4	25.8	15.5	39.2	10.4	153.5	66.2
1973	63.6	14.1	18.3	17.3	41.4	13.9	168.6	68.7
1974	72.5	17.2	21.4	21.4	46.0	11.9	190.4	70.8
1975	86.7	21.6	34.3	23.2	53.3	9.3	228.4	70.4
1976	97.2	26.3	43.5	26.7	53.7	10.1	257.5	70.7
1977	111.5	31.4	39.6	29.9	58.8	12.4	283.5	70.8
1978	122.8	35.9	36.9	35.4	76.9	15.8	323.7	72.2
1979	136.7	41.6	46.5	42.6	85.3	12.0	364.7	72.3
1980	156.5	49.0	47.0	52.5	103.2	16.2	424.4	73.6
1981	183.7	59.3	51.5	68.7	108.6	13.2	485.0	73.8
1982	201.8	65.6	53.2	85.0	121.5	15.1	542.1	74.4
1983	219.1	73.5	61.2	89.8	128.7	21.3	593.6	74.6
1984	228.3	79.9	49.2	111.1	145.3	10.3	624.1	73.3
1985	238.2	91.0	49.7	129.4	162.2	17.3	689.5	72.9
1986	252.8	97.8	52.0ª	136.0	181.3	25.5	745.4	76.2
1987	263.8	105.6	52.1	138.6	185.2	23.8	769.1	76.6
1988	279.6	114.7	53.7	151.7	186.8	20.9	807.4	76.5
1989	285.9	133.4	52.3	169.1	210.4	16.9	868.0	75.9
1990	304.8	155.8	57.4	184.2	231.6	12.0	945.8	75.6

Year								
1991	329.2	175.7	69.9	194.5	233.8	15.2	1,018.3	77.0
1992	349.7	208.5	84.7	199.4	233.8	15.2	1,091.3	79.0
1993	368.8	230.0	87.8	198.8	236.7	20.4	1,142.5	81.1
1994	386.6	251.9	75.0	203.0	228.2	15.1	1,159.8	79.4
1995 (est.)	405.4	272.3	79.9	234.2	240.2	14.4	1,246.4	81.0

Note: From time to time the Office of Management and Budget reclassifies or redefines uncontrollables; hence the figures in this table may not be consistent with those published in some budget documents.

[a] Includes unemployment compensation, assistance to students, food and nutrition, public assistance, and other uncontrollables.

Sources: For the 1967-1972 fiscal years, *The Budget of the United States Government Fiscal Year 1977*, table 16; for the 1973-1981 fiscal years, *The Budget of the United States Government Fiscal Year 1983*; for the 1982-1983 fiscal years, *The Budget of the United States Government Fiscal Year 1985*, table 20; for the 1984-1985 fiscal years, *The Budget of the United States Government Fiscal Year 1986*, table 18; for the 1986 fiscal year, *The Budget of the United States Government Fiscal Year 1987*, table 16; for the 1987 fiscal year, *The Budget of the United States Government Fiscal Year 1989*, table 16; for the 1988 and 1989 fiscal years, *The Budget of the United States Government Fiscal Year 1990*, table 14; for fiscal years 1990-1991, *The Budget of the United States Government Fiscal Year 1992*, tables 1-1 and 1-2; for fiscal years 1992-1993, *The Budget of the United States Government Fiscal Year 1994*, Appendix; for fiscal years 1994-1995, *The Budget of the United States Government, Analytical Perspectives*, table 6-2.

Table 7-5   President's Budget Requests and Congressional
Appropriations, 1968-1994 (thousands of dollars)

Year	Budget requests	Appropriations	Appropriations compared with requests
1968	147,908,613	133,339,869	−14,568,744
1969	142,701,346	134,431,463	−8,269,883
1970	147,765,358	144,273,529	−3,491,830
1971	167,874,625	165,225,662	−2,648,963
1972	185,431,805	178,960,107	−6,471,698
1973	177,959,504	174,901,434	−3,058,070
1974	213,667,190	204,012,312	−9,654,878
1975	267,224,774	259,852,322	−7,372,452
1976	282,142,432	282,536,695	394,263
1977	364,867,240	354,025,781	− 10,841,459
1978	348,506,125	337,859,467	− 10,646,658
1979	397,653,766	386,822,093	− 10,831,673
1980	340,339,447	333,695,164	−6,644,283
1981	440,398,235	442,215,128	1,816,893
1982	507,740,133	514,832,375	7,092,242
1983	542,956,652	551,620,505	8,663,853
1984	576,343,258	559,151,835	−17,191,422
1985	588,698,503	583,446,885	−5,251,618
1986	590,345,199	577,279,102	−13,066,097
1987	595,071,473	584,399,770	−10,671,703
1988	607,213,694	606,443,182[a]	−770,511
1989	652,138,432	666,211,681	14,073,249
1990	704,510,962	697,257,740	−7,253,222
1991[b]	720,178,246	712,696,380	−7,481,866
1992[b/c]	736,231,270	715,697,705	−20,533,566
1993	798,046,000	782,150,000	−15,896,000
1994	782,753,000	779,375,000	−3,378,000

Note: The years are calendar, not fiscal, years. The amounts shown are for budget authority provided in appropriations acts and do not include permanent appropriations or budget authority provided in legislative acts.

[a] Includes defense rescission of −3,531,030.

[b] Excludes Desert Shield/Desert Storm contributed funds.

[c] Includes rescission of Desert Shield/Desert Storm funds.

Source: House Committee on Appropriations.

Table 7-6 Supplemental Appropriations, Fiscal Years, 1964-1994

Fiscal year	Number of supplemental bills [a]	Amount of budget authority [b] (millions of dollars)
1964	1	290
1965	4	5,645
1966	4	21,889
1967	3	19,420
1968	5	8,218
1969	4	5,835
1970	2	5,993
1971	4	9,870
1972	7	11,599
1973	5	11,371
1974	5	14,796
1975	7	27,587
1976	5	24,636
1977	5	49,835
1978	9	16,053
1979	1	13,845
1980	6	19,683
1981	2	20,960
1982	4	27,442
1983	2	22,655
1984	4	16,307
1985	3	14,804
1986	3	8,191
1987	1	9,400
1988	1	672
1989	1	3,294
1990	1	4,344
1991	3	48,639
1992	2	9,786
1993	5	11,957
1994	2	9,291

[a] The number of supplemental bills does not include regular and continuing appropriations in which supplemental budget authority was provided.

[b] The amount of budget authority does include, for fiscal year 1976 and subsequent years, supplementals provided in regular or continuing appropriation bills. The figure represents supplemental spending after accounting for offsetting cuts.

Sources: For the 1964-1969 fiscal years, Louis Fisher, "Supplemental Appropriations History, Controls, Recent Record," Congressional Research Service, Library of Congress, Washington, D.C., April 12, 1979; for the 1970-1980 fiscal years, Congressional Budget Office, *Supplemental Appropriations in the 1970s,* Staff Working Paper, July 1981; for the 1981-1983 and 1987-1988 fiscal years, *Congressional Quarterly Almanac;* for the 1984-1988 fiscal years, House Committee on Appropriations; for 1989-1994, *Congressional Quarterly Weekly Report,* June 30, 1989, November 3, 1990, December 7, 1991, November 5, 1994; for 1992-1994, House Committee on Appropriations.

Table 7-7   House Amendments to Appropriation Bills, 1963-1982

Year	Total amendments	Amendments adopted	Limitation amendments[a]	Limitation amendments adopted
1963	47	15	17	7
1964	27	9	11	2
1965	26	9	11	1
1966	56	10	8	1
1967	70	15	16	4
1968	75	24	20	7
1969	89	27	20	10
1970	51	11	13	1
1971	83	34	23	7
1972	89	15	26	5
1973	99	31	31	12
1974	109	53	34	15
1975	106	52	34	12
1976	122	68	33	13
1977	107	54	44	24
1978	135	61	44	25
1979	165	74	52	31
1980	168	100	74	57
1981	143	87	47	33
1982	59	33	21	14

Note: The years are calendar, not fiscal, years. No new data available after 1982.

[a] Limitation amendments are amendments that bar the use of appropriated funds for specified purposes.

Sources: For 1963-1977, Democratic Study Group, Special Report No. 95-12 (Washington, D.C., February 14, 1978); for 1978-1982, Richard S. Beth, Daniel P. Strickland, and Stanley Bach, "Limitation and Other House Amendments to General Appropriation Bills: Fiscal Years 1979-1983," Congressional Research Service, Library of Congress, Washington, D.C., December 28, 1982. The two sources may not be completely consistent in their scope and definition of amendments.

Table 7-8   Continuing Appropriations, Fiscal Years, 1972-1995

Fiscal year	Regular appropriation bills not enacted by start of fiscal year [a]	Continuing resolutions enacted for fiscal year
1972	5	5
1973	4	5
1974	10	2
1975	6	4
1976	11	3
1977[b]	0[c]	2
1978	4	3
1979	8	1
1980	10	2
1981	12	2
1982	13	5
1983	12	2
1984	9	4
1985	9	4
1986	13	5
1987	13	1
1988	13	5
1989	0[d]	0
1990	13	3
1991	13	5
1992	10	3
1993	12	1
1994	11	3
1995	0	0

[a] In calendar year 1976, the start of the fiscal year was changed from July 1 to October 1.
[b] Although all regular appropriation bills were enacted by the start of the fiscal year, continuing appropriations were needed for certain items not provided for in these bills.
[c] The appropriation was signed into law on the first day of the fiscal year.
[d] Congress cleared and sent all bills to the president by the beginning of the fiscal year, but not all bills were signed until the following day.

Sources: Robert A. Keith, "An Overview of the Use of Continuing Appropriations," Congressional Research Service, Library of Congress, Washington, D.C., September 26, 1980; Congressional Budget Office, "Consideration of Appropriation Bills," unpublished memorandum, August 21, 1979; data for the 1980-1989 fiscal years are taken from the House calendars; for 1990-1995 *Congressional Quarterly Weekly Report*, November 20, 1989, November 3, 1990, November 16, 1991, October 31, 1992, December 11, 1993, November 5, 1994.

Table 7-9   Budget-related Roll Call Votes in the House, Selected Years, 1955-1994

Measure	1955	1960	1965	1970	1975	1980	1981	1983
Authorizations	27	28	78	77	147	105	70	129
Appropriations	6	16	21	39	94	111	85	112
Tax legislation	3	3	3	1	48	14	7	9
Budget resolutions	—	—	—	—	12	30	13	4
Reconciliation bills	—	—	—	—	—	6	12	2
Debt ceilings	1	2	2	2	11	7	2	3
Miscellaneous	0	1	0	2	8	4	7	3
Total budget-related roll calls	37	50	104	121	320	277	196	262
Total roll calls	76	93	201	266	612	604	353	498
Percentage budget-related	49	54	52	45	52	46	56	53

Sources: For 1955-1982, Allen Schick, "Legislation, Appropriations, and Budgets: The Development of Spending Decision-Making in Congress," Congressional Research Service, Library of Congress, Washington, D.C., 1984; for 1983-1986, House Appropriations Committee; for 1987-1994, based on Congressional Quarterly roll call vote index.

1985	1986	1987	1988	1989	1990	1991	1992	1993	1994
95	112	118	84	68	116	83	38	94	94
82	93	86	60	95	110	101	129	176	121
11	3	0	3	0	0	11	21	6	6
10	8	8	6	7	8	9	10	8	9
10	10	6	0	14	5	0	0	9	0
11	4	7	0	3	6	0	0	0	1
1	1	2	1	0	8	4	16	12	34
220	231	227	154	187	253	208	214	305	265
439	451	488	451	359	497	414	459	513	500
50	51	46	34	52	51	50	47	59	53

Table 7-10   Budget-related Roll Call Votes in the Senate, Selected Years, 1955-1994

Measure	1955	1960	1965	1970	1975	1980	1981	1983
Authorizations	22	48	87	83	96	82	55	58
Appropriations	12	28	27	77	87	128	130	107
Tax legislation	2	10	10	6	48	10	56	13
Budget resolutions	—	—	—	—	8	50	26	34
Reconciliation bills	—	—	—	—	—	4	63	2
Debt ceilings	0	2	1	3	3	6	12	15
Miscellaneous	1	0	0	1	4	3	2	9
Total budget-related roll calls	37	88	125	170	246	283	344	238
Total roll calls	87	207	258	418	602	531	483	381
Percentage budget-related	42	42	48	41	41	53	71	62

Sources: For 1955-1982, Schick, "Legislation, Appropriations, and Budgets"; for 1983-1986, Senate Appropriations Committee; for 1987-1994, based on Congressional Quarterly roll call vote index.

1985	1986	1987	1988	1989	1990	1991	1992	1993	1994
67	33	84	30	42	81	73	20	27	68
59	74	66	67	75	58	66	64	114	108
7	26	0	15	5	0	5	41	27	3
39	14	17	11	8	1	12	14	46	15
23	12	8	0	2	6	0	0	6	0
29	14	17	0	0	1	0	0	0	0
6	10	3	0	6	10	3	9	16	9
230	183	195	123	138	157	159	148	236	203
381	359	420	379	302	337	287	267	383	330
60	51	46	32	46	46	55	55	62	62

Table 7-11 Rescissions, Fiscal Years, 1975-1994

Fiscal year	Number of rescissions	Amount proposed ($ thousands)	Amount approved ($ thousands)	Amount rescinded (percent)	Proposals approved, wholly or in part (percent)
1975	91	3,328,500	391,295	12	43
1976[a]	50	3,608,363	138,331	4	14
1977	21	1,835,602	1,271,040	69	48
1978	8	644,055	55,255	9	38
1979	11	908,692	723,609	80	80
1980	59	1,618,061	778,127	48	58
1981	208	16,204,936	14,509,878	90	67
1982	34	9,484,941	5,974,966	63	21
1983	21	1,569,015	0	0	0
1985	244	1,855,000	212,000	11	39
1986	83	10,121,548	18,876,367[b]	188[b]	—
1987	73	5,835,800	36,090	1	3
1988	0	0	0	—	—
1989	6	143,096	2,053	1	17
1990	11	554,258	0	0	0
1991	30	4,859,300	0	0	0
1992	128	7,879,500	2,066,900	26	20
1993	7	356,000	2,411,587[c]	667	—
1994	65	3,172,180	3,667,895[d]	116	—

[a] Fiscal 1976 data include the transition quarter. A proposal to rescind or defer funds in both fiscal 1976 and the transition quarter counted as a single proposal. [b] The number is higher because Congress initiated thirty-three of its own rescissions. [c] The number is higher because Congress initiated seventy-four of its own rescissions equalling $2,205,337. [d] The number is higher because Congress initiated eighty-one of its own rescissions equalling $2,374,416.

Source: House Appropriations Committee; Senate Budget Committee.

Table 7-12   Deferrals, Fiscal Years, 1975-1994

Fiscal year	Number of deferrals	Amount proposed ($ thousands)	Amount disapproved ($ thousands)	Number of deferrals disapproved	Amount disapproved (percent)	Deferrals disapproved (percent)
1975	159	24,574,236	9,318,217	16	38	10
1976[a]	119	9,209,780	393,081	24[b]	4	20
1977	68	6,831,194	25,600	3	0.4	4
1978	66	4,910,114	69,531	6	1	9
1979	70	4,696,056	13,852	2	0.3	3
1980	73	9,846,235	3,663,448	2	37	3
1981	131	7,535,493	367,359	15	5	12
1982	267	7,562,078	386,347	15	5	6
1983	87	9,957,186	4,119,590	16	41	19
1985	78	8,476,000	0	0	0	0
1986	70	24,767,151	2,828,276	c	11.4	c
1987	57	11,494,600	174,300	c	1.5	c
1988	22	9,320,100	0	0	0	0
1989	14	9,156,174	0	0	0	0
1990	28	11,071,540	0	0	0	0
1991	11	10,347,800	0	0	0	0
1992	12	5,791,800	0	0	0	0
1993	12	2,921,080	0	0	0	0
1994	12	7,334,903	0	0	0	0

[a] Fiscal 1976 data include the transition quarter. A proposal to rescind or defer funds in both fiscal 1976 and the transition quarter counted as a single proposal.   [b] Two fiscal 1976 deferrals that were disapproved by both the House and the Senate are counted here once each.   [c] Figures cannot be listed because in many cases Congress deferred only partial amounts.

Source: House Appropriations Committee; Senate Budget Committee.

Voting Alignments 8

Three important elements of voting on the floor of the House and the Senate are support for the president, the cohesion of the parties, and the strength of the ideological coalitions that cut across party lines. This chapter provides a description of the dynamics of these forces in congressional decision making since the 1950s, using the measures compiled annually by Congressional Quarterly.

Presidential Success and Support

Table 8-1 shows the annual percentages of presidential victories on votes on which the president took clear-cut positions. Congressional Quarterly determines what the president wants in the way of legislative action by analyzing his messages to Congress, press conference remarks, and other public statements and documents. The measure combines the significant and the trivial, the controversial and the consensual; moreover, it reflects the position of the president at the time of a vote, even though that position may reflect a major concession from an earlier stand.

Despite these limitations, the measure does give a rough indication of the state of relations between the president and Congress. Table 8-1 provides an overall success score, as well as the president's success averages in the House and Senate. Presidential success is mainly a function of the number of seats in Congress held by the president's party. When one party controls both branches, success never drops below 75 percent; with divided government, presidents average well below that level of success.

With the Democrats in control of the House, Senate, and presidency during Bill Clinton's first two years in office, presidential success scores reached 86.4 percent, the highest level since Lyndon Johnson's Great Society. In 1993 the president and the Democratic Congress achieved many genuine legislative victories. But in 1994 the high rate of success can largely be attributed to the fact that most of the presidennt's controversial legislation became so stymied that it never reached a vote. During the next two years these high percentages are expected to drop sharply as a consequence of the Republican takeover of Congress, just as we have seen in the heavy partisan swings of past elections. President Eisenhower's score dropped twenty-four percentage points after the Democratic victory in the 1958 elections. President Johnson achieved a modern high of 93 percent in the session following the 1964 elections. And, after his smashing victory in 1980, President Reagan enjoyed a level of support seven percentage points higher than that of his predecessor's first year in office. But his success rate plummeted in the Senate after the Democrats regained control in the 1986 elections.

Over the course of his four years in office, George Bush won an average of 51.6 of the roll call votes on which he took a stand. This marked the lowest score of any first term president since Congressional Quarterly began keeping track in 1953. Bush's score reached a low point in 1992 when he lost the support of many Senate Republicans and could claim victory on only 43 percent of the votes where he held a clear position. Although higher, the scores of many of Bush's predecessors similarly reflect the struggle which often accompanies divided government (Ronald Reagan, 61.9 percent; Gerald Ford, 57.6 percent; Richard Nixon, 67.2 percent; Dwight D. Eisenhower after 1954, 67.7 percent). The anomaly is 1981, when the Republicans controlled the presidency and the Senate but not the House. Ronald Reagan's overall success score of 82.3 percent in 1981 ranks with presidents whose party has controlled both houses; his score in the Senate places him alongside Eisenhower in 1953 and Lyndon Johnson in 1964. After that initial year, however, Reagan's overall success dropped sharply, due almost entirely to the collapse of his support in the Democrat-controlled House.

Success rates usually deteriorate over the course of a presidency (Johnson, Nixon, Reagan, and Bush), but at times they remain relatively stable (Carter) or even increase (Kennedy). It should be noted that presidential success cannot be measured by the outcome of roll call votes alone. These do not account for the many other ways in which a president can influence the legislative process. For example, on numerous occasions President Bush effectively used the veto and the threat of vetoes to affect legislative outcomes. Clinton, who did not use the veto once during his first two years, is more likely to use this route of influence in the 104th Congress.

The base for computing presidential scores varies widely, from a low of 34 House votes in 1953 and 1956 to a high of 185 Senate votes in

1973. The average number of votes on which presidents have taken clear-cut positions has increased over time, but the percentage has declined. In 1979 President Carter made his position known on only 22 percent of all House recorded votes and 19 percent of Senate votes. The comparable figures for President Eisenhower's third year are 56 percent in the House and 59 percent in the Senate. The congressional liaison workload of the White House has increased, but so too has the relative independence of Congress.

Table 8-2 presents presidential support scores (adjusted to remove the effects of absences) for all Democrats, southern Democrats, and Republicans in the House and Senate. Senate Republicans have usually been more supportive of presidents, Republican and Democratic, than their House counterparts. No such consistent pattern is evident among Democrats. Whereas Democrats in the Senate were more supportive of Carter than their party colleagues in the House, the pattern was just the opposite under Presidents Kennedy and Johnson. The voting of southern Democrats is at least partly responsible for this change. Among southern Democratic members, President Kennedy fared better in the House than in the Senate, but President Carter received more support among these members in the Senate.

The sharpest trend in Table 8-2 is the decline in support for Republican presidents among southern Democrats, particularly in the House. The steady decline in success by President Reagan after 1981 mirrors the collapse in support for his proposals by House Democrats south of the Mason-Dixon line. While Bush regained some support among southern Democrats in both houses during his first year in office, that support eroded over time, and, in fact, reached a low point in the Senate in 1992. In 1993 Clinton received the highest support score recorded among Southern Democrats in the House and Senate. But the House score dropped almost fifteen percentage points in 1994, foreshadowing the Republican takeover of that region. Clinton's scores among Republicans were lower than for most Democratic presidents, though they did go up in 1994 (again because many controversial measures failed to come to a vote).

Party Unity

One important component of the structure of congressional voting is party-line voting. Table 8-3 presents for both the House and the Senate the percentage of all recorded votes on which a majority of voting Democrats opposed a majority of voting Republicans. In the House the trend in that measure had been downward beginning with Johnson's troubles with the war in Vietnam. Under Presidents Nixon and Ford, about 35 percent of all roll call votes produced a party split, down from an average of nearly 50 percent under President Eisenhower. The number rose to 40 percent during Carter's four years in office and then dropped back to 37 percent in Reagan's first year. By 1983, however, voting in the House had taken on a distinctively partisan cast. Four years later the percentage of party votes in the House reached its highest point in the postwar period, at 64 percent. After declining slightly over the next few years, party unity votes again reached that postwar high in 1992, and continued to rise in 1993 to 65 percent in the House (67 percent in the Senate) as the first Democratic White House and Congress in twelve years worked to advance several measures along partisan lines. Party unity scores then dropped in 1994, falsely giving the picture of a less partisan Congress. Actually, Congress was so split along party lines that many bills never made it to a House vote. How much partisanship will be carried over into the Republican-controlled 104th Congress remains to be seen.

There also appears to be an election year cycle in these figures, especially in recent years. The percentage of party votes increases in off years and declines in subsequent election years. This may reflect the efforts of congressional leaders during election years to avoid sharply partisan votes that may hurt members back home, or an effort by members to put party interests aside and vote with their constituents' interests in mind.

The Senate figures on party voting in Table 8-3 are less patterned than the House figures. The percentage of party votes grew under Carter and Reagan, reached new highs in 1990 under Bush and then skyrocketed to 67 percent—the highest percentage of any recent president—under Clinton.

Table 8-4 presents other information needed to gauge the level of party voting: the cohesion of the parties on those votes that elicit a party split. Party unity among Democrats declined after the Kennedy and the early Johnson years, more so in the House (about ten percentage points) than in the Senate (about five percentage points). A decline in party unity also was registered among Republicans during this period, although in the House they appear to have turned the corner by the late 1970s and in the Senate they rebounded in 1981 to a high of 85 percent. Party unity among House Democrats also increased after the election of Ronald Reagan, and Democratic cohesion in both the House and the Senate reached postwar highs during the last two years of his presidency. Cohesion among Democrats remained fairly consistent during the Bush presidency, while Republican unity increased steadily. Since 1992, GOP unity scores in both houses have been over 80 percent reaching 86 percent in 1993.

However important the decline in party voting during the 1960s and 1970s or the post-1980 resurgence, it pales in significance when compared with the long-term decline in party voting. During the years

1890-1910, two-thirds of all votes evoked a party split, and in several sessions more than half the roll calls found 90 percent of one party opposing 90 percent of the other. Since 1946 the percentage of votes showing such extreme partisan division has not gone above 10 percent.

Conservative Coalition

One reason for the decline in cohesion among the Democrats was the emergence in the late 1930s of a set of issues that brought together southern Democrats and Republicans and pitted them against northern Democrats. Since that time this "conservative coalition" has proved itself a formidable opponent to Democratic presidents.

Table 8-5 shows the percentage of all recorded votes in which the coalition has appeared (a majority of voting southern Democrats and a majority of voting Republicans oppose the stand taken by a majority of voting northern Democrats). It also shows the percentage of those votes won by the coalition.

Over the past several decades the conservative coalition appeared more often in the Senate than in the House, although its record of success was no greater in the Senate (with the important exception of the Reagan era of split-party control of Congress). Its percentage of success reached an all-time low in the House during the Eighty-ninth Congress, after the 1964 Democratic landslide, and a modern-day high in 1981, rivaling its record in the 1940s and 1950s.[1] But much more significant is the virtual disappearance of the conservative coalition during the last two years of the Reagan presidency. This trend has continued into the 1990s, with a coalition appearing on no more than 14 percent of roll call votes in either house since 1987. As one political scientist put it, "The conservative coalition as a working political force is really a statistical artifact."[2] While the percentage of conservative coalition votes dropped to its lowest level in 1993 and 1994, its success rate reached 98 percent in 1993.

The coalition's success after the 1980 elections was due both to the increase in the number of Republicans in both chambers and to the increasingly conservative cast of Senate Republicans. Conservative coalition support scores (adjusted for absences) for northern Democrats, southern Democrats, and Republicans are presented in Table 8-6. In the House there was a steady increase in the degree of support for the coalition among northern Democrats beginning in the early 1970s and running through 1981. That support waned somewhat during the 1980s, but was back above 30 percent by the end of 1992, and reached its highest level of 39 percent in 1994. Among northern Democrats in the Senate, support has remained fairly constant since the late 1970s. (By definition, the conservative coalition support among northern Democrats overall cannot exceed 50 percent.) Among southern Democrats in both houses, support declined after the late 1960s and early 1970s, although 1981 and 1982 saw a temporary increase in support.

Conservative coalition support scores are perhaps most useful for gauging how ideologically representative smaller groups of members are of their party and of the entire chamber. Tables 8-7 and 8-8 present the mean conservative coalition support scores for House and Senate committees between 1959 and 1993. Scores are presented for all committee members as well as for Democratic and Republican members separately. Overall scores reflecting the average conservative coalition support among all members in the chamber and in each party caucus provide a view of the relative conservatism of each committee. The absolute scores are less reliable than the relative standing of the committees and their parent chamber over time.

The ideological makeup of some committees has changed dramatically. In the House, the District of Columbia Committee, one of the most conservative committees in 1959, became one of the most liberal (with only a six percent support score among Democrats on the committee in 1991). Not surprisingly it was among the first committees to be eliminated by the Republicans when they took control after the 1994 elections. (Its duties have been folded into the new Government Reform and Oversight Committee.) A similar though less dramatic change occurred in the Ways and Means and Energy and Commerce committees, while Education and Labor grew more conservative. Other committees did not transform their philosophical base but moved further toward the ideological poles. Armed Services, always conservative, became the most conservative committee in the House. There have been dramatic changes in the ideological makeup of House committees in 1995, due to the Republican takeover and their reforms in committee sizes and jurisdiction.

Similar patterns can be discerned for Senate committees in Table 8-8, at least before the 1980 elections. Between 1959 and 1979 the Finance and the Appropriations committees moved from right to center, Energy and Public Works from left to center. Armed Services and Agriculture remained more conservative than the Senate; Foreign Relations and Labor continued to be more liberal. In 1981, after the infusion of conservative Republicans from the 1980 election, the Senate shifted distinctively to the right, upsetting many patterns of behavior, including those of its committees. Every committee shifted in a conservative direction.

In 1981 nine Senate committees were still more liberal than the average, but two-thirds of these were more conservative than the average in the preceding Congress. Even the liberal Labor and Human

Resources Committee had shifted by fifteen percentage points in a more conservative direction and its average score was more than 50 percent for the first time in at least three decades. The change came from the Republicans, with their great increase in numbers and the greater conservatism of the new members. The Democrats barely changed in ideology from the Ninety-sixth to the Ninety-seventh Congress, averaging in both Congresses 43 percent or 44 percent in conservative coalition support. Republican support, however, went up substantially, from an average of 74 percent to an average of 84 percent.

The partisan ideological gap within committees also grew. As Table 8-8 shows, the change was greater on some committees than others but was particularly significant among the most prestigious committees, such as Appropriations, Finance, Budget, and Foreign Relations. Some already polarized committees, like Labor and Banking, became even more polarized. Partisan conflict also increased in the important Energy and Environment committees.

The Senate chamber shifted back to the left after the Democrats regained majority control in the 1986 elections, and remained fairly consistent through 1993. Three-fourths of the committees either became more liberal or remained at their 1993 level in 1994. But the Republican takeover in the 104th Congress is sure to push the chamber to the right.

NOTES

1. John F. Manley, "The Conservative Coalition in Congress," *American Behavioral Scientist*, vol. 17, no. 2 (1973).
2. Quote by Burdett Loomis, *Congressional Quarterly Weekly Report*, December 28, 1991, 3759.

Table 8-1   Presidential Victories on Votes in Congress, 1953-1994

President and year	House and Senate (%)	House (%)	No. of Votes	Senate (%)	No. of Votes
Eisenhower					
1953	89.2	91.2	34	87.8	49
1954	82.8	n.a.	n.a.	n.a.	n.a.
1955	75.3	63.4	41	84.6	52
1956	69.7	73.5	34	67.7	65
1957	68.4	58.3	60	78.9	57
1958	75.7	74.0	50	76.5	98
1959	52.0	55.5	54	50.4	121
1960	65.1	65.0	43	65.1	86
Average	72.2				
Kennedy					
1961	81.5	83.1	65	80.6	124
1962	85.4	85.0	60	85.6	125
1963	87.1	83.1	71	89.6	115
Average	84.6				
Johnson					
1964	87.9	88.5	52	87.6	97
1965	93.1	93.8	112	92.6	162
1966	78.9	91.3	103	68.8	125
1967	78.8	75.6	127	81.2	165
1968	74.5	83.5	103	68.9	164
Average	82.6				
Nixon					
1969	74.8	72.3	47	76.4	72
1970	76.9	84.6	65	71.4	91
1971	74.8	82.5	57	69.5	82
1972	66.3	81.1	37	54.3	46
1973	50.6	48.0	125	52.4	185
1974	59.6	67.9	53	54.2	83
Average	67.2				
Ford					
1974	58.2	59.3	54	57.4	68
1975	61.0	50.6	89	71.0	93
1976	53.8	43.1	51	64.2	53
Average	57.6				
Carter					
1977	75.4	74.7	79	76.1	88
1978	78.3	69.6	112	84.8	151

(Table continues)

Table 8-1   (continued)

President and year	House and Senate (%)	House (%)	No. of Votes	Senate (%)	No. of Votes
1979	76.8	71.7	145	81.4	161
1980	75.1	76.9	117	73.3	116
Average	76.4				
Reagan					
1981	82.3	72.4	76	88.3	128
1982	72.4	55.8	77	83.2	119
1983	67.1	47.6	82	85.9	85
1984	65.8	52.2	113	85.7	77
1985	59.9	45.0	80	71.6	102
1986	56.5	34.1	88	81.2	80
1987	43.5	33.3	99	56.4	78
1988	47.4	32.7	104	64.8	88
Average	61.9				
Bush					
1989	62.6	50.0	86	73.3	101
1990	46.8	32.4	108	63.4	93
1991	54.2	43.0	111	69.0	81
1992	43.0	37.0	105	53.0	60
Average	51.6				
Clinton					
1993	86.4	87.2	102	85.4	89
1994	86.4	87.2	78	85.5	62

n.a. = not available.

Note: Percentages indicate number of congressional votes supporting the president divided by the total number of votes on which the president had taken a position.

The findings for 1956, 1981, 1982, and 1983 differ slightly from previous editions due to recalculation and corrections in the *Congressional Quarterly Almanac*. The *Congressional Quarterly Almanac* frequently rounds off House and Senate percentages of these votes, but figures in *Vital Statistics* are not rounded here.

Sources: Congressional Quarterly Almanac (Washington, D.C.: Congressional Quarterly, various years); *Congressional Quarterly Weekly Report*, January 2, 1982; December 31, 1983; October 27, 1984; January 11, 1986; October 25, 1986, 2690; January 16, 1988; November 19, 1988; December 30, 1989; January 6, 1990; December 22, 1990; December 28, 1991; December 19, 1992; December 18, 1993; December 31, 1994. Some percentages recalculated.

Figure 8-1 Presidential Victories on Votes in Congress, 1953–1994

Percent

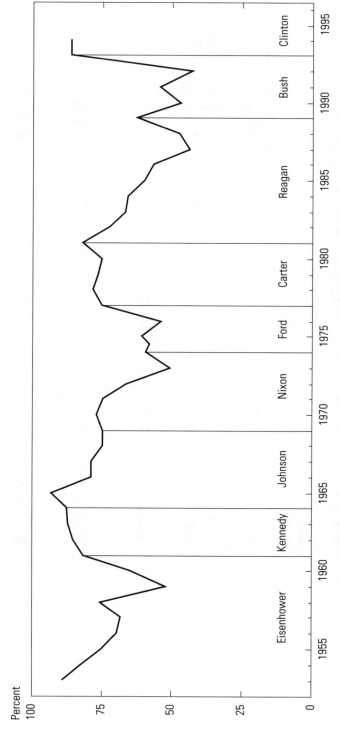

Note: Percentages indicate number of congressional votes supporting the president divided by the total number of votes on which the president has taken a position.
Source: Table 8-1.

Table 8-2   Congressional Voting in Support of the President's Position, 1954-1994 (percent)

President and year	House			Senate		
	All Demo-crats	Southern Demo-crats	Repub-licans	All Demo-crats	Southern Demo-crats	Repub-licans
Eisenhower						
1954	54	n.a.	n.a.	45	n.a.	82
1955	58	n.a.	67	65	n.a.	85
1956	58	n.a.	79	44	n.a.	80
1957	54	n.a.	60	60	n.a.	80
1958	63	n.a.	65	51	n.a.	77
1959	44	n.a.	76	44	n.a.	80
1960	49	n.a.	63	52	n.a.	76
Kennedy						
1961	81	n.a.	41	73	n.a.	42
1962	83	71	47	76	63	48
1963	84	71	36	77	65	52
Johnson						
1964	84	70	42	73	63	52
1965	83	65	46	75	60	55
1966	81	64	45	71	59	53
1967	80	65	51	73	69	63
1968	77	63	59	64	50	57
Nixon						
1969	56	55	65	55	56	74
1970	64	64	79	56	62	74
1971	53	69	79	48	59	76
1972	56	59	74	52	71	77
1973	39	49	67	42	55	70
1974	52	64	71	44	60	65
Ford						
1974	48	52	59	45	55	67
1975	40	48	67	53	67	76
1976	36	52	70	47	61	73
Carter						
1977	69	58	46	77	71	58
1978	67	54	40	74	61	47

Table 8-2   (continued)

President and year	House			Senate		
	All Democrats	Southern Democrats	Republicans	All Democrats	Southern Democrats	Republicans
1979	70	58	37	75	66	51
1980	71	63	44	71	69	50
Reagan						
1981	46	60	72	52	63	84
1982	43	55	70	46	57	77
1983	30	45	74	45	46	77
1984	37	47	64	45	58	81
1985	31	43	69	36	46	80
1986	26	37	69	39	56	90
1987	26	36	64	38	42	67
1988	27	34	61	51	58	73
Bush						
1989	38	49	72	56	66	84
1990	26	35	65	39	49	72
1991	35	43	74	42	53	83
1992	27	38	75	33	41	75
Clinton						
1993	80	81	39	87	84	30
1994	78	68	49	88	88	44

n.a. = not available.

Note: Percentages indicate number of congressional votes supporting the president divided by the total number of votes on which the president had taken a position. The percentages are normalized to eliminate the effects of absences, as follows: support = (support)/(support + opposition).

Sources: Congressional Quarterly Almanac, various years; *Congressional Quarterly Weekly Report,* January 2, 1982; October 27, 1984; January 11, 1986; October 25, 1986, 2690-2693; January 16, 1988; November 19, 1988; December 30, 1989; January 6, 1990; December 22, 1990; December 28, 1991; December 19, 1992; December 18, 1993; December 31, 1994.

Table 8-3   Party Unity Votes in Congress, 1953-1994
(percentage of all votes)

Year	House	Senate	Year	House	Senate
1953	52	n.a.	1974	29	44
1954	38	47	1975	48	48
1955	41	30	1976	36	37
1956	44	53	1977	42	42
1957	59	36	1978	33	45
1958	40	44	1979	47	47
1959	55	48	1980	38	46
1960	53	37	1981	37	48
1961	50	62	1982	36	43
1962	46	41	1983	56	44
1963	49	47	1984	47	40
1964	55	36	1985	61	50
1965	52	42	1986	57	52
1966	41	50	1987	64	41
1967	36	35	1988	47	42
1968	35	32	1989	55	35
1969	31	36	1990	49	54
1970	27	35	1991	55	49
1971	38	42	1992	64	53
1972	27	36	1993	65	67
1973	42	40	1994	62	52

n.a. = not available.

Note: Data indicate the percentage of all recorded votes on which a majority of voting Democrats opposed a majority of voting Republicans.

Sources: Congressional Quarterly Almanac, various years; *Congressional Quarterly Weekly Report,* January 9, 1982; January 15, 1983, 107; December 31, 1983, 2790; October 27, 1984, 2810; January 11, 1986, 87; November 15, 1986, 2902; January 16, 1988; November 19, 1988; December 30, 1989; December 22, 1990; December 28, 1991; December 19, 1992; December 18, 1993; December 31, 1994.

Table 8-4 Party Unity Scores in Congressional Voting, 1954-1994 (percent)

Year	House			Senate		
	All Democrats	Southern Democrats	Republicans	All Democrats	Southern Democrats	Republicans
1954	80	n.a.	84	77	n.a.	89
1955	84	68	78	82	78	82
1956	80	79	78	80	75	80
1957	79	71	75	79	81	81
1958	77	67	73	82	76	74
1959	85	77	85	76	63	80
1960	75	62	77	73	60	74
1961	n.a.	n.a.	n.a.	n.a.	n.a.	n.a.
1962	81	n.a.	80	80	n.a.	81
1963	85	n.a.	84	79	n.a.	79
1964	82	n.a.	81	73	n.a.	75
1965	80	55	81	75	55	78
1966	78	55	82	73	52	78
1967	77	53	82	75	59	73
1968	73	48	76	71	57	74
1969	71	47	71	74	53	72
1970	71	52	72	71	49	71
1971	72	48	76	74	56	75
1972	70	44	76	72	43	73
1973	75	55	74	79	52	74
1974	72	51	71	72	41	68
1975	75	53	78	76	48	71
1976	75	52	75	74	46	72
1977	74	55	77	72	48	75
1978	71	53	77	75	54	75
1979	75	60	79	76	62	73

(Table continues)

Table 8-4 (continued)

Year	House			Senate		
	All Democrats	Southern Democrats	Republicans	All Democrats	Southern Democrats	Republicans
1980	78	64	79	76	64	74
1981	75	57	80	77	64	85
1982	77	62	76	76	62	80
1983	82	67	80	76	70	79
1984	81	68	77	75	61	83
1985	86	76	80	79	68	81
1986	86	76	76	74	59	80
1987	88	78	79	85	80	78
1988	88	81	80	85	78	74
1989	86	77	76	79	69	79
1990	86	78	78	82	75	77
1991	86	78	81	83	73	83
1992	86	79	84	82	70	83
1993	88	84	87	87	78	86
1994	88	83	87	86	77	81

n.a. = not available.

Note: Data show percentage of members voting with a majority of their party on party unity votes. Party unity votes are those roll calls on which a majority of a party votes on one side of the issue and a majority of the other party votes on the other side. The percentages are normalized to eliminate the effects of absences, as follows: party unity = (unity)/(unity + opposition).

Sources: Congressional Quarterly Almanac, various years; Congressional Quarterly Weekly Report, January 9, 1982; January 15, 1983, 108; October 27, 1984, 2804-2805; January 11, 1986, 88; November 15, 1986, 2902-2906; January 16, 1988; November 19, 1988; December 30, 1989; January 6, 1990; December 22, 1990; December 28, 1991, 3790-3792; December 19, 1992, 3907-3909, December 18, 1993, 3481-3483; December 31, 1994, 3660-3662.

Table 8-5   Conservative Coalition Votes and Victories in Congress, 1957-1994 (percent)

	House		Senate	
Year	Votes	Victories	Votes	Victories
1957	16	81	11	100
1958	15	64	19	86
1959	13	91	19	65
1960	20	35	22	67
1961	30	74	32	48
1962	13	44	15	71
1963	13	67	19	44
1964	11	67	17	47
1965	25	25	24	39
1966	19	32	30	51
1967	22	73	18	54
1968	22	63	25	80
1969	25	71	28	67
1970	17	70	26	64
1971	31	79	28	86
1972	25	79	29	63
1973	25	67	21	54
1974	22	67	30	54
1975	28	52	28	48
1976	17	59	26	58
1977	22	60	29	74
1978	20	57	23	46
1979	21	73	18	65

(Table continues)

Table 8-5   (continued)

| | House | | Senate | |
Year	Votes	Victories	Votes	Victories
1980	16	67	20	75
1981	21	88	21	95
1982	16	78	20	90
1983	18	71	12	89
1984	14	75	17	94
1985	13	84	16	93
1986	11	78	20	93
1987	9	88	8	100
1988	8	82	10	97
1989	11	80	12	95
1990	10	74	11	95
1991	9	86	14	95
1992	10	88	14	87
1993	7	98	10	90
1994	7	92	10	72

Note: "Votes" is the percentage of all roll call votes on which a majority of voting southern Democrats and a majority of voting Republicans—the conservative coalition—opposed the stand taken by a majority of voting northern Democrats. "Victories" is the percentage of conservative coalition votes won by the coalition.

Sources: Congressional Quarterly Almanac, various years; *Congressional Quarterly Weekly Report*, January 9, 1982; January 15, 1983; December 31, 1983; October 27, 1984, 2821; January 11, 1986, 76-77, 81; November 15, 1986, 2908-2909; January 16, 1988; November 19, 1988; December 30, 1989; January 6, 1990; December 22, 1990; December 28, 1991; December 19, 1992; December 18, 1993, 3485; December 31, 1994, 3663.

Table 8-6 Voting in Support of the Conservative Coalition, 1959-1994 (percent)

	House			Senate		
	Northern Democrats	Southern Democrats	Republicans	Northern Democrats	Southern Democrats	Republicans
1959	17	85	87	23	69	80
1960	8	66	77	21	77	74
1961	15	69	83	15	74	75
1962	14	65	75	29	77	79
1963	13	70	78	20	73	76
1964	13	72	76	20	78	72
1965	10	69	81	19	71	81
1966	13	69	82	17	75	80
1967	15	75	81	24	76	72
1968	16	77	75	31	77	74
1969	21	79	75	24	77	73
1970	19	79	78	21	74	72
1971	25	76	80	38	80	79
1972	24	75	79	20	78	74
1973	22	69	77	17	74	76
1974	24	72	69	19	79	69
1975	22	69	81	19	79	69
1976	25	72	80	21	73	76
1977	25	68	82	26	75	80
1978	26	68	79	24	70	69

(Table continues)

Table 8-6 (continued)

	House			Senate		
	Northern Democrats	Southern Democrats	Republicans	Northern Democrats	Southern Democrats	Republicans
1979	29	70	85	29	75	74
1980	27	69	81	26	72	74
1981	30	75	82	29	76	84
1982	27	73	81	30	76	81
1983	22	68	81	30	69	81
1984	23	68	84	27	74	85
1985	23	67	84	30	72	82
1986	27	70	83	26	70	83
1987	27	71	87	30	70	79
1988	27	67	88	29	72	80
1989	27	68	87	31	69	84
1990	27	69	85	29	70	83
1991	30	69	90	33	71	84
1992	31	67	87	27	67	79
1993	31	63	87	31	70	84
1994	39	58	89	30	69	81

Note: Data indicate the percentage of conservative coalition votes on which members voted in agreement with the position of the conservative coalition. Conservative coalition votes are those on which a majority of northern Democrats voted against a majority of southern Democrats and Republicans—the conservative coalition. The percentages are normalized to eliminate the effects of not voting, as follows: conservative coalition support = (support)/(support + opposition).

Sources: Congressional Quarterly Almanac, various years; *Congressional Quarterly Weekly Report,* January 9, 1982; January 15, 1983, 102; October 27, 1984, 2821; January 11, 1986, 76; November 15, 1986, 2908-2912; January 16, 1988; November 19, 1988; December 30, 1989; January 6, 1990; December 22, 1990; December 28, 1991, 3795-3797; December 19, 1992, 3902-3904; December 18, 1993, 3486-3488; December 31, 1994, 3665-3667.

Table 8-7   House Committee Support of the Conservative Coalition, 1959-1993 (percent)

Committee	1959	1969	1977	1981	1983	1985	1987	1989	1991	1993
Agriculture										
All members	79	80	56	70	60	65	69	70	73	66
Democrats	69	72	44	58	48	52	56	58	62	51
Republicans	97	90	81	86	81	84	89	89	93	88
Appropriations										
All members	69	63	56	56	52	53	58	57	57	64
Democrats	55	54	42	42	37	36	41	39	39	47
Republicans	90	76	83	78	79	81	86	85	88	90
Armed Services										
All members	68	69	69	80	74	75	74	73	72	74
Democrats	55	63	59	71	65	67	63	62	59	61
Republicans	90	79	90	91	90	86	90	89	92	92
Banking, Finance, and Urban Affairs										
All members	44	50	45	52	50	52	58	56	57	50
Democrats	26	37	33	34	34	34	39	35	39	26
Republicans	75	68	68	77	76	79	86	87	88	85
Budget										
All members	n.a.	n.a.	43	63	50	55	56	56	60	59
Democrats	n.a.	n.a.	26	47	32	34	33	34	43	45
Republicans	n.a.	n.a.	79	87	85	87	89	88	88	81
District of Columbia										
All members	72	62	41	39	40	31	44	39	42	43
Democrats	65	54	37	17	15	15	17	7	6	14
Republicans	85	72	49	78	79	66	91	96	96	86
Education and Labor										
All members	39	40	42	44	39	42	49	44	46	48[a]
Democrats	16	17	26	25	25	21	28	19	23	26
Republicans	86	72	73	70	71	73	82	84	88	85[a]
Energy and Commerce										
All members	65	60	48	58	50	56	57	60	60	59
Democrats	49	41	31	38	31	35	36	39	41	39
Republicans	92	84	81	85	84	87	87	93	94	86

(Table continues)

Table 8-7   (continued)

Committee	1959	1969	1977	1981	1983	1985	1987	1989	1991	1993
Foreign Affairs										
All members	48	42	41	51	42	45	50	45	47	50
Democrats	32	20	25	38	25	21	28	22	24	29
Republicans	78	68	73	70	74	79	81	80	81	80
Government Operations										
All members	55	37	47	54	53	54	57	50	53	50
Democrats	37	25	32	37	40	31	40	30	36	28
Republicans	81	55	78	77	78	86	85	83	85	83
House Administration										
All members	61	55	49	58	49	53	52	57	55	61
Democrats	52	37	32	41	30	32	38	35	31	42
Republicans	78	79	87	83	82	88	92	94	95	94
Judiciary[b]										
All members	58	43	45	51	47	50	52	49	52	52
Democrats	45	28	36	30	26	26	26	24	30	30
Republicans	83	63	62	79	85	87	90	87	88	86
Merchant Marine and Fisheries										
All members	54	52	49	63	53	61	61	65	66	61
Democrats	39	41	29	51	39	47	46	52	50	45
Republicans	82	67	71	79	76	83	84	85	91	88
Natural Resources[c]										
All members	56	57	51	57	54	55	57	54	58	54
Democrats	36	36	33	34	33	30	36	31	37	32
Republicans	86	85	88	91	91	92	92	93	95	90
Post Office and Civil Service										
All members	57	49	43	49	47	42	40	38	42	51
Democrats	40	28	24	23	21	14	17	17	21	31
Republicans	88	77	84	83	87	83	78	71	79	81
Public Works and Transportation										
All members	58	63	62	66	56	54	60	67	67	64
Democrats	45	45	53	51	39	34	42	49	53	50
Republicans	82	86	80	87	83	83	86	90	91	85

Table 8-7   (continued)

Committee	1959	1969	1977	1981	1983	1985	1987	1989	1991	1993
Rules										
All members	63	54	47	54	48	45	53	48	52	55
Democrats	44	39	26	36	28	25	35	32	32	38
Republicans	100	85	56	94	92	92	95	87	98	94
Science, Space and Technology										
All members	52	58	56	58	55	60	64	62	69	67[a]
Democrats	34	46	47	49	43	47	52	52	58	56
Republicans	85	73	73	70	74	80	82	77	86	84[a]
Small Business										
All members	n.a.	n.a.	n.a.	59	55	60	63	61	61	59
Democrats	n.a.	n.a.	n.a.	44	47	43	48	46	43	39
Republicans	n.a.	n.a.	n.a.	79	71	84	88	85	91	89
Standards of Official Conduct										
All members	n.a.	n.a.	70	63	55	63	63	62	55	56
Democrats	n.a.	n.a.	67	57	29	37	38	38	22	31
Republicans	n.a.	n.a.	74	82	82	90	88	87	88	81
Veterans' Affairs										
All members	53	63	62	73	65	65	65	69	74	64
Democrats	46	54	53	65	53	51	52	56	62	47
Republicans	65	74	80	83	85	84	86	89	92	93
Ways and Means										
All members	62	56	54	60	54	53	55	55	55	54
Democrats	42	38	39	45	38	34	36	37	34	35
Republicans	95	83	86	87	85	87	87	86	91	86
Chamber average										
All members	59	56	51	61	55	56	60	56	60	60[a]
Democrats	44	42	38	45	39	36	41	37	42	42
Republicans	86	75	78	82	81	84	87	87	90	87[a]

n.a. = not available.

Note: Data indicate the percentage of conservative coalition votes on which members voted in agreement with the position of the conservative coalition. Conservative coalition votes are those on which a majority of northern Democrats voted against a majority of southern Democrats and Republicans—the conservative coalition. The percentages are normalized to eliminate the effects of not voting as follows: conservative coalition support = (support)/(support + opposition).

[a] Vacancy left by the death of Rep. Paul B. Henry (R-Mich.) on July 31, 1993. Henry was eligible for eighteen conservative coalition votes in 1993. Support score adjusted for absences was zero percent.

[b] Frederick Boucher (D-Va.) replaced Harold Washington (D-Ill.), who resigned from Congress to become mayor of Chicago, April 1983.

[c] In 1993 the Interior and Insular Affairs Committee was renamed Natural Resources. The figures for 1959-1991 are actually for the members of the Interior and Insular Affairs Committee.

Sources: Congressional Directory (Washington, D.C.: Government Printing Office, various years); *Congressional Quarterly Almanac,* various years; *Congressional Quarterly Weekly Report,* January 6, 1990; December 28, 1991; December 19, 1992; December 18, 1993, 3486-3487.

Figure 8-2   House Committee Support of the Conservative Coalition, 1959, 1977, 1981, 1989, 1991, and 1993

Note: Percentage of conservative coalition votes on which members voted in agreement with the position of the conservative coalition. Conservative coalition votes are those on which a majority of northern Democrats voted against a majority of southern Democrats and Republicans—the conservative coalition.

Source: Table 8-7.

Figure 8-2 (continued)   219

% 1981

100

80 ● Armed Services

● Veterans' Affairs

70 ● Agriculture

● Public Works

Chamber average (61)

●●● Standards of Official Conduct ● Budget
    ● Merchant Marine and Fisheries

60 ● Ways and Means
● Small Business
●●● Energy & Commerce ● Science ● House Admin.
● Interior and Insular Affairs
● Appropriations

●● Rules ● Government Operations

● Banking
50 ●● Foreign Affairs ● Judiciary

● Post Office and Civil Service

● Education and Labor

40

● District of Columbia

0

% 1989

100

80

● Armed Services

70 ● Agriculture
● Veterans' Affairs

● Public Works

● Merchant Marine

●● Science ● Standards of Official Con
● Small Business
60 ● Energy and Commerce

Chamber averag

●● Appropriations ● House Administrat
● Banking ● Budget
● Ways and Means
● Interior

50 ● Government Operations
● Judiciary
● Rules

● Foreign Affairs
● Education and Labor

40

● District of Columbia
● Post Office

0

Table 8-8 Senate Committee Support of the Conservative Coalition, 1959-1993 (percent)

Committee	1959	1969	1977	1981	1983	1985	1987	1989	1991	1993
Agriculture, Nutrition, and Forestry										
All members	63	81	67	77	75	72	72	67	70	68
Democrats	51	78	51	62	61	53	54	46	52	48
Republicans	85	83	91	90	86	90	92	90	93	93
Appropriations										
All members	65	67	50	68	66	66	59	57	62	62
Democrats	55	58	47	53	49	49	44	38	45	42
Republicans	85	79	55	83	83	81	76	81	83	86
Armed Services[a]										
All members	70	65	66	76	70	69	68	70	69	69
Democrats	68	55	47	58	46	47	56	55	54	53
Republicans	84	77	96	92	89	88	83	89	88	87
Banking, Housing, and Urban Affairs										
All members	49	49	46	55	59	60	58	58	60	59
Democrats	35	29	27	23	27	31	41	41	43	38
Republicans	76	57	74	83	84	85	80	82	85	89
Budget										
All members	n.a.	n.a.	53	69	63	65	67	64	64	60
Democrats	n.a.	n.a.	36	44	40	43	50	47	44	40
Republicans	n.a.	n.a.	82	89	81	83	87	86	89	87
Commerce, Science, and Transportation										
All members	55	52	58	72	58	70	61	73	72	70
Democrats	40	38	45	58	43	56	46	64	61	58
Republicans	83	72	80	84	71	83	78	84	85	85
Energy and Natural Resources[b]										
All members	45	52	54	62	58	65	62	64	67	69
Democrats	23	29	34	37	38	44	48	43	52	56
Republicans	75	78	76	83	71	82	77	87	86	85
Environment and Public Works										
All members	40	53	51	63	60	58	51	61	51	52
Democrats	22	36	35	38	38	35	37	46	34	33
Republicans	75	78	76	85	77	78	68	80	73	79
Finance										
All members	67	63	51	67	63	67	55	59	59	58
Democrats	53	47	35	51	49	53	43	40	47	43
Republicans	94	90	74	80	74	78	70	81	76	76

(Table continues)

Table 8-8 (continued)

Committee	1959	1969	1977	1981	1983	1985	1987	1989	1991	1993
Foreign Relations										
All members	44	45	36	55	52	54	50	56	55	51
Democrats	29	39	26	26	25	23	18	30	27	27
Republicans	71	55	51	78	76	82	86	85	89	84
Governmental Affairs[c]										
All members	55	55	48	61	60	63	64	58	59	61
Democrats	39	43	41	47	44	51	52	42	47	48
Republicans	88	71	55	73	73	73	79	78	78	83
Judiciary										
All members	53	55	42	63	61	63	49	55	55	53
Democrats	43	36	35	36	38	38	28	30	32	29
Republicans	74	72	69	85	80	83	76	88	87	84
Labor and Human Resources										
All members	35	34	36	54	56	53	41	48	46	43
Democrats	12	14	18	14	23	18	16	18	23	22
Republicans	71	62	62	85	82	81	74	86	78	74
Rules and Administration										
All members	56	71	51	64	60	62	56	60	63	60
Democrats	43	65	39	38	36	41	33	41	45	40
Republicans	82	79	74	82	77	79	86	84	88	87
Veterans' Affairs										
All members	n.a.	n.a.	n.a.	63	59	66	48	61	53	55
Democrats	n.a.	n.a.	n.a.	34	38	40	31	42	34	40
Republicans	n.a.	n.a.	n.a.	84	74	84	68	85	78	76
Chamber average										
All members	54	55	51	65	62	63	60	61	61	60
Democrats	41	42	37	44	42	41	43	42	44	41
Republicans	80	73	73	84	79	82	79	84	84	84

n.a. = not available.

Note: Data indicate the percentage of conservative coalition votes on which members voted in agreement with the position of the conservative coalition. Conservative coalition votes are those on which a majority of northern Democrats voted against a majority of southern Democrats and Republicans—the conservative coalition. The percentages are normalized to eliminate the effects of not voting as follows: conservative coalition support = (support)/(support + opposition).

[a] Alan Dixon (D-Ill.) filled the seat vacated by the death of Henry Jackson (D-Wash.), September 1, 1983.

[b] Daniel Evans (R-Wash.) replaced Henry Jackson (D-Wash.) in 1983.

[c] David Pryor (D-Ark.) replaced Henry Jackson (D-Wash.) in 1983.

Sources: Congressional Directory, various years; *Congressional Quarterly Almanac,* various years; *Congressional Quarterly Weekly Report,* January 6, 1990; December 28, 1991; December 19, 1992; December 18, 1993, 3488.

Figure 8-3   Senate Committee Support of the Conservative Coalition, 1959, 1977, 1981, 1989, 1991, and 1993

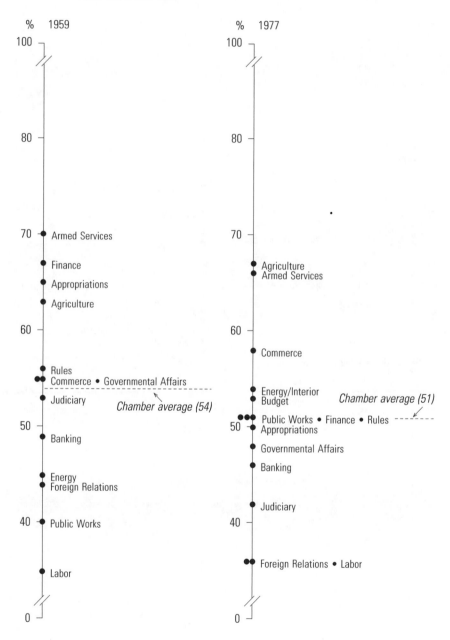

Note: Percentage of conservative coalition votes on which members voted in agreement with the position of the conservative coalition. Conservative coalition votes are those on which a majority of northern Democrats voted against a majority of southern Democrats and Republicans—the conservative coalition.

Source: Table 8-8.

Figure 8-3 (continued)

225

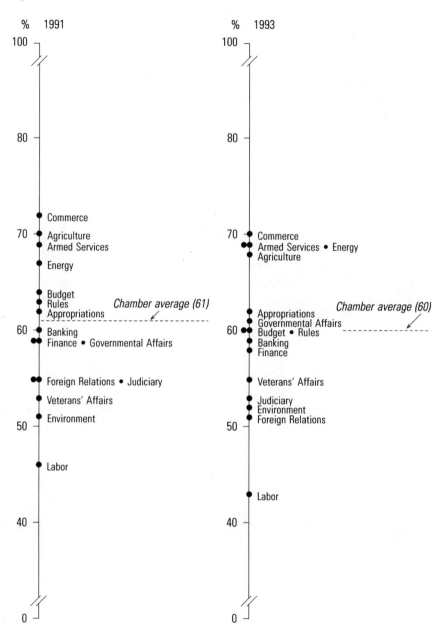

% 1991

100 –

80 –

70 – • Commerce
• Agriculture
• Armed Services
• Energy

• Budget
• Rules
• Appropriations   *Chamber average (61)*

60 – • Banking
• Finance • Governmental Affairs

• Foreign Relations • Judiciary

• Veterans' Affairs

• Environment
50 –

• Labor

40 –

0 –

% 1993

100 –

80 –

70 – • Commerce
• Armed Services • Energy
• Agriculture

• Appropriations
• Governmental Affairs   *Chamber average (60)*
60 – • Budget • Rules
• Banking
• Finance

• Veterans' Affairs

• Judiciary
• Environment
50 – • Foreign Relations

• Labor

40 –

0 –

Appendix

The appendix contains data on individual members of the 104th and 103d Congresses. Tables A-1 and A-3 show years of service, age, returns for the most recent election participated in (for House members, 1994), and various voting ratings for each member of the 104th House (A-1) and Senate (A-3) all based on the year 1994. Tables A-2 and A-4 give comparable data on members of the 103d Congress, based on the year 1992. The following abbreviations are used throughout the tables in the appendix:

ACU	American Conservative Union
ADA	Americans for Democratic Action
AL	at large
CC	conservative coalition
conv.	nominated by convention
D	Democrat
I	Independent
PU	party unity
PS	presidential support
R	Republican
unopp.	unopposed

Note that the conservative coalition, party unity, and presidential support scores, all derived from Congressional Quarterly measures, have been recalculated to eliminate the effect of absences. Americans for Democratic Action and American Conservative Union scores have not been so altered.

Table A-1 House of Representatives, 104th Congress, 1995

State, district	Representative	Party	Years of service[a]	Age	% vote in 1994 Primary	% vote in 1994 General	1994 voting ratings CC	PU	PS	ADA	ACU	ACU (career)
Alabama												
1	S. Callahan	R	10	62	unopp.	67.3	100	88	41	5	100	94
2	T. Everett	R	2	57	unopp.	73.6	97	80	44	0	100	98
3	G. Browder	D	6	51	84	63.6	94	76	77	25	62	8
4	T. Bevill	D	28	73	unopp.	98.5	94	85	88	35	50	53
5	R.E. "Bud" Cramer	D	4	47	unopp.	50.5	97	81	86	40	38	39
6	S. Bachus	R	2	47	unopp.	79.0	97	94	44	15	95	98
7	E. F. Hilliard	D	2	52	unopp.	76.9	39	94	75	80	29	17
Alaska												
AL	D. Young	R	22	61	unopp.	56.9	97	83	45	10	100	72
Arizona												
1	M. Salmon	R	—	36	39	56.0	—	—	—	—	—	7
2	E. Pastor	D	4	51	74	62.3	42	95	84	80	14	96
3	B. Stump	R	18	67	unopp.	70.1	94	99	27	0	100	—
4	J. Shadegg	R	—	45	43	60.2	—	—	—	—	—	81
5	J. Kolbe	R	10	52	80	67.7	82	83	51	15	80	—
6	J. Hayworth	R	—	36	45	54.6	—	—	—	—	—	—
Arkansas												
1	B. Lambert	D	2	34	unopp.	53.4	67	79	73	60	10	18
2	R. Thornton	D	10	66	unopp.	57.4	71	93	90	75	19	19
3	T. Hutchinson	R	2	45	unopp.	67.7	86	95	38	5	95	98
4	J. Dickey	R	2	55	unopp.	51.8	91	93	92	0	95	98

California

District	Member	Party										
1	F. Riggs	R	—	44	63	53.3	—	—	—	—	—	—
2	W. Herger	R	8	49	unopp.	64.2	94	97	39	5	100	99
3	V. Fazio	D	16	52	75	49.8	50	95	87	75	14	6
4	J. T. Doolittle	R	4	44	unopp.	61.3	97	99	36	5	100	100
5	R. T. Matsui	D	16	53	unopp.	68.5	37	98	93	75	11	6
6	L. Woolsey	D	2	57	unopp.	58.1	8	99	77	100	0	2
7	G. Miller	D	20	49	unopp.	69.7	3	98	79	90	0	24
8	N. Pelosi	D	7	54	92	81.8	0	99	79	90	0	1
9	R. V. Dellums	D	24	59	unopp.	72.2	0	99	74	100	5	6
10	B. Baker	R	2	54	77	59.3	97	98	41	0	100	98
11	R. W. Pombo	R	2	33	unopp.	62.1	100	87	40	5	100	100
12	T. Lantos	D	14	66	unopp.	67.4	46	95	84	70	24	8
13	P. Stark	D	22	63	77	64.6	0	98	78	95	0	5
14	A. G. Eshoo	D	2	52	87	60.6	11	98	81	95	0	2
15	N. Y. Mineta	D	20	63	unopp.	59.9	15	98	90	90	10	4
16	Z. Lofgren	D	—	47	45	65.0	—	—	—	—	—	—
17	S. Farr[b]	D	2	53	80	52.2	13	99	84	90	0	4
18	G. A. Condit	D	6	46	unopp.	65.5	66	59	66	45	38	42
19	G. P. Radanovich	R	—	39	51	56.8	—	—	—	—	—	—
20	C. Dooley	D	4	40	unopp.	56.7	71	82	74	55	22	19
21	B. Thomas	R	16	53	70	68.1	94	90	51	10	84	78
22	A. Seastrand	R	—	53	59	49.3	—	—	—	—	—	—
23	E. Gallegly	R	8	50	unopp.	66.2	100	94	54	10	95	91
24	A. C. Beilenson	D	18	62	87	49.4	19	97	85	95	0	7
25	H. P. "Buck" McKeon	R	2	55	82	64.9	100	96	48	5	95	99
26	H. L. Berman	D	12	43	76	62.6	15	98	84	90	0	6
27	C. J. Moorhead	R	22	72	77	53.0	97	97	41	0	100	96
28	D. Dreier	R	14	42	unopp.	67.1	100	99	38	5	100	95

(Table continues)

Table A-1 (continued)

State, district	Representative	Party	Years of service[a]	Age	% vote in 1994 Primary	% vote in 1994 General	CC	PU	PS	ADA	ACU	ACU (career)
29	H. A. Waxman	D	20	55	80	68.0	3	98	77	90	0	5
30	X. Becerra	D	2	36	81	66.2	13	98	78	100	0	2
31	M. G. Martinez	D	13	65	56	59.1	63	94	86	70	15	8
32	J. C. Dixon	D	16	60	90	77.6	15	99	91	75	10	5
33	L. Roybal-Allard	D	2	53	79	81.5	14	99	87	100	0	2
34	E. E. Torres	D	12	64	unopp.	61.7	27	98	93	75	10	3
35	M. Waters	D	4	56	unopp.	78.1	6	97	75	100	10	4
36	J. Harman	D	2	49	unopp.	48.0	74	83	88	60	19	18
37	W. R. Tucker III	D	2	37	84	77.4	25	97	77	90	11	8
38	S. Horn	R	2	63	76	58.5	85	69	69	30	57	60
39	E. Royce	R	2	43	unopp.	66.4	82	97	34	10	95	96
40	J. Lewis	R	16	60	69	70.7	91	81	55	0	88	85
41	J. C. Kim	R	2	55	41	62.1	100	96	44	5	95	94
42	G. E. Brown Jr.	D	30	74	unopp.	51.1	27	96	89	80	10	6
43	K. Calvert	R	2	41	51	54.7	100	91	58	5	90	93
44	S. Bono	R	—	59	49	55.6	—	—	—	—	—	—
45	D. Rohrabacher	R	6	47	unopp.	69.1	69	97	29	10	86	93
46	R. K. Dornan	R	16	61	unopp.	57.1	97	97	36	0	100	97
47	C. Cox	R	6	42	85	71.7	89	98	37	0	100	98
48	R. Packard	R	12	63	81	73.4	97	91	45	0	95	93
49	B. P. Bilbray	R	—	43	51	48.5	—	—	—	—	—	—
50	B. Filner	D	2	52	unopp.	56.7	17	98	79	100	0	4
51	R. "Duke" Cunningham	R	4	53	86	66.9	94	91	55	15	95	96
52	D. Hunter	R	14	46	unopp.	64.0	94	93	33	0	100	95

Colorado													
1	P. Schroeder	D	22	54	85	80.0	14	83	74	100	5	12
2	D. E. Skaggs	D	8	51	unopp.	56.7	20	97	90	80	10	9
3	S. McInnis	R	2	41	unopp.	69.6	88	86	43	15	81	84
4	W. Allard	R	4	51	unopp.	72.3	94	97	40	5	95	95
5	J. Hefley	R	8	59	unopp.	100.0	89	96	33	0	100	97
6	D. Schaefer	R	12	58	unopp.	59.8	92	96	35	10	90	89
Connecticut													
1	B. B. Kennelly	D	13	58	unopp.	73.4	42	96	90	85	10	5
2	S. Gejdenson	D	14	46	unopp.	42.6	17	99	87	80	10	4
3	R. DeLauro	D	4	51	unopp.	63.4	31	97	86	90	5	4
4	C. Shays	R	7	49	unopp.	74.4	42	67	56	55	38	40
5	G. A. Franks	R	4	41	unopp.	52.2	86	74	71	20	70	83
6	N. L. Johnson	R	12	59	unopp.	63.9	66	62	68	30	52	50
Delaware													
AL	M. N. Castle	R	2	55	unopp.	70.7	92	82	71	20	67	71
Florida													
1	J. Scarborough	R	—	31	54	61.6	—	—	—	—	—	—
2	P. Peterson	D	4	59	unopp.	61.3	84	87	84	50	38	23
3	C. Brown	D	2	48	67	57.7	47	95	90	85	24	14
4	T. Fowler	R	2	52	unopp.	unopp.	94	89	62	15	90	87
5	K. L. Thurman	D	2	43	unopp.	57.2	69	81	73	65	19	18
6	C. Stearns	R	6	53	unopp.	99.1	89	99	35	0	100	92
7	J. L. Mica	R	2	51	unopp.	73.4	97	94	42	10	95	96
8	B. McCollum	R	14	50	unopp.	99.7	93	91	44	0	95	91
9	M. Bilirakis	R	12	64	unopp.	99.9	94	89	50	20	86	85
10	C. W. Bill Young	R	24	64	unopp.	unopp.	85	87	55	25	81	84

(Table continues)

Table A-1 (continued)

State, district	Representative	Party	Years of service[a]	Age	% vote in 1994 Primary	% vote in 1994 General	CC	PU	PS	ADA	ACU	ACU (career)
11	S. M. Gibbons	D	32	74	unopp.	51.6	51	94	90	70	16	31
12	C. T. Canady	R	2	40	unopp.	65.0	100	94	54	5	90	95
13	D. Miller	R	2	52	81	unopp.	82	96	42	20	90	89
14	P. J. Goss	R	6	56	unopp.	unopp.	89	94	51	10	86	87
15	D. Weldon	R	—	41	54	53.7	—	—	—	—	—	—
16	M. Foley	R	—	40	60	58.1	—	—	—	—	—	—
17	C. P. Meek	D	2	68	unopp.	100.0	32	97	86	95	10	10
18	I. Ros-Lehtinen	R	6	42	unopp.	unopp.	72	78	61	25	65	75
19	H. A. Johnston	D	6	63	unopp.	66.1	14	97	83	90	5	12
20	P. Deutsch	D	2	37	unopp.	61.2	49	92	84	60	19	16
21	L. Diaz-Balart	R	2	40	unopp.	100.0	80	71	61	25	71	73
22	E. Clay Shaw Jr.	R	14	55	78	63.4	94	89	64	15	74	85
23	A. L. Hastings	D	2	58	unopp.	unopp.	21	97	78	80	7	6
Georgia												
1	J. Kingston	R	2	39	unopp.	76.6	97	89	43	5	100	100
2	S. D. Bishop Jr.	D	2	47	67	66.2	70	92	90	75	25	19
3	M. Collins	R	2	50	unopp.	65.5	86	92	36	0	95	98
4	J. Linder	R	2	52	unopp.	57.9	100	96	46	0	95	98
5	J. Lewis	D	8	54	unopp.	69.1	60	97	73	100	5	2
6	N. Gingrich	R	16	51	77	64.2	100	95	45	5	100	88
7	B. Barr	R	—	46	57	51.9	—	—	—	—	—	—
8	S. Chambliss	R	—	51	unopp.	62.7	—	—	—	—	—	—
9	N. Deal[c]	D	2	52	unopp.	57.9	91	63	64	15	67	64

	Name	Party										
10	C. Norwood	R	—	53	51	65.2	—	—	—	—	—	—
11	C. A. McKinney	D	2	39	unopp.	65.6	3	99	77	100	0	0
Hawaii												
1	N. Abercrombie	D	4	56	67	53.6	17	98	72	100	0	0
2	P. T. Mink	D	17	67	85	70.1	3	99	74	100	0	1
Idaho												
1	H. Chenoweth	R	—	56	48	55.4	—	—	—	—	—	—
2	M. D. Crapo	R	2	43	unopp.	75.0	97	96	40	5	90	93
Illinois												
1	B. L. Rush	D	2	48	unopp.	75.7	6	97	74	100	5	3
2	M. Reynolds	D	2	42	57	98.1	21	99	86	85	0	2
3	W. O. Lipinski	D	12	57	unopp.	54.2	71	77	74	45	38	38
4	L. V. Gutierrez	D	2	41	64	75.2	6	96	69	90	0	2
5	M. P. Flanagan	R	—	32	39	54.4	—	—	—	—	—	—
6	H. J. Hyde	R	20	70	82	73.5	86	87	54	5	90	88
7	C. Collins	D	22	63	unopp.	79.6	3	96	70	95	6	3
8	P. M. Crane	R	25	64	40	64.9	81	98	29	5	100	99
9	S. R. Yates	D	44	85	75	66.1	0	98	72	100	0	4
10	J. Edward Porter	R	15	59	66	75.1	61	73	55	30	52	64
11	J. Weller	R	—	37	32	60.6	—	—	—	—	—	—
12	J. F. Costello	D	7	45	unopp.	65.9	72	76	73	50	38	31
13	H. W. Fawell	R	10	65	unopp.	73.1	78	85	51	25	81	81
14	D. Hastert	R	8	52	80	76.5	94	95	47	5	95	90
15	T. W. Ewing	R	4	59	unopp.	68.2	94	94	43	10	90	95
16	D. Manzullo	R	2	50	unopp.	70.6	94	94	46	5	95	98
17	L. Evans	D	12	43	unopp.	54.5	6	99	77	100	0	3
18	R. LaHood	R	—	49	50	60.2	—	—	—	—	—	—

(Table continues)

Table A-1 (continued)

State, district	Representative	Party	Years of service[a]	Age	% vote in 1994		1994 voting ratings					
					Primary	General	CC	PU	PS	ADA	ACU	ACU (career)
19	G. Poshard	D	6	49	unopp.	58.4	69	65	63	55	38	31
20	R. J. Durbin	D	12	50	unopp.	54.8	22	98	78	95	0	9
Indiana												
1	P. J. Visclosky	D	10	45	77	56.5	36	96	91	75	19	8
2	D. M. McIntosh	R	—	36	43	54.5	—	—	—	—	—	—
3	T. Roemer	D	4	38	86	55.2	69	86	83	65	14	3
4	M. E. Souder	R	—	44	40	55.4	—	—	—	—	—	—
5	S. Buyer	R	2	36	unopp.	69.5	97	94	50	0	100	100
6	D. Burton	R	12	56	87	77.0	97	99	29	0	100	97
7	J. T. Myers	R	28	67	54	65.1	92	75	42	5	100	83
8	J. Hostettler	R	—	33	35	52.4	—	—	—	—	—	—
9	L. H. Hamilton	D	30	63	82	52.0	69	78	82	60	38	22
10	A. Jacobs Jr.	D	28	62	58	53.5	40	62	71	85	30	26
Iowa												
1	J. Leach	R	18	52	unopp.	60.2	69	69	64	40	33	41
2	J. Nussle	R	4	34	unopp.	56.0	81	94	43	25	70	79
3	J. Ross Lightfoot	R	10	56	unopp.	57.8	94	89	51	5	95	85
4	G. Ganske	R	—	45	78	52.5	—	—	—	—	—	—
5	T. Latham	R	—	46	62	60.8	—	—	—	—	—	—
Kansas												
1	P. Roberts	R	14	58	unopp.	77.4	97	96	40	0	100	86
2	S. Brownback	R	—	38	48	65.6	—	—	—	—	—	—

		Party										
3	J. Meyers	R	10	66	59	56.6	78	75	70	30	65	71
4	T. Tiahrt	R	—	43	54	52.9	—	—	—	—	—	—
Kentucky												
1	E. Whitfield	R	—	51	52	51.0	—	—	—	—	—	—
2	R. Lewis[d]	R	1	48	55	59.8	89	96	40	n.a.	86	86
3	M. Ward	D	—	43	27	94.4	—	—	—	—	—	—
4	J. Bunning	R	8	63	unopp.	74.1	83	96	31	5	95	95
5	H. Rogers	R	14	57	unopp.	79.4	86	81	49	15	89	83
6	S. Baesler	D	2	53	unopp.	58.8	83	83	85	45	33	36
Louisiana												
1	R. L. Livingston	R	18	51	81	e	94	84	43	0	95	88
2	W. J. Jefferson	D	4	47	78	e	29	97	89	90	15	5
3	W. J. "Billy" Tauzin	D	15	51	76	e	92	51	56	15	76	69
4	C. Fields	D	2	32	70	e	25	97	76	90	5	5
5	J. McCrery	R	7	45	80	e	92	86	56	5	90	89
6	R. H. Baker	R	8	46	81	e	100	94	47	0	100	93
7	J. Hayes	D	8	48	53	e	94	57	60	20	83	60
Maine												
1	J. B. Longley Jr.	R	—	43	42	51.9	—	—	—	—	—	—
2	J. Baldacci	D	—	39	27	45.7	—	—	—	—	—	—
Maryland												
1	W. T. Gilchrest	R	4	47	65	67.7	78	72	64	30	62	65
2	B. Ehrlich Jr.	R	—	37	57	62.7	—	—	—	—	—	—
3	B. L. Cardin	D	8	51	87	71.0	31	96	79	75	10	4
4	A. R. Wynn	D	2	43	84	75.0	26	97	98	95	0	2
5	S. H. Hoyer	D	14	55	82	58.8	57	95	86	70	24	8
6	R. G. Bartlett	R	2	68	84	65.9	100	99	40	0	100	100

(Table continues)

Table A-1 (continued)

State, district	Representative	Party	Years of service[a]	Age	% vote in 1994		1994 voting ratings					
					Primary	General	CC	PU	PS	ADA	ACU	ACU (career)
7	K. Mfume	D	8	46	unopp.	81.5	9	96	73	95	0	4
8	C. A. Morella	R	8	63	70	70.3	51	46	78	70	29	24
Massachusetts												
1	J. W. Olver	D	4	58	unopp.	99.4	3	99	78	100	0	2
2	R. E. Neal	D	6	45	unopp.	58.6	26	98	79	95	0	8
3	P. I. Blute	R	2	38	unopp.	54.6	78	77	68	20	67	71
4	B. Frank	D	14	54	86	99.5	0	98	69	100	0	4
5	M. T. Meehan	D	2	38	77	69.9	12	91	70	85	16	17
6	P. G. Torkildsen	R	2	36	unopp.	50.5	78	69	73	15	67	71
7	E. J. Markey	D	18	48	unopp.	64.4	30	99	76	85	0	4
8	J. P. Kennedy II	D	8	42	unopp.	99.0	20	98	78	90	5	5
9	J. Moakley	D	22	67	86	69.8	25	99	78	95	0	7
10	G. E. Studds	D	22	57	77	68.7	0	99	82	95	0	4
Michigan												
1	B. Stupak	D	2	42	unopp.	56.9	67	85	72	70	24	21
2	P. Hoekstra	R	2	41	unopp.	75.3	81	94	40	20	86	87
3	V. J. Ehlers[f]	R	1	60	unopp.	73.9	81	77	47	25	81	81
4	D. Camp	R	4	41	unopp.	73.1	89	92	51	20	95	88
5	J. A. Barcia	D	2	42	unopp.	65.5	75	70	64	50	43	43
6	F. Upton	R	8	41	unopp.	73.5	64	83	49	35	67	71
7	N. Smith	R	2	60	67	65.1	91	93	47	5	95	92
8	D. Chrysler	R	—	52	unopp.	51.6	—	—	—	—	—	—
9	D. E. Kildee	D	18	65	unopp.	51.2	25	93	77	60	5	7

District	Name	Party										
10	D. E. Bonior	D	18	49	unopp.	62.2	11	99	79	95	5	4
11	J. Knollenberg	R	2	61	unopp.	68.2	94	96	44	0	100	98
12	S. M. Levin	D	12	63	80	52.0	28	95	84	85	5	3
13	L. N. Rivers	D	—	38	56	51.9	—	—	—	—	—	—
14	J. Conyers Jr.	D	30	65	50	81.5	13	98	74	100	5	5
15	B. Collins	D	4	55	unopp.	84.1	3	99	69	100	0	0
16	J. D. Dingell	D	39	68	unopp.	59.1	41	94	82	70	15	8
Minnesota												
1	G. Gutknecht	R	—	43	57	55.2	—	—	—	—	—	20
2	D. Minge	D	2	52	unopp.	52.0	61	72	68	60	14	20
3	J. Ramstad	R	4	48	unopp.	73.2	72	82	55	30	62	71
4	B. F. Vento	D	18	54	unopp.	54.9	6	98	78	100	0	3
5	M. Olav Sabo	D	16	56	unopp.	61.9	6	99	83	95	10	3
6	W. P. "Bill" Luther	D	—	49	57	49.9	—	—	—	—	—	—
7	C. C. Peterson	D	4	50	unopp.	51.2	74	59	58	45	52	32
8	J. L. Oberstar	D	20	60	unopp.	65.7	14	96	74	80	15	7
Mississippi												
1	R. Wicker	R	—	43	53	63.1	—	—	—	—	—	13
2	B. Thompson[8]	D	2	46	unopp.	53.7	37	96	88	80	20	13
3	G. V. "Sonny" Montgomery	D	28	74	unopp.	67.6	97	76	79	35	57	79
4	M. Parker	D	6	45	59	68.5	100	62	68	20	67	68
5	G. Taylor	D	6	41	unopp.	60.1	97	37	60	15	67	79
Missouri												
1	W. L. Clay	D	26	63	53	63.4	9	86	71	85	14	4
2	J. M. Talent	R	2	38	unopp.	67.3	97	95	51	5	95	96
3	R. A. Gephardt	D	18	53	77	57.7	21	99	91	80	5	11
4	I. Skelton	D	18	63	unopp.	67.8	100	70	78	35	62	53
5	K. McCarthy	D	—	47	41	56.6	—	—	—	—	—	—

(Table continues)

Table A-1 (continued)

State, district	Representative	Party	Years of service[a]	Age	% vote in 1994		1994 voting ratings					
					Primary	General	CC	PU	PS	ADA	ACU	ACU (career)
6	P. Danner	D	2	60	77	66.1	77	81	70	70	29	27
7	M. Hancock	R	6	65	unopp.	57.3	89	98	29	10	95	99
8	B. Emerson	R	14	57	unopp.	70.1	100	88	47	0	10	88
9	H. L. Volkmer	D	18	63	68	50.5	83	78	74	50	48	34
Montana												
AL	P. Williams	D	16	57	unopp.	48.7	54	88	74	75	19	10
Nebraska												
1	D. Bereuter	R	16	55	unopp.	62.6	83	78	55	15	71	71
2	J. Christensen	R	—	31	53	49.9	—	—	—	—	—	—
3	B. Barrett	R	4	65	unopp.	78.7	97	95	47	5	95	90
Nevada												
1	J. Ensign	R	—	36	83	48.5	—	—	—	—	—	—
2	B. F. Vucanovich	R	12	73	78	63.5	100	88	53	0	100	93
New Hampshire												
1	B. Zeliff	R	4	58	unopp.	65.6	94	93	50	5	86	88
2	C. Bass	R	—	42	29	51.4	—	—	—	—	—	—
New Jersey												
1	R. E. Andrews	D	4	37	unopp.	72.3	72	69	71	45	26	25
2	F. A. LoBiondo	R	—	48	55	64.6	—	—	—	—	—	—
3	H. James Saxton	R	10	51	unopp.	66.4	89	83	63	15	67	79
4	C. H. Smith	R	14	41	unopp.	67.9	74	66	54	30	70	56

District	Name	Party										
5	M. Roukema	R	14	65	77	74.2	67	69	67	35	50	51
6	F. Pallone Jr.	D	6	43	unopp.	60.4	39	89	71	70	14	23
7	B. Franks	R	2	43	unopp.	59.6	69	77	55	25	62	65
8	B. Martini	R	—	47	unopp.	49.9	—	—	—	—	—	—
9	R. G. Torricelli	D	12	43	91	62.5	50	90	78	65	6	9
10	D. M. Payne	D	6	60	unopp.	75.9	3	98	74	95	10	4
11	R. Frelinghuysen	R	—	48	conv.	71.2	—	—	—	—	—	—
12	D. Zimmer	R	4	50	unopp.	58.3	67	81	44	25	57	69
13	R. Menendez	D	2	41	unopp.	70.9	31	96	79	90	5	7
New Mexico												
1	S. H. Schiff	R	6	47	unopp.	73.9	89	81	53	15	80	75
2	J. Skeen	R	14	67	unopp.	63.3	100	83	53	0	95	82
3	B. Richardson	D	12	47	unopp.	63.6	57	94	89	55	26	19
New York												
1	M. P. Forbes	R	—	42	56	52.5	—	—	—	—	—	—
2	R. A. Lazio	R	2	36	unopp.	68.2	83	77	72	20	57	64
3	P. T. King	R	2	50	71	59.2	83	92	45	5	81	87
4	D. Frisa	R	—	39	51	50.2	—	—	—	—	—	—
5	G. L. Ackerman	D	12	52	unopp.	55.0	28	96	81	90	0	3
6	F. H. Flake	D	8	49	unopp.	80.4	16	99	84	95	0	2
7	T. J. Manton	D	10	62	unopp.	87.1	49	94	86	70	15	11
8	J. Nadler	D	2	47	62	82.0	6	96	74	100	5	7
9	C. E. Schumer	D	14	44	unopp.	72.6	31	94	83	90	5	4
10	E. Towns	D	12	60	unopp.	89.0	16	98	81	85	5	2
11	M. R. Owens	D	12	58	unopp.	88.9	4	97	73	90	0	3
12	N. M. Velazquez	D	2	41	79	92.3	6	98	71	100	0	0
13	S. Molinari	R	5	36	unopp.	71.4	83	84	60	20	71	69
14	C. B. Maloney	D	2	46	78	64.2	22	94	76	100	0	2

(Table continues)

Table A-1 (continued)

State, district	Representative	Party	Years of service[a]	Age	% vote in 1994		1994 voting ratings					
					Primary	General	CC	PU	PS	ADA	ACU	ACU (career)
15	C. B. Rangel	D	24	64	58	96.5	12	98	80	95	5	5
16	J. E. Serrano	D	5	51	unopp.	96.3	9	98	73	95	0	1
17	E. L. Engel	D	6	47	61	77.6	11	97	80	100	0	7
18	N. M. Lowey	D	6	57	unopp.	57.3	11	98	82	85	10	6
19	S. W. Kelly	R	—	58	23	52.1	—	—	—	—	—	—
20	B. A. Gilman	R	22	72	unopp.	67.5	69	45	71	35	52	44
21	M. R. McNulty	D	6	47	unopp.	67.0	60	84	75	55	42	23
22	G. B. H. Solomon	R	16	64	unopp.	73.4	88	97	35	0	95	89
23	S. Boehlert	R	12	58	unopp.	70.5	63	58	71	50	38	34
24	J. M. McHugh	R	2	46	unopp.	78.6	89	94	51	10	90	87
25	J. T. Walsh	R	6	47	unopp.	57.6	86	74	70	20	67	6
26	M. D. Hinchey	D	2	56	unopp.	49.1	14	99	79	95	5	5
27	B. Paxon	R	6	40	unopp.	74.5	92	98	35	0	100	92
28	L. M. Slaughter	D	8	65	unopp.	56.6	14	99	82	95	0	7
29	J. J. LaFalce	D	20	55	80	55.2	53	89	88	80	15	14
30	J. Quinn	R	2	43	unopp.	67.0	83	82	64	30	76	80
31	A. Houghton	R	8	68	unopp.	84.8	82	61	72	20	68	60
North Carolina												
1	E. Clayton	D	2	60	unopp.	61.1	22	98	82	100	0	0
2	D. Funderburk	R	—	50	54	56.0	—	—	—	—	—	—
3	W. B. Jones Jr.	R	—	51	unopp.	52.7	—	—	—	—	—	—
4	F. K. Heineman	R	—	65	51	50.4	—	—	—	—	—	—
5	R. M. Burr	R	—	39	unopp.	57.3	—	—	—	—	—	—
6	H. Coble	R	10	63	unopp.	100.0	83	97	28	5	95	88

District	Name	Party				%						
7	C. Rose	D	22	55	unopp.	51.6	57	94	81	75	14	20
8	W. G. "Bill" Hefner	D	20	64	66	52.4	71	93	79	65	19	31
9	S. Myrick	R	—	53	68	65.0	—	—	—	—	—	—
10	C. Ballenger	R	8	68	unopp.	71.5	91	98	36	5	90	89
11	C. H. Taylor	R	4	53	unopp.	60.1	94	94	36	5	100	94
12	M. Watt	D	2	49	unopp.	65.8	3	98	73	100	10	5
North Dakota												
AL	E. Pomeroy	D	2	42	unopp.	52.3	72	86	79	65	14	18
Ohio												
1	S. Chabot	R	—	41	unopp.	56.1	—	—	—	—	—	—
2	R. Portman[h]	R	2	39	unopp.	77.4	88	94	45	10	86	90
3	T. P. Hall	D	16	52	unopp.	59.3	46	91	81	85	19	15
4	M. G. Oxley	R	14	50	74	100.0	91	92	48	0	95	89
5	P. E. Gillmor	R	6	55	unopp.	73.4	89	68	64	15	86	80
6	F. A. Cremeans	R	2	51	50	50.9	—	—	—	—	—	—
7	D. L. Hobson	R	4	58	unopp.	100.0	83	82	58	20	67	77
8	J. A. Boehner	R	4	45	unopp.	99.9	97	98	38	5	100	98
9	M. Kaptur	D	12	48	unopp.	75.3	58	89	80	60	20	11
10	M. R. Hoke	R	2	42	unopp.	51.9	88	88	45	15	80	82
11	L. Stokes	D	26	69	unopp.	77.2	9	98	72	100	10	6
12	J. R. Kasich	R	12	42	80	66.5	86	81	47	10	76	84
13	S. Brown	D	2	42	unopp.	49.1	36	92	64	75	14	12
14	T. Sawyer	D	8	49	69	51.9	30	98	92	90	5	3
15	D. Pryce	R	2	43	unopp.	70.7	88	90	55	15	67	78
16	R. Regula	R	22	70	86	75.0	89	76	59	15	86	54
17	J. A. Traficant Jr.	D	10	53	unopp.	77.4	67	80	68	65	33	14
18	B. Ney	R	unopp.	40	69	54.0	—	—	—	—	—	—

(Table continues)

Table A-1 (continued)

| State, district | Representative | Party | Years of service[a] | Age | % vote in 1994 | | 1994 voting ratings | | | | | |
					Primary	General	CC	PU	PS	ADA	ACU	ACU (career)
19	S. LaTourette	R	—	40	54	48.5	—	—	—	—	—	—
Oklahoma												
1	S. Largent	R	—	39	51	62.7	—	—	—	—	—	—
2	T. Coburn	R	—	46	64	52.1	—	—	—	—	—	—
3	B. Brewster	D	4	53	71	73.8	91	73	75	30	60	54
4	J. C. Watts	R	—	37	52	51.6	—	—	—	—	—	—
5	E. Jim Istook Jr.	R	2	44	unopp.	78.1	91	96	38	5	95	98
6	F. D. Lucas[i]	R	1	34	unopp.	70.2	100	93	49	0	100	100
Oregon												
1	E. Furse	D	2	58	unopp.	47.7	22	96	81	95	5	5
2	W. Cooley	R	—	62	23	57.3	—	—	—	—	—	—
3	R. Wyden	D	14	45	unopp.	72.5	33	96	81	80	0	10
4	P. A. DeFazio	D	8	47	unopp.	66.8	34	90	62	70	29	8
5	J. Bunn	R	—	38	43	49.8	—	—	—	—	—	—
Pennsylvania												
1	T. M. Foglietta	D	14	66	69	81.5	9	99	81	95	0	3
2	C. Fattah	D	—	38	58	85.9	—	—	—	—	—	—
3	R. A. Borski	D	12	46	86	62.7	46	95	86	65	29	13
4	R. Klink	D	2	43	unopp.	64.2	53	83	72	50	43	34
5	W. F. Clinger	R	16	65	80	99.9	97	73	59	15	95	63
6	T. Holden	D	2	37	unopp.	56.7	72	75	68	45	43	41
7	C. Weldon	R	8	47	80	69.7	81	81	65	10	74	65
8	J. C. Greenwood	R	2	43	unopp.	66.1	78	71	69	20	70	77

District	Name	Party										
9	B. Shuster	R	22	62	unopp.	99.7	94	93	45	0	100	93
10	J. M. McDade	R	32	63	unopp.	65.7	94	73	69	20	83	58
11	P. E. Kanjorski	D	10	57	unopp.	66.5	47	88	82	55	29	21
12	J. P. Murtha	D	21	62	unopp.	68.9	78	88	85	50	38	38
13	J. D. Fox	R	—	47	36	49.4	—	—	—	100	—	—
14	W. J. Coyne	D	14	58	unopp.	64.1	3	99	75	45	0	3
15	P. McHale	D	2	44	unopp.	47.8	69	84	78	45	24	25
16	R. S. Walker	R	18	52	unopp.	69.7	94	98	31	0	100	92
17	G. W. Gekas	R	12	64	unopp.	99.9	97	93	41	10	95	85
18	M. Doyle	D	—	41	20	54.8	—	—	—	—	—	—
19	B. Goodling	R	20	67	unopp.	99.5	85	90	46	10	90	73
20	F. R. Mascara	D	—	64	50	53.1	—	—	—	—	—	—
21	P. English	R	—	38	66	49.5	—	—	—	—	—	—
Rhode Island												
1	P. J. Kennedy	D	—	27	78	54.1	—	—	—	85	—	—
2	J. Reed	D	4	45	unopp.	68.0	28	97	91	85	5	5
South Carolina												
1	M. Sanford	R	—	34	52	66.3	—	—	—	—	—	—
2	F. D. Spence	R	24	66	unopp.	99.8	92	89	53	5	95	89
3	L. Graham	R	—	39	50	60.1	—	—	—	—	—	—
4	B. Inglis	R	2	35	unopp.	73.5	92	86	38	5	100	100
5	J. M. Spratt Jr.	D	12	52	unopp.	52.1	78	91	82	65	24	25
6	J. E. Clyburn	D	2	54	86	63.8	37	96	89	75	15	4
South Dakota												
AL	T. Johnson	D	8	48	unopp.	59.8	62	90	82	55	24	24
Tennessee												
1	J. H. Quillen	R	32	78	78	72.9	94	77	49	5	95	86

(Table continues)

Table A-1 (continued)

State, district	Representative	Party	Years of service[a]	Age	% vote in 1994 Primary	% vote in 1994 General	CC	PU	PS	ADA	ACU	ACU (career)
2	J. J. "Jimmy" Duncan Jr.	R	6	47	unopp.	90.5	67	95	25	20	76	86
3	Z. Wamp	R	—	37	68	52.3	—	—	—	—	—	—
4	V. Hilleary	R	—	35	58	56.6	—	—	—	—	—	—
5	B. Clement	D	7	51	unopp.	60.2	82	84	83	35	35	26
6	B. Gordon	D	10	45	68	50.6	79	85	76	55	24	16
7	E. Bryant	R	—	46	35	60.2	—	—	—	—	—	—
8	J. Tanner	D	6	50	unopp.	63.8	94	69	74	30	67	47
9	H. E. Ford	D	20	49	78	57.8	24	96	83	75	0	5
Texas												
1	J. Chapman	D	10	49	unopp.	55.3	94	74	73	45	45	34
2	C. Wilson	D	22	61	68	59.0	86	82	75	55	53	44
3	S. Johnson	R	4	64	89	91.0	97	98	37	0	100	99
4	R. M. Hall	D	14	71	79	58.8	97	37	54	10	95	78
5	J. Bryant	D	12	47	unopp.	50.1	50	95	82	80	5	11
6	J. L. Barton	R	10	45	90	75.6	97	95	38	0	100	95
7	B. Archer	R	24	66	unopp.	100.0	94	99	33	0	100	98
8	J. Fields	R	14	42	unopp.	92.0	100	97	39	0	100	96
9	S. Stockman	R	—	38	73	51.9	—	—	—	—	—	—
10	L. Doggett	D	—	48	83	56.3	94	76	82	45	38	37
11	C. Edwards	D	4	43	unopp.	59.2	97	58	69	15	67	65
12	P. Geren	D	6	42	unopp.	68.7	—	—	—	—	—	—
13	W. M. "Mac" Thornberry	R	—	36	75	55.4	—	—	—	—	—	—
14	G. Laughlin	D	6	52	unopp.	55.6	87	74	77	50	60	56

15	E. "Kika" de la Garza	D	30	67	60	59.0	86	81	78	50	45	41
16	R. D. Coleman	D	12	53	62	57.1	62	96	88	80	19	18
17	C. W. Stenholm	D	16	56	unopp.	53.7	97	42	53	5	90	80
18	S. Jackson-Lee	D	—	44	63	73.5	—	—	—	—	—	—
19	L. Combest	R	10	49	unopp.	100.0	97	86	40	0	100	98
20	H. B. Gonzalez	D	33	78	unopp.	62.5	22	96	80	75	15	15
21	L. Smith	R	8	47	82	90.0	94	96	43	5	95	92
22	T. DeLay	R	10	47	unopp.	73.7	94	98	31	0	100	98
23	H. Bonilla	R	2	40	unopp.	62.6	100	93	44	0	95	96
24	M. Frost	D	16	53	unopp.	52.8	82	89	86	55	25	18
25	K. Bentsen	D	—	35	64	52.3	—	—	—	—	—	—
26	D. Armey	R	10	54	unopp.	76.4	94	99	38	0	100	98
27	S. P. Ortiz	D	12	57	unopp.	59.4	82	79	79	45	48	32
28	F. Tejeda	D	2	49	unopp.	70.9	86	81	78	50	43	38
29	G. Green	D	2	47	55	73.4	56	90	78	80	16	15
30	E. Bernice Johnson	D	2	59	unopp.	72.6	29	96	86	85	19	10
Utah												
1	J. V. Hansen	R	14	62	unopp.	64.5	100	95	37	0	95	94
2	E. G. Waldholtz	R	—	36	unopp.	45.8	—	—	—	—	—	—
3	B. Orton	D	4	46	unopp.	59.0	86	58	61	25	79	63
Vermont												
AL	B. Sanders[j]	I	4	53	unopp.	49.9	11	—	73	100	0	7
Virginia												
1	H. H. Bateman	R	12	66	conv.	74.3	86	69	60	10	90	81
2	O. B. Pickett	D	8	64	unopp.	59.0	91	70	78	35	48	45
3	R. C. Scott	D	2	47	conv.	79.4	28	96	87	80	24	16
4	N. Sisisky	D	12	67	conv.	61.6	91	72	81	35	48	41
5	L. F. Payne Jr.	D	7	49	conv.	53.3	89	76	77	25	57	47

(Table continues)

Table A-1 (continued)

| State, district | Representative | Party | Years of service[a] | Age | % vote in 1994 | | 1994 voting ratings | | | | | |
					Primary	General	CC	PU	PS	ADA	ACU	ACU (career)
6	R. W. Goodlatte	R	2	42	conv.	99.9	86	96	39	10	90	93
7	T. J. Bliley Jr.	R	14	62	conv.	84.0	97	92	44	0	100	91
8	J. P. Moran	D	4	49	conv.	59.3	53	91	88	55	29	15
9	R. Boucher	D	12	48	conv.	58.8	65	91	80	65	30	14
10	F. R. Wolf	R	14	55	conv.	87.3	89	87	53	0	86	83
11	T. M. Davis III	R	—	45	conv.	52.9	—	—	—	—	—	—
Washington												
1	R. White	R	—	41	27	51.7	—	—	—	—	—	—
2	J. Metcalf	R	—	67	25	54.7	—	—	—	—	—	—
3	L. Smith	R	—	44	27	52.0	—	—	—	—	—	—
4	R. "Doc" Hastings	R	—	53	49	53.3	—	—	—	—	—	—
5	G. Nethercutt	R	—	50	30	50.9	—	—	—	—	—	—
6	N. Dicks	D	18	54	59	58.3	58	94	91	65	14	12
7	J. McDermott	D	6	58	72	75.1	15	98	79	95	5	2
8	J. Dunn	R	2	53	70	76.1	97	91	55	5	86	89
9	R. Tate	R	—	29	52	51.8	—	—	—	—	—	—
West Virginia												
1	A. B. Mollohan	D	12	51	unopp.	70.3	58	89	75	60	38	32
2	B. Wise	D	12	46	unopp.	63.7	71	94	82	75	30	13
3	N. J. Rahall II	D	18	45	unopp.	63.9	47	87	65	75	24	15
Wisconsin												
1	M. W. Neumann	R	—	40	unopp.	49.4	—	—	—	—	—	—

246

2	S. L. Klug	R	4	41	unopp.	69.2	61	80	51	45	43	53
3	S. Gunderson	R	14	43	63	55.7	86	86	53	10	81	66
4	G. D. Kleczka	D	11	51	unopp.	53.7	35	94	87	85	5	7
5	T. M. Barrett	D	2	41	unopp.	62.4	22	90	77	90	0	7
6	T. Petri	R	16	54	unopp.	99.5	81	93	41	25	76	73
7	D. R. Obey	D	26	56	unopp.	54.3	16	97	72	80	10	6
8	T. Roth	R	16	56	68	63.7	77	93	35	15	81	86
9	F. James Sensenbrenner Jr	R	16	51	unopp.	99.8	69	96	21	20	76	85
Wyoming												
AL	B. Cubin	R	—	48	39	53.2	—	—	—	—	—	—

Note: In compiling this table, the conservative coalition, party unity, and presidential support scores were calculated to eliminate the effects of absences, as follows: support = support/(support + opposition).

[a] Service beginning in or after November in a given year is not counted as a year of service.

[b] Sam Farr was elected on June 8, 1993, to replace Leon Panetta (D) who was confirmed as director of the Office of Management and Budget on January 13, 1993.

[c] On April 10, 1994, Nathan Deal switched from the Democratic to the Republican Party.

[d] Ron Lewis was elected on May 24, 1994, to replace William Natcher (D) who died on March 29, 1994.

[e] Louisiana has a two-step election process in which candidates of all parties run against one another in a September primary. If no candidate wins 50 percent or more of the vote at that time, the top two candidates run against each other in November. If a clear winner emerges from the September primary, no candidates compete in the November election.

[f] Vernon Ehlers was elected on December 7, 1993, to replace Paul Henry (R) who died on July 31, 1993.

[g] Bennie Thompson was elected on April 13, 1993, to replace Mike Espy (D) who was confirmed as secretary of Agriculture on January 14, 1993.

[h] Rob Portman was elected on May 4, 1993, to replace Willis Gradison Jr. (R) who resigned in January 1993.

[i] Frank Lucas was elected on May 10, 1994, to replace Glenn English (D) who resigned in January 1994.

[j] Bernard Sanders voted as an Independent. Had he voted as a Democrat, his party unity score, adjusted for absences, would have been 96 percent.

Sources: Congressional Quarterly Almanac, various years; *Congressional Directory*, various years; *Congressional Quarterly Weekly Report*, various years; American Conservative Union; Americans for Democratic Action.

Table A-2 House of Representatives, 103d Congress, 1993

State, district	Representative	Party	Years of service[a]	Age	% vote in 1992 Primary	% vote in 1992 General	1992 voting ratings CC	PU	PS	ADA	ACU	ACU (career)
Alabama												
1	S. Callahan	R	8	60	unopp.	60.2	100	87	83	5	96	92
2	T. Everett	R	—	55	58.3	49.5	—	—	—	—	—	—
3	G. Browder	D	4	49	unopp.	60.3	87	77	45	45	48	53
4	T. Bevill	D	26	71	unopp.	68.5	87	82	42	55	32	54
5	R. E. "Bud" Cramer	D	2	45	unopp.	65.6	85	76	40	55	44	41
6	S. Bachus	R	—	45	59.2	52.3	—	—	—	—	—	—
7	E. F. Hilliard	D	—	50	50.5	69.5	—	—	—	—	—	—
Alaska												
AL	D. Young	R	20	59	53.0	46.8	89	79	77	25	84	69
Arizona												
1	S. Coppersmith	D	—	37	73.5	51.3	26	—	—	—	—	—
2	E. Pastor	D	2	49	unopp.	66.0	94	91	21	85	12	6
3	B. Stump	R	16	65	67.5	61.5	96	99	85	0	100	96
4	J. Kyl	R	6	50	unopp.	59.2	81	96	90	5	92	96
5	J. Kolbe	R	8	50	65.1	66.5	—	87	79	25	76	79
6	K. English	D	—	43	44.0	53.0	—	—	—	—	—	—
Arkansas												
1	B. Lambert	D	—	32	61.2	69.8	—	—	—	—	—	—
2	R. Thornton	D	8	64	unopp.	74.2	74	88	36	85	8	11
3	T. Hutchinson	R	—	43	53.0	50.2	—	—	—	—	—	—
4	J. Dickey	R	—	53	unopp.	52.3	—	—	—	—	—	—

California

1	D. Hamburg	D	—	44	unopp.	47.6	—	—	—	—	—	—
2	W. Herger	R	6	47	88.8	65.2	91	96	82	5	95	98
3	V. Fazio	D	14	50	unopp.	51.2	48	91	29	90	8	6
4	J. T. Doolittle	R	2	42	71.1	49.8	96	97	81	5	100	
5	R. T. Matsui	D	14	51	unopp.	68.6	30	94	26	80	8	5
6	L. Woolsey	D	—	55	26.1	65.2	—	—	—	—	—	—
7	G. Miller	D	18	47	unopp.	70.3	14	94	16	85	0	26
8	N. Pelosi	D	5	52	unopp.	82.5	2	99	13	90	0	1
9	R. V. Dellums	D	22	57	unopp.	71.9	4	95	13	95	0	6
10	B. Baker	R	—	52	63.9	52.0	—	—	—	—	—	—
11	R. W. Pombo	R	12	31	35.8	47.6	31	94	19	95	8	7
12	T. Lantos	D	20	64	81.8	68.8	5	93	15	95	4	6
13	P. Stark	D	—	61	unopp.	60.2	—	—	—	—	—	—
14	A. G. Eshoo	D	18	50	40.5	56.7	19	95	17	100	0	3
15	N. Y. Mineta	D	30	61	unopp.	63.5	10	97	13	100	0	4
16	D. Edwards	D	16	77	71.5	62.0	28	90	23	90	4	12
17	L. Panetta	D	4	54	85.8	72.0	58	63	38	55	48	41
18	G. A. Condit	D	10	44	unopp.	84.7	70	81	31	60	19	6
19	R. H. Lehman	D	2	44	75.8	46.9	57	81	32	75	20	15
20	C. Dooley	D	14	38	unopp.	64.9	90	90	79	15	90	78
21	B. Thomas	R	—	51	65.6	65.2	—	—	—	—	—	—
22	M. Huffington	R	6	45	48.6	52.5	96	93	81	15	84	90
23	E. Gallegly	R	16	48	63.3	54.3	16	90	28	85	9	7
24	A. C. Beilenson	D	—	60	unopp.	55.5	—	—	—	—	—	—
25	H. P. "Buck" McKeon	R	10	53	39.6	51.9	17	94	21	85	8	6
26	H. L. Berman	D	20	51	unopp.	61.0	98	98	86	5	100	96
27	C. J. Moorhead	R	20	70	61.7	49.7	100	92	86	0	100	95
28	D. Dreier	R	12	40	unopp.	58.4						

(Table continues)

Table A-2 (continued)

State, district	Representative	Party	Years of service[a]	Age	% vote in 1992		1992 voting ratings					
					Primary	General	CC	PU	PS	ADA	ACU	ACU (career)
29	H. A. Waxman	D	18	53	84.4	61.3	13	95	17	95	0	5
30	X. Becerra	D	—	34	31.8	58.4	—	—	—	—	—	—
31	M. G. Martinez	D	11	63	57.4	62.6	35	94	17	95	4	6
32	J. C. Dixon	D	14	58	unopp.	87.2	24	94	19	80	4	4
33	L. Roybal-Allard	D	—	51	74.5	63.0	—	—	—	—	—	—
34	E. E. Torres	D	10	62	unopp.	61.3	20	95	22	85	4	2
35	M. Waters	D	2	54	89.2	82.5	11	96	13	95	0	0
36	J. Harman	D	—	47	45.3	48.4	—	—	—	—	—	—
37	W. R. Tucker III	D	—	35	39.1	85.7	—	—	—	—	—	—
38	S. Horn	R	—	61	29.8	48.6	—	—	—	—	—	—
39	E. Royce	R	—	41	unopp.	57.3	—	—	—	—	—	—
40	J. Lewis	R	14	58	unopp.	63.1	93	82	84	10	83	85
41	J. C. Kim	R	—	53	30.1	59.6	—	—	—	—	—	—
42	G. E. Brown Jr.	D	28	72	unopp.	50.7	30	95	21	95	5	6
43	K. Calvert	R	—	39	27.6	46.7	—	—	—	—	—	—
44	A. McCandless	R	10	65	61.2	54.2	96	91	78	10	88	90
45	D. Rohrabacher	R	4	45	47.9	54.5	88	95	74	20	96	97
46	R. K. Dornan	R	14	59	59.6	50.2	100	95	85	5	100	97
47	C. Cox	R	4	40	67.8	64.9	100	93	84	5	100	96
48	R. Packard	R	10	61	63.8	61.1	98	89	86	0	100	92
49	L. Schenk	D	—	47	53.3	51.1	—	—	—	—	—	—
50	B. Filner	D	—	50	26.0	56.6	—	—	—	—	—	—
51	R. "Duke" Cunningham	R	2	51	51.8	56.1	98	96	86	5	96	95
52	D. Hunter	R	12	44	59.8	52.9	98	94	81	15	100	94

State / District	Member	Party											
Colorado													
1	P. Schroeder	D	20	52	unopp.	68.8	30	78	21	95	4	12	
2	D. E. Skaggs	D	6	49	79.4	60.7	38	89	30	90	8	8	
3	S. McInnis	R	—	39	unopp.	54.7	—		85	5	92	95	
4	W. Allard	R	2	49	unopp.	57.8	83	96	85	5	92	95	
5	J. Hefley	R	6	57	unopp.	71.1	91	95	75	20	92	96	
6	D. Schaefer	R	10	56	unopp.	60.9	98	97	83	5	88	88	
Connecticut													
1	B. B. Kennelly	D	11	56	unopp.	67.1	29	94	22	100	4	4	
2	S. Gejdenson	D	12	44	unopp.	50.8	17	96	16	90	12	3	
3	R. DeLauro	D	2	49	unopp.	65.7	26	94	17	90	4	2	
4	C. Shays	R	5	47	unopp.	67.3	42	62	40	65	40	37	
5	G. A. Franks	R	2	39	unopp.	43.7	85	86	75	20	88	85	
6	N. L. Johnson	R	10	57	unopp.	69.7	77	67	63	40	58	48	
Delaware													
AL	M. N. Castle	R	—	53	55.6	55.4	—	—	—	—	—	—	
Florida													
1	E. Hutto	D	14	66	68.5	52.0	91	46	68	15	83	75	
2	P. Peterson	D	2	57	68.8	73.4	72	84	28	75	19	15	
3	C. Brown	D	—	46	63.8	59.3	—	—	—	—	—	—	
4	T. Fowler	R	—	50	unopp.	56.7	—	—	—	—	—	—	
5	K. L. Thurman	D	4	41	75.9	49.2	94	96	81	5	92	89	
6	C. Stearns	R	—	51	unopp.	65.4	—	—	—	—	—	—	
7	J. L. Mica	R	12	49	52.7	56.4	98	92	77	15	92	90	
8	B. McCollum	R	10	48	79.5	68.5	85	88	65	20	80	85	
9	M. Bilirakis	R	22	62	66.7	58.9	91	84	65	15	76	84	
10	C. W. Bill Young	R		62	unopp.	56.6							

(Table continues)

Table A-2 (continued)

State, district	Representative	Party	Years of service[a]	Age	% vote in 1992 Primary	% vote in 1992 General	CC	PU	PS	ADA	ACU	ACU (career)
11	S. M. Gibbons	D	30	72	unopp.	52.8	62	85	32	65	22	32
12	C. T. Canady	R	—	38	unopp.	52.1	—	—	—	—	—	—
13	D. Miller	R	—	50	52.7	57.8	—	—	—	—	—	—
14	P. J. Goss	R	4	54	unopp.	82.1	85	91	75	5	88	86
15	J. Bacchus	D	2	43	65.6	50.7	58	81	26	70	29	24
16	T. Lewis	R	10	68	64.1	60.8	98	94	72	10	96	87
17	C. P. Meek	D	—	66	82.5	unnop.	—	—	—	—	—	—
18	I. Ros-Lehtinen	R	4	40	unopp.	66.8	81	75	63	25	78	78
19	H. A. Johnston	D	4	61	unopp.	63.1	34	90	19	90	12	14
20	P. Deutsch	D	—	35	62.6	55.1	—	—	—	—	—	—
21	L. Diaz-Balart	R	—	38	68.6	unopp.	—	—	—	—	—	—
22	E. Clay Shaw Jr.	R	12	53	unopp.	52.0	94	79	76	15	84	85
23	A. L. Hastings	D	—	56	57.5	58.5	—	—	—	—	—	—
Georgia												
1	J. Kingston	R	—	37	81.3	57.8	—	—	—	—	—	—
2	S. D. Bishop Jr.	D	—	45	53.1	63.7	—	—	—	—	—	—
3	M. Collins	R	—	48	54.6	54.8	—	—	—	—	—	—
4	J. Linder	R	—	50	62.0	50.5	—	—	—	—	—	—
5	J. Lewis	D	6	52	76.3	72.1	7	99	12	95	0	2
6	N. Gingrich	R	14	49	50.7	57.7	98	94	88	10	100	86
7	G. "Buddy" Darden	D	9	49	unopp.	57.3	79	83	31	70	32	51
8	J. Roy Rowland	D	10	66	67.6	55.7	89	71	46	50	48	49
9	N. Deal	D	—	50	55.1	59.2	—	—	—	—	—	—

10	D. Johnson	D	—	44	52.8	53.8	—	—	—	—	—	—	—
11	C. A. McKinney	D	—	37	56.4	73.1	—	—	—	—	—	—	—
Hawaii													
1	N. Abercrombie	D	2	54	unopp.	72.9	2	98	9	95	0	0
2	P. T. Mink	D	15	65	83.1	72.6	14	97	15	100	0	7
Idaho													
1	L. LaRocco	D	2	46	unopp.	58.1	56	86	29	80	24	18
2	M. D. Crapo	R	—	41	68.0	60.8	—	—	—	—	—	—
Illinois													
1	B. L. Rush	D	—	46	42.2	82.8	—	—	—	—	—	—
2	M. Reynolds	D	—	40	62.5	78.1	—	—	—	—	—	—
3	W. O. Lipinski	D	10	55	58.1	63.5	68	77	40	50	48	39
4	L. V. Gutierrez	D	—	38	59.6	77.6	—	—	—	—	—	—
5	D. Rostenkowski	D	34	65	57.2	57.3	37	94	20	95	0	8
6	H. J. Hyde	R	18	68	unopp.	65.5	93	81	81	15	94	88
7	C. Collins	D	20	61	88.2	81.1	16	97	11	85	0	3
8	P. M. Crane	R	23	62	55.4	55.7	93	98	87	0	100	99
9	S. R. Yates	D	42	83	64.5	68.0	4	97	16	95	0	4
10	J. Edward Porter	R	13	57	60.1	64.5	66	76	65	30	74	64
11	G. E. Sangmeister	D	4	61	unopp.	55.7	48	86	29	70	24	20
12	J. F. Costello	D	5	43	unopp.	71.2	50	81	33	60	44	30
13	H. W. Fawell	R	8	63	73.0	68.4	75	87	71	25	84	80
14	D. Hastert	R	6	51	unopp.	67.3	88	90	80	5	92	88
15	T. W. Ewing	R	2	57	unopp.	59.3	72	82	75	25	88	94
16	D. Manzullo	R	—	48	56.4	55.6	—	—	—	—	—	—
17	L. Evans	D	10	41	81.8	60.1	6	95	12	95	4	3
18	R. H. Michel	R	36	69	unopp.	57.8	95	87	93	10	87	86

(Table continues)

Table A-2 (continued)

State, district	Representative	Party	Years of service[a]	Age	% vote in 1992		1992 voting ratings					
					Primary	General	CC	PU	PS	ADA	ACU	ACU (career)
19	G. Poshard	D	4	47	61.8	69.1	48	80	30	65	36	27
20	R. J. Durbin	D	10	48	unopp.	56.5	21	95	13	90	4	9
Indiana												
1	P. J. Visclosky	D	8	43	71.8	69.4	38	91	22	85	16	6
2	P. R. Sharp	D	18	50	unopp.	57.1	41	84	21	85	25	22
3	T. Roemer	D	2	36	87.7	57.4	71	71	41	55	40	35
4	J. L. Long	D	4	40	86.6	62.1	44	89	26	80	24	25
5	S. Buyer	R	—	34	unopp.	51.0	—	—	—	—	—	—
6	D. Burton	R	10	54	80.5	72.2	89	96	77	10	100	96
7	J. T. Myers	R	26	65	61.3	59.5	90	72	81	0	84	82
8	F. McCloskey	D	10	53	unopp.	52.5	28	95	18	95	12	13
9	L. H. Hamilton	D	28	61	unopp.	69.7	74	80	34	80	32	21
10	A. Jacobs Jr.	D	26	60	89.0	64.0	38	60	21	85	20	26
Iowa												
1	J. Leach	R	16	50	unopp.	68.1	58	66	53	60	40	41
2	J. Nussle	R	2	32	unopp.	50.2	65	90	71	25	76	81
3	J. Ross Lightfoot	R	8	54	58.3	48.9	91	86	84	15	87	83
4	N. Smith	D	34	72	unopp.	61.6	49	89	38	75	17	15
5	F. Grandy	R	6	44	unopp.	99.3	80	84	80	15	88	65
Kansas												
1	P. Roberts	R	12	56	unopp.	68.3	96	96	88	10	88	84
2	J. Slattery	D	10	44	unopp.	56.2	56	76	31	75	28	28

3	J. Meyers	R	8	64	56.3	58.0	74	79	63	30	72	65
4	D. Glickman	D	16	48	unopp.	51.7	60	79	27	75	32	25
Kentucky												
1	T. Barlow	D	—	52	48.1	60.5	—	—	—	—	—	—
2	W. H. Natcher	D	39	83	70.9	61.4	60	89	38	85	16	29
3	R. L. Mazzoli	D	22	60	75.9	52.7	38	90	28	70	28	25
4	J. Bunning	R	6	61	unopp.	61.6	91	94	79	10	90	94
5	H. Rogers	R	12	55	unopp.	54.6	88	81	69	25	80	82
6	S. Baesler	D	—	51	81.7	60.7	—	—	—	—	—	—
Louisiana												
1	R. L. Livingston	R	16	49	72.7	#	92	79	86	10	95	87
2	W. J. Jefferson	D	2	45	73.5	#	28	95	16	85	0	0
3	W. J. "Billy" Tauzin	D	13	49	81.7	#	89	60	57	40	71	68
4	C. Fields	D	—	30	47.8	73.9	—	—	—	—	—	—
5	J. McCrery	R	5	43	44.1	63.0	98	93	93	5	91	88
6	R. H. Baker	R	6	44	33.1	50.6	98	95	90	0	100	91
7	J. Hayes	D	6	46	73.0	#	89	64	52	30	65	54
Maine												
1	T. H. Andrews	D	2	39	unopp.	65.0	13	92	14	100	4	1
2	O. J. Snowe	R	14	45	unopp.	49.1	69	59	41	50	60	49
Maryland												
1	W. T. Gilchrest	R	2	46	47.1	51.6	72	71	57	30	64	67
2	H. Delich Bentley	R	8	69	87.1	65.1	91	80	66	25	80	74
3	B. L. Cardin	D	6	49	84.5	73.5	28	95	17	95	4	3
4	A. R. Wynn	D	—	41	28.0	75.2	—	—	—	—	—	—
5	S. H. Hoyer	D	12	53	84.1	53.0	52	92	27	90	17	6
6	R. G. Bartlett	R	—	66	42.4	54.2	—	—	—	—	—	—

(Table continues)

Table A-2 (continued)

State, district	Representative	Party	Years of service[a]	Age	% vote in 1992 Primary	% vote in 1992 General	CC	PU	PS	ADA	ACU	ACU (career)
7	K. Mfume	D	6	44	84.4	85.3	13	94	13	95	0	4
8	C. A. Morella	R	6	61	unopp.	72.5	50	49	41	70	35	20
Massachusetts												
1	J. W. Olver	D	2	56	unopp.	51.5	10	95	12	100	0	0
2	R. E. Neal	D	4	43	47.7	53.1	15	95	14	90	0	10
3	P. I. Blute	R	—	36	48.8	50.4	—	—	—	—	—	—
4	B. Frank	D	12	52	unopp.	67.7	4	95	17	100	0	4
5	M. T. Meehan	D	—	36	65.2	52.2	—	—	—	—	—	—
6	P. G. Torkildsen	R	—	34	55.7	54.8	—	—	—	—	—	—
7	E. J. Markey	D	16	46	unopp.	62.1	9	97	12	100	0	4
8	J. P. Kennedy II	D	6	40	80.6	83.1	17	93	16	95	8	5
9	J. Moakley	D	20	65	unopp.	69.2	13	97	18	85	4	8
10	G. E. Studds	D	20	55	60.5	60.8	8	96	14	100	0	4
Michigan												
1	B. Stupak	D	—	40	48.6	53.9	—	—	—	—	—	—
2	P. Hoekstra	R	—	39	46.1	63.0	—	—	—	—	—	—
3	P. B. Henry	R	8	50	unopp.	61.3	73	80	60	35	80	61
4	D. Camp	R	2	39	unopp.	62.5	73	86	70	5	84	80
5	J. A. Barcia	D	—	40	46.2	60.3	—	—	—	—	—	—
6	F. Upton	R	6	39	unopp.	61.8	73	78	57	30	72	72
7	N. Smith	R	—	58	43.1	87.6	—	—	—	—	—	—
8	B. Carr	D	16	49	unopp.	47.6	60	81	31	70	22	20
9	D. E. Kildee	D	16	63	unopp.	53.7	8	96	16	90	4	7

District	Name	Party										
10	D. E. Bonior	D	16	47	unopp.	53.1	13	97	15	80	0	4
11	J. Knollenberg	R	—	59	43.1	57.6	—	—	—	—	—	3
12	S. M. Levin	D	10	61	unopp.	52.6	30	96	18	95	4	6
13	W. D. Ford	D	28	65	unopp.	51.9	20	97	14	95	0	5
14	J. Conyers Jr.	D	28	63	64.0	82.4	5	94	13	90	0	0
15	B. Collins	D	2	53	67.8	80.5	13	97	14	95	0	0
16	J. D. Dingell	D	37	66	unopp.	65.1	36	94	20	90	0	8
Minnesota												
1	T. J. Penny	D	10	41	91.6	73.9	48	62	41	45	53	31
2	D. Minge	D	—	50	53.4	47.8	—	—	—	—	—	—
3	J. Ramstad	R	2	46	unopp.	63.6	56	78	53	30	68	76
4	B. F. Vento	D	16	52	unopp.	57.5	6	96	13	100	0	3
5	M. Olav Sabo	D	14	54	67.4	62.8	8	98	16	100	0	3
6	R. Grams	R	—	44	68.6	44.4	—	—	—	—	—	—
7	C. C. Peterson	D	2	48	71.3	50.4	45	83	36	65	24	19
8	J. L. Oberstar	D	18	58	78.3	59.0	15	95	17	90	4	6
Mississippi												
1	J. L. Whitten	D	51	82	81.9	59.5	74	85	42	50	29	47
2	B. Thompson	D	6	39	Unopp.	55.2	36	91	21	75	20	13
3	G. V. "Sonny" Montgomery	D	16	72	85.2	81.2	88	65	66	30	64	81
4	M. Parker	D	4	43	unopp.	67.3	88	63	63	30	68	68
5	G. Taylor	D	4	39	unopp.	63.2	83	58	58	30	76	82
Missouri												
1	W. L. Clay	D	24	61	68.2	68.1	12	90	9	95	0	4
2	J. M. Talent	R	—	36	58.1	50.4	—	—	—	—	—	—
3	R. A. Gephardt	D	16	51	76.2	64.0	36	96	18	85	0	11
4	I. Skelton	D	16	61	78.9	70.4	85	68	60	45	65	53
5	A. Wheat	D	10	41	58.3	59.1	11	97	12	95	0	1

(*Table continues*)

Table A-2 (continued)

State, district	Representative	Party	Years of service[a]	Age	% vote in 1992 — Primary	% vote in 1992 — General	CC	PU	PS	ADA	ACU	ACU (career)
6	P. Danner	D	—	58	52.3	55.4	—	—	—	—	—	—
7	M. Hancock	R	4	63	77.1	61.6	96	98	81	10	96	99
8	B. Emerson	R	12	55	69.3	63.0	92	85	76	20	92	86
9	H. L. Volkmer	D	16	61	57.1	47.7	85	73	42	50	40	33
Montana												
AL	P. Williams	D	14	55	unopp.	50.5	37	85	19	85	8	9
Nebraska												
1	D. Bereuter	R	14	53	unopp.	59.7	74	79	70	20	79	70
2	P. Hoagland	D	4	51	84.7	51.2	61	89	31	85	24	23
3	B. Barrett	R	2	63	unopp.	71.7	87	92	85	10	84	89
Nevada												
1	J. Bilbray	D	6	54	unopp.	57.9	67	81	32	70	33	32
2	B. F. Vucanovich	R	10	71	69.5	47.9	89	86	87	5	96	91
New Hampshire												
1	B. Zeliff	R	2	56	50.0	53.1	92	93	82	20	92	86
2	D. Swett	D	2	35	65.5	61.7	50	76	28	85	32	36
New Jersey												
1	R. E. Andrews	D	2	35	unopp.	67.3	51	81	40	70	32	23
2	W. J. Hughes	D	18	60	unopp.	55.9	28	83	23	80	20	19
3	H. James Saxton	R	8	49	89.3	59.2	89	82	75	15	80	69
4	C. H. Smith	R	12	39	unopp.	61.8	83	62	62	40	68	54

5	M. Roukema	R	12	63	62.2	71.5	61	69	52	50	68	51
6	F. Pallone Jr.	D	4	41	54.7	52.3	33	82	29	90	28	28
7	B. Franks	R	—	41	#	53.3	—	—	—	—	—	—
8	H. Klein	D	—	62	38.8	47.0	—	—	—	—	—	—
9	R. G. Torricelli	D	10	41	79.6	58.3	55	89	27	85	16	9
10	D. M. Payne	D	4	58	73.9	78.4	4	97	11	95	0	3
11	D. A. Gallo	R	8	57	unopp.	70.1	89	75	74	25	76	67
12	D. Zimmer	R	2	48	unopp.	63.9	67	83	58	40	76	71
13	R. Menendez	D	—	39	68.0	64.3	—	—	—	—	—	—
New Mexico												
1	S. H. Schiff	R	4	45	unopp.	62.6	85	74	68	25	72	70
2	J. Skeen	R	12	65	unopp.	56.4	92	68	76	20	76	81
3	B. Richardson	D	10	45	unopp.	67.4	49	90	31	75	33	19
New York												
1	G. J. Hochbrueckner	D	6	54	unopp.	51.7	23	95	18	95	4	7
2	R. A. Lazio	R	—	34	unopp.	53.2	—	—	—	—	—	—
3	P. T. King	R	—	48	68.4	49.6	—	—	—	—	—	—
4	D. A. Levy	R	—	39	52.8	50.2	—	—	—	—	—	—
5	G. L. Ackerman	D	10	50	61.8	52.4	11	99	19	70	0	2
6	F. H. Flake	D	6	47	75.3	81.0	11	97	12	90	0	2
7	T. J. Manton	D	8	60	unopp.	56.9	43	91	33	85	8	10
8	J. Nadler	D	—	45	#	unopp.	—	—	—	—	—	—
9	C. E. Schumer	D	12	42	unopp.	88.6	13	95	19	95	0	4
10	E. Towns	D	10	58	62.3	95.8	15	95	15	80	0	2
11	M. R. Owens	D	10	56	unopp.	93.6	6	96	12	85	0	3
12	N. M. Velazquez	D	—	39	33.1	76.5	—	—	—	—	—	—
13	S. Molinari	R	3	34	70.9	56.1	81	78	66	35	64	64
14	C. B. Maloney	D	—	44	65.3	50.4	—	—	—	—	—	—

(Table continues)

Table A-2 (continued)

State, district	Representative	Party	Years of service[a]	Age	% vote in 1992 Primary	General	CC	PU	PS	ADA	ACU	ACU (career)
15	C. B. Rangel	D	22	62	80.7	94.9	15	96	13	95	0	5
16	J. E. Serrano	D	3	49	unopp.	91.4	4	97	9	95	0	0
17	E. L. Engel	D	4	45	73.9	80.1	26	95	18	95	4	9
18	N. M. Lowey	D	4	55	unopp.	55.6	15	97	13	100	0	4
19	H. Fish Jr.	R	24	66	unopp.	60.1	67	59	56	40	48	43
20	B. A. Gilman	R	20	70	unopp.	66.1	56	43	41	75	32	43
21	M. R. McNulty	D	4	45	unopp.	62.7	54	90	27	90	12	18
22	G. B.H. Solomon	R	14	62	unopp.	65.4	87	91	73	15	96	88
23	S. Boehlert	R	10	56	unopp.	63.6	60	51	42	75	40	33
24	J. M. McHugh	R	—	44	69.7	60.8	—	—	—	—	—	—
25	J. T. Walsh	R	4	45	unopp.	55.7	87	66	64	25	72	64
26	M. D. Hinchey	D	—	54	54.5	50.4	—	—	—	—	—	—
27	B. Paxon	R	4	38	unopp.	63.5	96	95	80	10	92	88
28	L. M. Slaughter	D	6	63	unopp.	55.2	17	97	16	95	4	9
29	J. J. LaFalce	D	18	53	unopp.	54.5	31	91	27	85	12	14
30	J. Quinn	R	—	41	unopp.	51.7	—	—	—	—	—	—
31	A. Houghton	R	6	66	unopp.	70.6	81	66	67	30	68	56
North Carolina												
1	E. Clayton	D	—	58	54.7	67.0	—	—	—	—	—	—
2	T. Valentine	D	10	66	unopp.	53.7	67	68	39	45	48	48
3	H. Martin Lancaster	D	6	49	unopp.	54.4	75	75	47	45	58	45
4	D. Price	D	6	52	unopp.	64.6	52	92	25	85	12	16
5	S. L. Neal	D	18	58	unopp.	52.7	64	80	27	65	27	32
6	H. Coble	R	8	61	unopp.	70.8	75	92	75	10	92	86

District	Representative	Party										
7	C. Rose	D	20	53	unopp.	56.7	50	91	25	95	4	21
8	W. G. "Bill" Hefner	D	18	62	66.7	57.9	64	89	20	40	6	33
9	A. McMillan	R	8	60	unopp.	67.3	94	86	82	15	84	81
10	C. Ballenger	R	6	66	unopp.	63.4	89	94	72	10	92	89
11	C. H. Taylor	R	2	51	unopp.	54.7	89	92	80	15	87	89
12	M. Watt	D	—	47	47.0	70.4	—	—	—	—	—	—
North Dakota												
AL	E. Pomeroy	D	—	40	unopp.	56.8	—	—	—	—	—	—
Ohio												
1	D. Mann	D	—	53	34.3	51.3	—	—	—	—	—	—
2	R. Portman	R	18	64	unopp.	70.1	88	79	76	20	72	69
3	T. P. Hall	D	14	50	unopp.	59.7	41	88	29	60	25	14
4	M. G. Oxley	R	12	48	unopp.	61.3	98	90	88	5	96	88
5	P. E. Gillmor	R	4	53	unopp.	unopp.	93	78	74	20	80	78
6	T. Strickland	D	—	51	54.6	50.7	—	—	—	—	—	—
7	D. L. Hobson	R	2	56	unopp.	71.3	88	85	67	15	80	80
8	J. A. Boehner	R	2	43	unopp.	74.0	94	97	88	5	96	95
9	M. Kaptur	D	10	46	unopp.	73.6	51	89	23	75	8	9
10	M. R. Hoke	R	—	40	33.5	56.8	—	—	—	—	—	—
11	L. Stokes	D	24	67	unopp.	69.2	6	98	11	95	0	6
12	J. R. Kasich	R	10	40	unopp.	71.2	81	74	74	15	84	87
13	S. Brown	D	—	40	45.4	53.3	—	—	—	—	—	—
14	T. Sawyer	D	6	47	75.4	67.8	15	97	17	95	4	1
15	D. Pryce	R	—	41	unopp.	44.1	—	—	—	—	—	—
16	R. Regula	R	20	68	unopp.	63.7	81	73	56	35	72	57
17	J. A. Traficant Jr.	D	8	51	91.5	84.2	42	91	21	85	8	11
18	D. Applegate	D	16	64	unopp.	68.3	38	80	28	70	12	32

(Table continues)

Table A-2 (continued)

State, district	Representative	Party	Years of service[a]	Age	% vote in 1992		1992 voting ratings					
					Primary	General	CC	PU	PS	ADA	ACU	ACU (career)
19	E. D. Fingerhut	D	—	33	24.2	52.6	—	—	—	—	—	—
Oklahoma												
1	J. M. Inhofe	R	6	58	67.7	52.8	96	96	83	10	96	95
2	M. Synar	D	14	42	53.1	55.5	21	93	19	95	0	11
3	B. K. Brewster	D	2	51	unopp.	75.1	85	77	43	60	48	45
4	D. McCurdy	D	12	42	unopp.	70.7	79	74	45	70	32	38
5	E. Jim Istook Jr.	R	—	42	56.3	53.4	—	—	—	—	—	—
6	G. English	D	18	52	unopp.	67.8	85	65	52	55	56	67
Oregon												
1	E. Furse	D	—	56	59.9	52.0	—	—	—	—	—	—
2	B. Smith	R	10	61	unopp.	67.1	91	95	85	5	92	84
3	R. Wyden	D	12	43	unopp.	77.1	19	92	17	95	0	11
4	P. A. DeFazio	D	6	45	unopp.	71.4	22	93	13	90	9	4
5	M. Kopetski	D	2	43	unopp.	63.9	22	93	25	85	4	5
Pennsylvania												
1	T. M. Foglietta	D	12	64	unopp.	80.9	14	97	18	80	0	3
2	L. E. Blackwell	D	1	61	53.8	76.8	6	96	13	90	0	0
3	R. A. Borski	D	10	44	unopp.	58.9	40	92	28	80	16	11
4	R. Klink	D	—	41	45.4	78.5	—	—	—	—	—	—
5	W. F. Clinger	R	14	63	unopp.	unopp.	91	75	80	10	90	59
6	T. Holden	D	—	35	39.4	52.1	—	—	—	—	—	—
7	C. Weldon	R	6	45	77.4	66.0	83	84	68	25	80	62
8	J. C. Greenwood	R	—	41	79.4	51.9	—	—	—	—	—	—

District	Member	Party										
9	B. Shuster	R	20	60	unopp.	unopp.	92	89	74	5	100	92
10	J. M. McDade	R	30	61	unopp.	90.4	84	66	72	15	76	56
11	P. E. Kanjorski	D	8	55	unopp.	67.1	46	85	31	80	16	20
12	J. P. Murtha	D	19	60	unopp.	unopp.	71	86	42	65	24	39
13	M. Margolies-Mezvinsky	D	—	50	79.3	50.3	—	—	—	—	—	—
14	W. J. Coyne	D	12	56	76.5	72.3	19	97	19	95	4	3
15	P. McHale	D	—	42	73.9	52.2	—	—	—	—	—	—
16	R. S. Walker	R	16	50	unopp.	64.8	96	96	84	10	96	91
17	G. W. Gekas	R	—	62	unopp.	69.5	87	93	79	15	88	83
18	R. Santorum	R	2	34	unopp.	60.6	79	83	72	20	83	80
19	B. Goodling	R	18	65	unopp.	45.3	81	86	72	10	83	71
20	A. J. Murphy	D	16	65	36.1	50.7	33	67	24	65	33	28
21	T. Ridge	R	10	47	unopp.	68.0	73	77	52	30	68	48
Rhode Island												
1	R. K. Machtley	R	4	44	unopp.	70.1	72	60	48	55	44	39
2	J. Reed	D	2	43	76.4	70.7	17	95	14	90	4	2
South Carolina												
1	A. Ravenel Jr.	R	6	65	unopp.	66.1	85	64	59	40	80	71
2	F. D. Spence	R	22	64	unopp.	87.6	98	83	76	15	92	88
3	B. Derrick	D	18	56	unopp.	61.1	67	88	31	80	28	35
4	B. Inglis	R	—	33	70.8	50.3	—	—	—	—	—	—
5	J. M. Spratt Jr.	D	10	50	unopp.	61.2	79	85	34	75	28	25
6	J. E. Clyburn	D	—	52	56.1	65.3	—	—	—	—	—	—
South Dakota												
AL	T. Johnson	D	6	46	unopp.	69.1	40	83	29	70	32	24
Tennessee												
1	J. H. Quillen	R	30	76	99.9	67.5	84	75	77	5	92	85

(Table continues)

Table A-2 (continued)

State, district	Representative	Party	Years of service[a]	Age	% vote in 1992 Primary	% vote in 1992 General	1992 voting ratings CC	PU	PS	ADA	ACU	ACU (career)
2	J. J. "Jimmy" Duncan Jr.	R	4	45	unopp.	72.2	71	88	63	25	84	87
3	M. Lloyd	D	18	64	81.1	48.8	90	70	47	45	50	59
4	J. Cooper	D	10	38	84.8	64.1	76	77	43	70	32	26
5	B. Clement	D	5	49	66.3	66.8	60	83	27	65	39	24
6	B. Gordon	D	8	43	83.1	56.6	68	89	26	70	25	14
7	D. Sundquist	R	10	56	unopp.	61.7	92	89	79	5	96	85
8	J. Tanner	D	4	48	unopp.	83.7	79	73	40	65	50	41
9	H. E. Ford	D	18	47	64.6	57.9	16	91	13	85	5	5
Texas												
1	J. Chapman	D	8	47	unopp.	unopp.	80	82	33	75	24	34
2	C. Wilson	D	20	59	70.8	56.1	80	77	41	65	45	44
3	S. Johnson	R	2	62	83.1	86.1	100	91	87	10	100	100
4	R. M. Hall	D	12	69	66.2	58.1	92	49	63	40	76	76
5	J. Bryant	D	10	45	unopp.	58.9	63	89	21	80	14	12
6	J. L. Barton	R	8	43	79.1	71.9	95	94	85	5	100	94
7	B. Archer	R	22	64	unopp.	unopp.	95	89	86	0	100	98
8	J. Fields	R	12	40	unopp.	77.0	95	95	84	5	96	95
9	J. Brooks	D	40	70	unopp.	53.6	60	89	33	75	23	23
10	J. Pickle	D	29	79	82.2	67.7	73	79	42	65	33	40
11	C. Edwards	D	2	41	unopp.	67.4	85	77	43	55	40	37
12	P. Geren	D	4	40	unopp.	62.8	91	61	58	45	60	62
13	B. Sarpalius	D	4	44	unopp.	60.3	85	66	57	40	64	69
14	G. Laughlin	D	4	50	unopp.	68.1	79	74	46	45	52	56

15	E. "Kika" de la Garza	D	28	65	unopp.	60.4	66	86	38	70	19	41
16	R. D. Coleman	D	10	51	63.8	51.9	60	89	30	85	12	18
17	C. W. Stenholm	D	14	54	unopp.	66.1	89	53	70	30	72	79
18	C. Washington	D	3	51	unopp.	64.7	7	95	6	90	0	4
19	L. Combest	R	8	47	unopp.	77.4	94	83	79	10	100	98
20	H. B. Gonzalez	D	31	76	unopp.	unopp.	38	94	23	80	4	15
21	L. Smith	R	6	45	unopp.	72.2	98	91	79	20	88	91
22	T. DeLay	R	8	45	unopp.	68.9	94	93	83	5	100	98
23	H. Bonilla	R	—	39	63.3	59.1	—	—	—	—	—	—
24	M. Frost	D	14	51	unopp.	59.8	71	88	32	75	25	17
25	M. A. Andrews	D	10	48	82.5	56.0	83	75	39	70	38	34
26	D. Armey	R	8	52	unopp.	73.1	96	99	86	0	100	98
27	S. P. Ortiz	D	10	55	unopp.	55.5	71	84	40	60	40	29
28	F. Tejeda	D	—	47	unopp.	87.1	—	—	—	—	—	—
29	G. Green	D	—	45	51.5	64.9	—	—	—	—	—	—
30	E. Bernice Johnson	D	—	57	91.6	71.5	—	—	—	—	—	—
Utah												
1	J. V. Hansen	R	12	60	unopp.	65.3	91	90	92	5	100	94
2	K. Shepherd	D	—	52	unopp.	50.5	—	—	—	—	—	—
3	B. Orton	D	12	44	unopp.	58.9	68	58	57	55	56	63
Vermont												
AL	B. Sanders	I	2	51	unopp.	57.8	8	92	12	95	0	7
Virginia												
1	H. H. Bateman	R	10	64	conv.	57.5	83	72	83	10	84	79
2	O. B. Pickett	D	6	62	unopp.	56.0	76	70	65	35	52	43
3	R. C. Scott	D	—	45	67.0	78.6	—	—	—	—	—	—
4	N. Sisisky	D	10	65	unopp.	68.4	94	72	50	55	48	40
5	L. F. Payne Jr.	D	5	47	conv.	68.9	77	77	44	65	32	46

(Table continues)

Table A-2 (continued)

State, district	Representative	Party	Years of service[a]	Age	% vote in 1992 Primary	% vote in 1992 General	CC	PU	PS	ADA	ACU	ACU (career)
6	R. W. Goodlatte	R	—	40	conv.	60.0	—	—	—	—	—	—
7	T. J. Bliley Jr.	R	12	60	conv.	82.9	96	92	87	15	96	90
8	J. P. Moran	D	2	47	conv.	56.1	49	89	31	80	13	10
9	R. Boucher	D	10	46	conv.	63.1	44	90	21	90	8	12
10	F. R. Wolf	R	12	53	unopp.	63.6	96	86	78	20	84	82
11	L. L. Byrne	D	—	46	conv.	50.0	—	—	—	—	—	—
Washington												
1	M. Cantwell	D	—	34	52.5	54.9	—	—	—	—	—	—
2	A. Swift	D	14	57	43.5	52.1	35	93	24	90	4	6
3	J. Unsoeld	D	4	61	51.7	56.0	12	96	13	90	0	5
4	J. Inslee	D	—	41	22.6	50.8	—	—	—	n	—	—
5	T. S. Foley	D	28	63	52.7	55.2	0	100	10	80	0	9
6	N. Dicks	D	16	52	57.6	64.2	56	89	37	80	8	12
7	J. McDermott	D	4	56	73.0	78.4	13	96	18	95	0	1
8	J. Dunn	R	—	51	31.9	60.4	—	—	—	—	—	—
9	M. Kreidler	D	—	49	23.4	52.1	—	—	—	—	—	—
West Virginia												
1	A. B. Mollohan	D	10	49	61.5	unopp.	60	85	37	70	21	32
2	B. Wise	D	10	44	unopp.	70.9	51	91	19	80	17	10
3	N. J. Rahall II	D	16	43	unopp.	65.6	37	82	27	70	20	14
Wisconsin												
1	L. Aspin	D	22	54	unopp.	57.6	57	88	30	90	12	12

2	S. L. Klug	R	2	39	unopp.	62.6	67	75	55	40	56	55
3	S. Gunderson	R	12	41	unopp.	56.4	77	68	63	40	64	63
4	G. D. Kleczka	D	9	49	unopp.	65.8	35	96	20	80	4	7
5	T. M. Barrett	D	—	39	41.1	69.3	—	—	—	—	—	—
6	T. Petri	R	14	52	unopp.	52.9	74	73	67	25	76	72
7	D. R. Obey	D	24	54	unopp.	64.4	15	95	15	100	0	6
8	T. Roth	R	14	54	unopp.	70.1	79	85	71	15	83	86
9	F. James Sensenbrenner Jr	R	14	49	unopp.	69.7	65	91	70	15	92	85
Wyoming												
AL	C. Thomas	R	4	59	unopp.	57.8	83	87	78	20	79	87

Note: In compiling this table, the conservative coalition, party unity, and presidential support scores were calculated to eliminate the effects of absences, as follows: support = support/(support + opposition).

a Service beginning in or after November in a given year is not counted as a year of service.

b Ed Pastor was elected on September 24, 1991. He succeeded Morris K. Udall who resigned on May 4, 1991.

c Leon Panetta was confirmed as director of the Office of Management and Budget on January 13, 1993.

d Thomas W. Ewing was elected on July 2, 1991. He succeeded Edward Madigan who was confirmed as secretary of Agriculture on March 7, 1991.

e Louisiana has a two-step election process in which candidates of all parties run against one another in a September primary. If no candidate wins 50 percent or more of the vote at that time, the top two candidates run against each other in November. If a clear winner emerges from the September primary, no candidates compete in the November election.

f John Olver was elected on June 4, 1991. He succeeded Silvio O. Conte who died on February 8, 1991.

g Mike Espy was confirmed as secretary of Agriculture on January 14, 1993.

h Bob Franks was chosen by Republican Party officials to replace incumbent Rep. Matthew J. Rinaldo who announced his retirement after winning the GOP primary.

i Jerrold Nadler was chosen by Democratic Party leaders to replace incumbent Rep.Ted Weiss who died the day before the September 15, 1992, primary.

j Willis Gradison resigned from the House on January 31, 1993.

k Lucien E. Blackwell was elected on November 5, 1991. He succeeded William H. Gray III, who resigned on September 11, 1991.

l Sam Johnson was elected on May 18, 1991. He succeeded Steve Bartlett who resigned on March 11, 1991.

m Bernard Sanders voted as an Independent. Had he voted as a Democrat, his party unity score, adjusted for absences, would have been 92 percent.

n The ADA did not rate House Speaker Thomas Foley in 1992.

o Les Aspin was confirmed as secretary of Defense on January 7, 1993.

Sources: Congressional Quarterly Almanac, various years; *Congressional Directory*, various years; *Congressional Quarterly Weekly Report*, various years; American Conservative Union; Americans for Democratic Action.

Table A-3 Senate, 104th Congress, 1995

State, senator	Party	Years of service[a]	Age	Previous Senate election			1994 Voting ratings					
				Year	Primary (%)	General (%)	CC	PU	PS	ADA	ACU	ACU (career)
Alabama												
Howell Heflin	D	16	73	1990	81.0	61.0	88	66	85	55	28	26
Richard C. Shelby[b]	R	8	60	1992	61.5	64.8	96	50	67	30	55	59
Alaska												
Ted Stevens	R	26	71	1990	59.0	66.0	87	73	52	25	77	57
Frank H. Murkowski	R	14	61	1992	80.5	53.0	90	92	34	10	96	78
Arizona												
John McCain	R	8	58	1992	unopp.	55.8	73	91	44	10	96	87
Jon Kyl[c]	D	—	52	1994	unopp.	53.7	94	96	44	5	90	95
Arkansas												
Dale Bumpers	D	20	69	1992	64.5	60.2	63	86	95	80	4	16
David Pryor	D	16	60	1990	unopp.	unopp.	62	84	95	80	4	15
California												
Dianne Feinstein	D	2	61	1994	74.0	46.8	44	89	92	70	8	11
Barbara Boxer	D	2	54	1992	43.7	47.9	19	92	87	95	0	4
Colorado												
Hank Brown	R	4	54	1990	unopp.	56.0	77	93	21	30	92	91
Ben Nighthorse Campbell[d]	R	2	61	1992	45.5	51.8	48	78	83	55	25	24

Connecticut												
Christopher J. Dodd	D	14	50	1992	unopp.	58.8	24	90	95	80	0	10
Joseph I. Lieberman	D	6	52	1994	unopp.	67.0	45	76	88	65	8	21
Delaware												
William V. Roth Jr.	R	24	73	1994	unopp.	55.8	66	77	56	35	68	68
Joseph R. Biden Jr.	D	22	52	1990	unopp.	63.0	31	92	89	80	0	13
Florida												
Bob Graham	D	8	58	1992	84.3	65.4	53	85	92	75	8	25
Connie Mack	R	6	54	1994	unopp.	70.5	94	89	40	10	96	94
Georgia												
Sam Nunn	D	22	56	1990	unopp.	unopp.	91	66	89	50	33	45
Paul Coverdell	R	2	55	1992	50.5	50.7	90	95	35	5	100	96
Hawaii												
Daniel K. Inouye	D	32	70	1992	76.0	57.3	42	92	95	75	0	7
Daniel K. Akaka	D	5	70	1994	unopp.	71.8	31	94	97	85	0	2
Idaho												
Larry E. Craig	R	4	49	1990	59.0	61.0	94	98	30	0	100	98
Dirk Kempthorne	R	2	43	1992	57.4	56.5	94	98	31	0	100	100
Illinois												
Paul Simon	D	10	66	1990	unopp.	65.0	17	96	85	95	4	5
Carol Moseley-Braun	D	2	47	1992	38.3	53.3	13	91	86	85	4	2
Indiana												
Richard G. Lugar	R	18	62	1994	unopp.	67.4	78	78	45	10	76	82
Daniel R. Coats	R	6	51	1992	unopp.	57.3	91	89	42	5	92	92

(Table continues)

Table A-3 (continued)

State, senator	Party	Years of service[a]	Age	Previous Senate election Year	Previous Senate election Primary (%)	Previous Senate election General (%)	1994 Voting ratings CC	PU	PS	ADA	ACU	ACU (career)
Iowa												
Charles E. Grassley	R	14	61	1992	unopp.	69.6	69	87	34	15	92	78
Tom Harkin	D	10	55	1990	unopp.	54.0	10	97	92	100	0	5
Kansas												
Bob Dole	R	26	71	1992	80.4	62.7	97	96	35	0	100	82
Nancy Landon Kassebaum	R	16	62	1990	87.0	74.0	63	61	74	45	48	56
Kentucky												
Wendell H. Ford	D	20	70	1992	unopp.	62.9	61	82	92	60	24	27
Mitch McConnell	R	10	52	1990	89.0	52.0	87	92	37	5	92	87
Louisiana												
J. Bennett Johnston	D	22	62	1990	54.0	e	74	78	85	55	22	42
John B. Breaux	D	8	50	1992	73.1	e	78	78	85	55	17	32
Maine												
William S. Cohen	R	16	54	1990	unopp.	61.0	65	96	63	40	45	51
Olympia J. Snowe[c]	R	—	47	1994	unopp.	60.2	79	67	60	30	57	51
Maryland												
Paul S. Sarbanes	D	18	61	1994	79.0	59.1	13	98	95	95	0	4
Barbara A. Mikulski	D	8	58	1992	76.8	71.0	29	90	93	85	0	4

Massachusetts													
Edward M. Kennedy	D	32	62	1994	unopp.	58.1	19	94	95	90	0	3	
John Kerry	D	10	51	1990	unopp.	57.0	16	94	90	95	0	5	
Michigan													
Carl Levin	D	16	60	1990	unopp.	57.0	16	92	90	95	0	8	
Spencer Abraham	R	—	42	1994	52.0	51.9	—	—	—	—	—	—	
Minnesota													
Paul Wellstone	D	4	50	1990	60.0	50.0	3	94	82	100	4	4	
Rod Grams[c]	R	—	46	1994	58.0	49.1	97	99	39	0	100	100	
Mississippi													
Thad Cochran	R	16	57	1990	unopp.	unopp.	94	82	45	10	92	79	
Trent Lott	R	6	53	1994	95.0	68.8	100	97	40	5	100	95	
Missouri													
Christopher S. Bond	R	8	55	1992	82.7	51.9	90	78	49	20	83	82	
John Ashcroft	R	—	52	1994	83.0	59.7	—	—	—	—	—	—	
Montana													
Max Baucus	D	16	53	1990	83.0	68.0	50	86	89	85	0	11	
Conrad Burns	R	6	59	1994	unopp.	62.4	94	84	43	5	92	90	
Nebraska													
Jim Exon	D	16	73	1990	unopp.	59.0	63	78	84	65	25	45	
Bob Kerrey	D	6	51	1994	unopp.	54.8	47	83	90	80	24	11	
Nevada													
Harry Reid	D	8	55	1992	52.8	51.0	41	88	90	85	4	22	
Richard H. Bryan	D	6	57	1994	unopp.	50.9	48	85	85	75	12	26	

(Table continues)

Table A-3 (continued)

State, senator	Party	Years of service[a]	Age	Previous Senate election			1994 Voting ratings					
				Year	Primary (%)	General (%)	CC	PU	PS	ADA	ACU	ACU (career)
New Hampshire												
Robert C. Smith	R	4	53	1990	65.0	65.0	88	96	20	5	100	96
Judd Gregg	R	2	47	1992	50.4	48.2	78	84	42	15	79	86
New Jersey												
Bill Bradley	D	16	51	1990	92.0	50.0	7	84	80	85	4	11
Frank R. Lautenberg	D	12	70	1994	81.0	50.3	19	84	82	95	4	7
New Mexico												
Pete V. Domenici	R	22	62	1990	unopp.	73.0	94	78	53	25	84	68
Jeff Bingaman	D	12	51	1994	unopp.	54.0	53	84	89	60	16	15
New York												
Daniel Patrick Moynihan	D	18	67	1994	74.0	55.2	16	92	84	100	0	6
Alfonse M. D'Amato	R	14	57	1992	unopp.	49.0	84	82	34	20	92	55
North Carolina												
Jesse Helms	R	22	73	1990	84.0	53.0	87	95	19	0	100	99
Lauch Faircloth	R	2	66	1992	47.7	50.4	100	98	24	5	100	100
North Dakota												
Kent Conrad[f]	D	8	46	1994	unopp.	58.0	53	85	89	85	12	23
Byron L. Dorgan	D	2	52	1992	unopp.	59.0	44	86	81	85	8	19

State / Senator	Party			Year									
Ohio													
John Glenn	D	20	73	1992	unopp.	51.0	23	90	95	80	4	13
Mike DeWine	R	—	47	1994	52.0	53.4	—	—	—	—	—	—
Oklahoma													
Don Nickles	R	14	46	1992	unopp.	58.5	88	94	25	5	100	95
James M. Inhofe[c]	R	—	60	1994	78.0	55.2	97	99	45	0	100	96
Oregon													
Mark O. Hatfield	R	28	72	1990	78.0	54.0	34	34	77	80	29	26
Bob Packwood	R	26	62	1992	59.1	52.1	47	63	55	50	67	42
Pennsylvania													
Arlen Specter	R	14	64	1992	65.1	49.1	61	56	56	55	46	39
Rick Santorum[c]	R	—	36	1994	81.0	49.4	94	83	56	15	81	79
Rhode Island													
Claiborne Pell	D	34	76	1990	unopp.	62.0	28	92	98	95	0	7
John H. Chafee	R	18	72	1994	69.0	64.5	42	46	80	65	30	28
South Carolina													
Strom Thurmond	R	40	92	1990	unopp.	64.0	97	93	39	5	96	90
Ernest F. Hollings	D	28	73	1992	unopp.	50.1	71	80	86	50	22	0
South Dakota													
Larry Pressler	R	16	52	1990	unopp.	52.0	84	89	34	0	96	78
Tom Daschle	D	8	47	1992	unopp.	64.9	38	91	94	80	4	14
Tennessee													
Bill Frist	R	—	42	1994	44.0	56.4	—	—	—	—	—	—
Fred Thompson	R	—	52	1944	62.0	60.4	—	—	—	—	—	—

(Table continues)

Table A-3 (continued)

State, senator	Party	Years of service[a]	Age	Previous Senate election			1994 Voting ratings					
				Year	Primary (%)	General (%)	CC	PU	PS	ADA	ACU	ACU (career)
Texas												
Phil Gramm	R	10	52	1990	unopp.	60.0	93	94	36	5	100	96
Kay Bailey Hutchison	R	2	51	1994	unopp.	60.8	94	94	38	10	96	95
Utah												
Orrin G. Hatch	R	18	60	1994	unopp.	68.9	94	95	37	5	100	93
Robert F. Bennett	R	2	61	1992	51.4	55.4	94	91	38	5	100	94
Vermont												
Patrick J. Leahy	D	20	54	1992	unopp.	54.2	6	96	89	95	0	5
James M. Jeffords	R	6	60	1994	unopp.	50.3	25	32	79	85	12	25
Virginia												
John W. Warner	R	16	67	1990	unopp.	81.0	84	77	60	20	80	78
Charles S. Robb	D	6	55	1994	58.0	45.6	45	82	85	60	12	25
Washington												
Slade Gorton	R	12	66	1994	52.0	55.7	84	76	48	30	80	66
Patty Murray	D	2	44	1992	28.3	54.0	13	98	94	90	0	0
West Virginia												
Robert C. Byrd	D	36	77	1994	85.0	69.0	69	73	74	75	40	28
John D. Rockefeller IV	D	10	57	1990	85.0	68.0	34	90	97	95	0	11

Wisconsin												
Herb Kohl	D	6	59	1994	90.0	58.3	41	75	81	90	12	16
Russell D. Feingold	D	2	41	1992	69.7	52.6	9	84	65	100	4	8
Wyoming												
Alan K. Simpson	R	16	63	1990	84.0	64.0	100	86	40	15	88	91
Craig Thomas[c]	R	—	61	1994	unopp.	58.9	97	92	42	5	89	87

Note: In compiling this table, the conservative coalition, party unity, and presidential support scores were calculated to eliminate the effects of absences, as follows: support = support/(support + opposition).

[a] Service beginning in or after November in a given year is not counted as a year of service.

[b] Richard C. Shelby switched from the Democratic to the Republican Party on November 9, 1994, the day after the election.

[c] These former House members are serving their first term in the 104th Senate. Their scores are compiled from votes in the 103d House.

[d] Ben Nighthorse Campbell switched from the Democratic to the Republican Party on March 3, 1995.

[e] Louisiana has a two-step election process in which candidates of all parties run against one another in a September primary. If no candidate wins 50 percent or more of the vote at that time, the top two candidates run against each other in November. If a clear winner emerges from the September primary, no candidates compete in the November election.

[f] Kent Conrad won a special election on December 4, 1992, to fill the seat formerly held by Quentin N. Burdick who died on September 8, 1992. Conrad had announced his retirement in April 1992, but decided to seek the open seat after Burdick's death.

Sources: *Congressional Quarterly Almanac,* various years; *Congressional Directory,* various years; *Congressional Quarterly Weekly Report,* various years; American Conservative Union; Americans for Democratic Action.

Table A-4 Senate, 103d Congress, 1993

State, senator	Party	Years of service[a]	Age	Previous Senate election			1992 Voting ratings					
				Year	Primary (%)	General (%)	CC	PU	PS	ADA	ACU	ACU (career)
Alabama												
Howell Heflin	D	14	71	1990	81.0	61.0	89	52	53	40	48	59
Richard C. Shelby	D	6	58	1992	61.5	64.8	89	45	65	30	63	58
Alaska												
Ted Stevens	R	24	69	1990	59.0	66.0	89	81	80	20	74	55
Frank H. Murkowski	R	12	59	1992	80.5	53.0	86	88	73	25	70	76
Arizona												
Dennis DeConcini	D	16	55	1988	unopp.	57.0	53	70	30	75	20	35
John McCain	R	6	56	1992	unopp.	55.8	86	87	75	20	85	86
Arkansas												
Dale Bumpers	D	18	67	1992	64.5	60.2	71	71	28	90	15	17
David Pryor	D	14	58	1990	unopp.	unopp.	66	78	27	90	15	16
California												
Dianne Feinstein	D	—	59	1992	57.8	54.3	—	—	—	—	—	—
Barbara Boxer[b]	D	—	52	1992	43.7	47.9	14	92	8	60	0	3
Colorado												
Hank Brown	R	2	52	1990	unopp.	56.0	92	95	75	20	89	90
Ben Nighthorse Campbell[b]	D	—	59	1992	45.5	51.8	71	79	37	55	38	30

Connecticut												
Christopher J. Dodd	D	12	48	1992	unopp.	58.8	34	83	32	75	11	11
Joseph I. Lieberman	D	4	50	1988	unopp.	50.0	37	77	37	70	22	25
Delaware												
William V. Roth Jr.	R	22	71	1988	unopp.	62.0	81	85	75	25	75	73
Joseph R. Biden Jr.	D	20	50	1990	unopp.	63.0	19	92	29	100	0	14
Florida												
Bob Graham	D	6	56	1992	84.3	65.4	53	73	35	75	15	29
Connie Mack	R	4	52	1988	62.0	50.0	86	91	84	10	96	94
Georgia												
Sam Nunn	D	20	54	1990	unopp.	unopp.	73	69	41	65	30	46
Paul Coverdell	R	—	53	1992	50.5	50.7	—	—	—	—	—	—
Hawaii												
Daniel K. Inouye	D	30	68	1992	76.0	57.3	35	87	41	65	4	7
Daniel K. Akaka	D	3	68	1990	91.0	54.0	26[d]	92[d]	30[d]	90	0	3
Idaho												
Larry E. Craig	R	2	47	1990	59.0	61.0	97	99	85	0	100	93
Dirk Kempthorne	R	—	41	1992	57.4	56.5	—	—	—	—	—	—
Illinois												
Paul Simon	D	8	64	1990	unopp.	65.0	16	90	27	95	7	6
Carol Moseley-Braun	D	—	45	1992	38.3	53.3	—	—	—	—	—	—
Indiana												
Richard G. Lugar	R	16	60	1988	unopp.	68.0	78	88	90	10	85	83
Daniel R. Coats	R	4	49	1992	unopp.	57.3	87	92	78	10	93	94

(Table continues)

Table A-4 (continued)

State, senator	Party	Years of service[a]	Age	Previous Senate election			1992 Voting ratings					
				Year	Primary (%)	General (%)	CC	PU	PS	ADA	ACU	ACU (career)
Iowa												
Charles E. Grassley	R	12	59	1992	unopp.	69.6	68	81	70	30	74	76
Tom Harkin	D	8	53	1990	unopp.	54.0	7	95	23	85	0	7
Kansas												
Bob Dole	R	24	69	1992	80.4	62.7	92	94	88	5	93	81
Nancy Landon Kassebaum	R	14	60	1990	87.0	74.0	74	77	72	25	67	56
Kentucky												
Wendell H. Ford	D	18	68	1992	unopp.	62.9	84	70	35	75	15	27
Mitch McConnell	R	8	50	1990	89.0	52.0	92	92	77	15	89	87
Louisiana												
J. Bennett Johnston	D	20	60	1990	54.0	c	79	67	53	70	23	43
John B. Breaux	D	6	48	1992	73.1	c	78	70	42	60	30	36
Maine												
William S. Cohen	R	14	52	1990	unopp.	61.0	45	61	63	40	48	49
George J. Mitchell	D	13	59	1988	unopp.	81.0	21	93	25	95	0	11
Maryland												
Paul S. Sarbanes	D	16	59	1988	86.0	62.0	11	96	27	100	0	4
Barbara A. Mikulski	D	6	56	1992	76.8	71.0	24	90	23	100	0	4

State / Senator	Party											
Massachusetts												
Edward M. Kennedy	D	30	60	1988	unopp.	65.0	5	97	25	100	0	3
John Kerry	D	8	49	1990	unopp.	57.0	8	92	23	100	0	5
Michigan												
Donald W. Riegle Jr.	D	16	54	1988	unopp.	60.0	26	91	29	95	4	7
Carl Levin	D	14	58	1990	unopp.	57.0	22	92	32	100	0	8
Minnesota												
Dave Durenberger	R	14	58	1988	93.0	56.0	63	58	66	25	42	41
Paul Wellstone	D	2	48	1990	60.0	50.0	8	95	24	100	0	4
Mississippi												
Thad Cochran	R	14	55	1990	unopp.	unopp.	92	94	84	10	85	78
Trent Lott	R	4	51	1988	unopp.	54.0	97	96	83	10	100	95
Missouri												
John C. Danforth	R	16	56	1988	unopp.	68.0	79	79	78	25	74	57
Christopher S. Bond	R	6	53	1992	82.7	51.9	74	84	75	25	76	82
Montana												
Max Baucus	D	14	51	1990	83.0	68.0	45	83	35	95	4	12
Conrad Burns	R	4	57	1988	85.0	52.0	95	94	85	5	89	88
Nebraska												
Jim Exon	D	14	71	1990	unopp.	59.0	55	74	43	75	26	47
Bob Kerrey	D	4	49	1988	91.0	57.0	24	89	30	90	0	8
Nevada												
Harry Reid	D	6	53	1992	52.8	51.0	45	78	37	80	23	25
Richard H. Bryan	D	4	55	1988	79.0	50.0	49	78	32	80	19	29

(Table continues)

Table A-4 (continued)

State, senator	Party	Years of service[a]	Age	Previous Senate election			1992 Voting ratings					
				Year	Primary (%)	General (%)	CC	PU	PS	ADA	ACU	ACU (career)
New Hampshire												
Robert C. Smith	R	2	51	1990	65.0	65.0	89	92	73	5	96	93
Judd Gregg	R	—	45	1992	50.4	48.2	—	—	—	—	—	—
New Jersey												
Bill Bradley	D	14	49	1990	92.0	50.0	20	89	25	85	4	11
Frank R. Lautenberg	D	10	68	1988	78.0	54.0	5	92	22	100	4	5
New Mexico												
Pete V. Domenici	R	20	60	1990	unopp.	73.0	89	89	82	15	78	68
Jeff Bingaman	D	10	49	1988	unopp.	63.0	42	75	44	75	4	14
New York												
Daniel Patrick Moynihan	D	16	65	1988	unopp.	67.0	34	90	35	100	0	6
Alfonse M. D'Amato	R	12	55	1992	unopp.	49.0	48	62	60	30	52	49
North Carolina												
Jesse Helms	R	20	71	1990	84.0	53.0	96	96	80	5	100	99
Lauch Faircloth	R	—	64	1992	47.7	50.4	—	—	—	—	—	—
North Dakota												
Kent Conrad[d]	D	6	44	1992	conv.	63.2	62	71	32	90	12	25
Byron L. Dorgan[b]	D	—	50	1992	unopp.	59.0	44	79	25	70	28	20

Ohio												
John Glenn	D	18	71	1992	unopp.	51.0	39	83	31	80	11	13
Howard M. Metzenbaum	D	17	75	1988	84.0	57.0	5	94	26	90	0	6
Oklahoma												
David L. Boren	D	14	51	1990	84.0	83.0	77	63	38	60	35	57
Don Nickles	R	12	44	1992	unopp.	58.5	89	95	79	0	96	95
Oregon												
Mark O. Hatfield	R	26	70	1990	78.0	54.0	47	46	53	70	23	25
Bob Packwood	R	24	60	1992	59.1	52.1	51	50	62	60	33	40
Pennsylvania												
Arlen Specter	R	12	62	1992	65.1	49.1	39	41	45	65	30	36
Harris Wofford[e]	D	2	66	1991	conv.	55.0	22	92	29	100	0	11
Rhode Island												
Claiborne Pell	D	32	74	1990	unopp.	62.0	11	90	29	80	8	7
John H. Chafee	R	16	70	1988	unopp.	55.0	55	60	62	40	44	27
South Carolina												
Strom Thurmond	R	38	90	1990	unopp.	64.0	95	94	78	10	89	90
Ernest F. Hollings	D	26	71	1992	unopp.	50.1	55	58	38	35	63	51
South Dakota												
Larry Pressler	R	14	50	1990	unopp.	52.0	84	91	73	20	85	75
Tom Daschle	D	6	45	1992	unopp.	64.9	37	82	25	95	22	15
Tennessee												
Jim Sasser	D	16	56	1988	unopp.	65.0	59	86	35	95	7	16
Harlan Mathews[f]	D	—	65	—	appt.	—	—	—	—	—	—	—

(Table continues)

Table A-4 (continued)

State, senator	Party	Years of service[a]	Age	Previous Senate election			1992 Voting ratings					
				Year	Primary (%)	General (%)	CC	PU	PS	ADA	ACU	ACU (career)
Texas												
Phil Gramm	R	8	50	1990	unopp.	60.0	94	98	90	0	93	95
Kay Bailey Hutchison[g]	R	—	49	1993	29.0	67.3	—	—	—	—	—	—
Utah												
Orrin G. Hatch	R	16	58	1988	unopp.	67.0	95	95	88	5	96	93
Robert F. Bennett	R	—	59	1992	51.4	55.4	—	—	—	—	—	—
Vermont												
Patrick J. Leahy	D	18	52	1992	unopp.	54.2	5	96	24	100	0	5
James M. Jeffords	R	4	58	1988	61.0	68.0	40	39	47	65	27	25
Virginia												
John W. Warner	R	14	65	1990	unopp.	81.0	79	87	73	20	74	78
Charles S. Robb	D	4	53	1988	unopp.	71.0	50	74	42	60	30	33
Washington												
Slade Gorton	R	10	64	1988	36.0	51.0	72	81	71	25	72	64
Patty Murray	D	—	42	1992	28.3	54.0	—	—	—	—	—	—
West Virginia												
Robert C. Byrd	D	34	75	1988	81.0	65.0	61	75	27	100	19	28
John D. Rockefeller IV	D	8	55	1990	85.0	68.0	28	89	28	100	7	11

Wisconsin												
Herb Kohl	D	4	57	1988	47.0	52.0	26	79	30	95	11	14
Russell D. Feingold	D	—	39	1992	69.7	52.6	—	—	—	—	—	—
Wyoming												
Malcolm Wallop	R	16	59	1988	83.0	50.0	100	96	81	10	100	91
Alan K. Simpson	R	14	61	1990	84.0	64.0	92	91	83	15	89	81

Note: In compiling this table, the conservative coalition, party unity, and presidential support scores were calculated to eliminate the effects of absences, as follows: support = support/(support + opposition).

[a] Service beginning in or after November in a given year is not counted as a year of service.

[b] These former House members are serving their first term in the 103d Senate. Their scores are compiled from votes in the 102d House.

[c] Louisiana has a two-step election process in which candidates of all parties run against one another in a September primary. If no candidate wins 50 percent or more of the vote at that time, the top two candidates run against each other in November. If a clear winner emerges from the September primary, no candidates compete in the November election.

[d] Kent Conrad won a special election on December 4, 1992, to fill the seat formerly held by Quentin N. Burdick who died on September 8, 1992. Conrad had announced his retirement in April 1992, but decided to seek the open seat after Burdick's death.

[e] Harris Wofford won a special election on November 5, 1991, to fill the seat formerly held by John Heinz who died on April 4, 1991. Wofford had been appointed in May 1991 to serve until the November special election.

[f] Harlan Mathews was sworn in on January 5, 1993, to fill the seat of Albert Gore, Jr., who was elected vice president of the United States on November 3, 1992. Mathews will serve through 1994 when a replacement will be chosen to complete Gore's unexpired term.

[g] Kay Bailey Hutchison was elected on June 5, 1993, in a runoff of a special election to fill the seat vacated by Lloyd Bentsen. Bentsen was confirmed as secretary of the Treasury on January 20, 1993.

Sources: Congressional Quarterly Almanac, various years; *Congressional Directory*, various years; *Congressional Quarterly Weekly Report*, various years; American Conservative Union; Americans for Democratic Action.

Index